The Transition Handbook

The Transition Handbook
Strategies High School
Teachers Use that Work!

by

Carolyn Hughes, Ph.D.
Vanderbilt University
Nashville, Tennessee

and

Erik W. Carter, M.Ed.
North East Transition School
San Antonio, Texas

·P A U L·H·
BROOKES
PUBLISHING C⁰

Baltimore • London • Toronto • Sydney

Paul H. Brookes Publishing Co.
Post Office Box 10624
Baltimore, Maryland 21285-0624

www.brookespublishing.com

Typeset by Brushwood Graphics, Inc., Baltimore, Maryland.
Manufactured in the United States of America by
Bang Printing, Brainerd, Minnesota.

The case studies in this book are completely fictional. Any similarity to actual individuals or circumstances is coincidental, and no implications should be inferred.

Library of Congress Cataloging-in-Publication Data

Hughes, Carolyn, 1946–
    The transition handbook : strategies high school teachers use that work!/ by Carolyn Hughes and Erik W. Carter.
        p. cm.
    Includes bibliographical references and indexes.
    ISBN 1-55766-439-0
    1. Handicapped youth—Education (Secondary)—United States. 2. Handicapped youth—Education (Middle school)—United States. 3. Handicapped youth—Services for—United States. 4. School-to-work transition—United States. 5. Community and school—United States. I. Carter, Erik W. II. Title.

    LC4019 .H84 2000
    371.9'0473--dc21
                                                                                99-052427

British Library Cataloguing in Publication data are available from the British Library.

Contents

APPENDIX

About the Authors

Carolyn Hughes, Ph.D., is an associate professor in the Department of Special Education at Vanderbilt University in Nashville, Tennessee, and Project Director of the federally funded Metropolitan Nashville Peer Buddy Program. In 1990, she received her doctoral degree in special education from the University of Illinois at Urbana-Champaign, specializing in the areas of secondary transition and employment and self-management strategies. At Vanderbilt University, Dr. Hughes teaches courses in behavior management and the transition from school to adult life and manages several federally funded research and personnel preparation grants. She conducts research and publishes widely in the areas of self-instruction and self-determination, supporting the transition from school to adult life, and social interaction and social inclusion of high school students. Dr. Hughes is a co-author of *Teaching Self-Determination to Students with Disabilities: Basic Skills for Successful Transition* (Paul H. Brookes Publishing Co., 1998) and is on the editorial boards of the *American Journal on Mental Retardation, Education and Training in Mental Retardation and Developmental Disabilities, Journal of The Association for Persons with Severe Handicaps, Journal of Behavioral Education,* and *Journal of Positive Behavior Interventions.* In addition, Dr. Hughes taught general and special education classes in public schools in Montana for 10 years.

Erik W. Carter, M.Ed., is a transition teacher at the North East Transition School in San Antonio, Texas. In 1998, he received his master's degree in special education at Vanderbilt University in Nashville, Tennessee, where he specialized in the areas of severe, profound, and multiple disabilities. While attending Vanderbilt University, Mr. Carter was a research assistant at the Metropolitan Nashville Peer Buddy Program where he provided technical assistance, project evaluation, and outreach services to teachers and students participating in a districtwide peer mentoring program. He has presented at state conferences in Tennessee on the topic of peer mentoring among high school students.

Foreword

As we move into the year 2000, the unemployment of young adults with disabilities continues to be one of the most pressing national problems in the country. Despite 20 years of significant progress in special education, assistive technology, and vocational rehabilitation as well as an excellent U.S. economy, young people with disabilities continue to be unemployed and underemployed at unconscionably high rates. The efforts of Congress have been significant on behalf of people with disabilities. In order to eradicate this problem, important laws have been passed, such as the Americans with Disabilities Act of 1990, the Rehabilitation Act Amendments of 1992, the Individuals with Disabilities Education Act of 1990 and its subsequent Amendments of 1991 and 1997, and the School-to-Work Opportunities Act of 1994. These are very meaningful statutes that have provided regulations and funds for helping young adults with disabilities.

Unfortunately, something continues to be missing. There is little doubt that individuals with disabilities have much more potential than is being utilized. Clearly society, businesses, and local communities continue to need more education and understanding of individuals' potential. Furthermore, many people with disabilities and their families need to use the potential skills that they have and much more aggressively pursue careers in the business industry, enroll in postsecondary education, and make perhaps a much greater effort at taking their rightful place in society.

When all is said and done, however, there continue to be at least two major human services issues on which much greater work and effort must be conducted. First, we need a truly seamless system for moving from secondary education to postsecondary adult life. Specifically, there needs to be a much better system of supports established in community colleges, vocational technical centers, 4-year colleges, and alliances within business and industry. These supports need to be targeted for people who are at risk for failure; often, these are people with disabilities. No individuals with disabilities who want to move into higher education or work should have to miss out on such an opportunity; yet, in most communities, this type of seamless system is virtually nonexistent. There are waiting lists, there are referrals, there are placements into dead-end centers and nursing homes, and there are programs that sound good on paper but have no meaningful outcomes associated with them.

So, the first issue of human services needs that we professionals should address is the establishment of a seamless system for moving from secondary education to postsecondary environments at a local community level. The second major human services issue that needs to be addressed is what goes on in a classroom for teenagers with disabilities. *The Transition Handbook* is the first book that directly addresses what should be happening in the classroom. Hughes and Carter have identified a rich array of transition support strategies for high school teachers and their associates to utilize in helping individuals with disabilities maximize their potential.

In this book, transition support applies, for the first time, to the same general philosophical principles of support that have been developed and applied to supported employment and supported living arrangements. Supported employment began in the late 1970s and was expanded to the more active utilization of coworkers and others in the natural work environment. But, with the paradigm shift in 1980 toward eliminating services in segregated programs, such as sheltered work centers to competitive worksites, the door opened for more empowering and liberating ways to help people with disabilities. Support was designed to meet the individual needs of people—not to try to "fix" them or "cure" them of disability. In a similar exciting way, Hughes and Carter are now applying these same principles to supporting transition activities in the classroom and community. *Transition support* is a new concept that helps to build on what we have learned that works well from previous experience and research.

Historically, there has been an overemphasis on trying to teach specific skills to people with disabilities. This approach has been too narrow. Many people with disabilities lack a large number of skills and competencies. Yet, there are only a certain number of these competencies that will be critical to adult adjustment. Creating an array of person-driven supports to catapult the student into the world of adulthood is a much more broad-based approach to helping people reach their potential. The theory behind the older approach has been to calibrate teaching skills to specific problems or issues; the transition support approach is a much more environmental-specific approach that takes into account the multiple variables in the home, community, and worksite.

The Transition Handbook specifically gives strategies for how to implement training techniques and support strategies in the context of community and social living. There are many pictures, cases, and vignettes so that the average high school teacher should be able to readily adapt this information directly into his or her daily lesson plans. There is a strong emphasis on self-determination and inclusion in general education environments, both of which are two key philosophies in the formulation of effective transition. Furthermore, the language and formatting of this book is extremely reader friendly. It truly is a handbook for *how* to design and implement transition supports and as such is a must for all secondary teachers.

Paul Wehman
Professor of Physical Medicine and Rehabilitation
Virginia Commonwealth University

REFERENCES

Americans with Disabilities Act (ADA) of 1990, PL 101-336, 42 U.S.C. §§ 12101 *et seq.*

Individuals with Disabilities Education Act (IDEA) of 1990, PL 101-476, 20 U.S.C. §§ 1400 *et seq.*

Individuals with Disabilities Education Act (IDEA) Amendments of 1991, PL 102-119, 20 U.S.C. §§ 1400 *et seq.*

Individuals with Disabilities Education Act (IDEA) Amendments of 1997, PL 105-17, 20 U.S.C. §§ 1400 *et seq.*

Rehabilitation Act Amendments of 1992, PL 102-569, 29 U.S.C. §§ 701 *et seq.*

School-to-Work Opportunities Act of 1994, PL 103-239, 20 U.S.C. §§ 6101 *et seq.*

Preface
A New Day Is Dawning

As we enter the new millennium, there is an increased awareness that it really is a small world, after all. Like it or not, we are "in each others' faces" much more than we ever used to be with rapid transit, overpopulation, telecommunications, urbanization, instant Internet access, and dwindling resources. A contemporary Buddhist spiritual teacher, John Daido Loori (1991), urges that "we need to know how to live together in peace and harmony with all the diversity on this great earth or we won't survive the twenty-first century—there won't be a twenty-second century. We have to have *mu tai:* no conflict!" Although in the past, we may have liked to think of ourselves as "rugged individualists" fending for ourselves, the truth is that none of us is self-sufficient. Our continued survival on this planet rests not only with our personal competence and individual set of skills that we take into a situation but also on each other—our mutual support, how we treat each other and the planet on which we live, and our ability to get along with each other. Our dependence on each other for support and survival is a lesson that relates directly to all students as they make the transition from school to adult life.

STUDENT SUPPORT AND TRANSITION

A successful transition from high school requires support from a variety of sources—parents, friends, teachers, and members of the community. In addition, the supports a student needs relate to her personal competence, preferences, and expectations.

Sources of Support

One of the most important factors that relates to a student's choices and success as she leaves high school to enter her adult life is the support of family, friends, and others. How do most of us get our jobs? Through our network of family and friends. How do many of us learn about a particular college or other postsecondary educational program we may be interested in attending? Often, through word of mouth from a friend who is familiar with the program, a tip from a guidance counselor at school, or from a family member who is an alumnus of the program. And, where do we often meet those important others with whom we may develop lasting, intimate relationships? Of course! It's through our interactions with our families, friends, or members of groups to which we belong. In addition, we may develop a love for boxing, hot air ballooning, or ballroom dancing because someone we know liked to watch or engage in these activities. Or, we may shop at a particular store or mall because it was recommended by an acquaintance or move to a new town or apartment complex because a friend may like the place. We may try out for a soccer team, go to a certain church, or join a social club mainly because we like the members.

Personal Competence and Preferences

Our personal competence and skills in relation to what is required by a particular situation also help determine the activities in which we become involved as do our personal preferences. For example, if we don't speak Russian, we are probably less likely to join a Russian conversation club, or if we don't like country music, we may not spend time going to the annual Country Music Awards ceremonies. However, "success" in our everyday lives—whether we are bank presidents, students, homemakers, social activists, street vendors, service station attendants, or artists and whether we spend our free time eating out, exercising, knitting, watching television, training dogs, or bird calling—is as much a factor of our interactions with others as it is of our personal array of skills. And, how well we like our jobs, our schools, our free-time activities, or our communities is, to a large extent, influenced by our interactions with others with whom we may come in contact.

When Typical Supports Are Not Enough

Some students may have ample supports that complement their particular set of skills and competencies as they make the transition from school to adult life. For example, a supportive parent, a helpful guidance counselor, an interested teacher, and an older brother already in college may be all that are needed to help a student choose which colleges to apply to when getting ready to graduate from high school. Or, a friend who works as a mechanic may help another student find a job at a service station or show a friend how to check the want ads in the local newspaper.

Other students, however, require support beyond that which they are receiving from their families, friends, community, and schools to make a successful transition to adult life. Without additional support, these students may join the growing number of high school dropouts, unemployed or financially dependent adults, unskilled or entry-level workers, or socially isolated citizens (Wagner, 1995). In some cases, additional support may simply mean helping a student learn how to gain access to resources that are already available in his environment, such as a nearby bus stop or a downtown employment agency. In other cases, a student's support needs may be more extensive, such as a personal care assistant, a computerized communication system, or a supported living apartment. In either case, support should ideally match a student's strengths, skills, needs, interests, and preferences in relation to improving her postschool outcomes as she makes the transition from school to adult life.

THE TRANSITION HANDBOOK: A TRANSITION SUPPORT MODEL

Sounds nice—but, how do you do it? How *do* you match support to a student's particular needs? That's what this book is all about—a model of transition support for students who need help making the transition from school to adult life. And, it's not just a *theoretical* model that sounds nice but leaves you thinking "Looks good, but how do I do it?" No, we offer you a *practical* model that you can *use* in everyday life. It's true—a new day *is* dawning and in more than one way! Researchers are now learning to listen to practitioners and to include them in building models and developing educational programs, rather than simply telling them what to do in terms of "recommended practices." After all, who likes to be told what to do? No one! Instead, we like to be consulted, to be asked to provide our input, to help devise new strategies, and to have ownership in model program development. That's exactly what we've done in *The Transition Handbook*. In developing the *Handbook*, we've interacted with both researchers *and* practitioners to come up with a resource you can begin to use immediately to support those students who are *not* making a successful transition to adult life. We have provided a resource that is full of strategies that are practical, easy to learn, and ready to use. To ensure that the support strategies in the *Handbook* are ones you can actually use, rather than simply read about, we have included only those strategies that teachers tell us have worked!

PUTTING THE MODEL TO WORK: SUPPORTING STUDENTS IN THE TRANSITION TO ADULT LIFE

So, jump in and get started. To make the *Handbook* even more accessible, we don't require or even suggest that you read it from cover to cover. Instead, we've arranged the strategies in a user-friendly menu format from which you can pick and choose strategies on a case-by-case basis. We've displayed the strategies in short snippets rather than lengthy text to make them easy on your eyes, and we've added headings and logos to guide you in finding the right strategies for a particular case. And, best of all, we've illustrated the *Handbook* with photos and humorous drawings to liven up our presentation!

As you look through *The Transition Handbook*, you'll see that Chapter 1 describes the purpose of the *Handbook* in more detail, how it was developed, and the "Transition Support Model" on which it is based. Chapter 2 tells you how the *Handbook* is organized and how to use it most effectively. Chapters 3–9 contain more than 500 teacher-suggested transition support strategies, arranged according to *The Transition Handbook's* "Transition Support Model." Chapter 10 wraps it up and provides the impetus for you to get started in providing support to students in transition!

Yes, a new day is dawning, and, like it or not, we are a part of a changing world. Many people share one globe, which is seemingly becoming increasingly smaller. Yes, we need to learn to live together with *mu tai*—"no conflict." We do this by realizing our mutual dependence on each other and the mutual support we offer one another. Let's put our support into practice for those who are about to become our nation's—not *future*, but *current*—leaders: the high school students of today.

REFERENCES

Loori, J.D. (Speaker). (1991). *Neither discarding nor attaching* [Cassette recording]. Mt. Tremper, NY: Dharma Communications.

Wagner, M. (1995). *Transition from high school to employment and post-secondary education: Interdisciplinary implications for youths with mental retardation.* Paper presented at the 119th annual meeting of the American Association on Mental Retardation, San Francisco, CA.

Acknowledgments

Acknowledging the many contributors to this text elicits waves of gratitude for us! All along, developing this text has been a collaborative affair, and many more people have had input into it than can even be mentioned.

First is the doctoral advisor of one of us (CH), Frank R. Rusch, who got us thinking about a model of transition support and who suggested we actually ask researchers and practitioners what they thought!

Second are the many researchers who had input in developing our model and particularly those who responded to our lengthy survey.

Third are the transition teachers throughout Tennessee who voluntarily shared their transition support strategies, which became the substance of this text—without them, *The Transition Handbook* would never have happened!

Fourth are the teachers and students of the 11 academic/vocational high schools in Nashville, Tennessee, who have participated in the Metropolitan Nashville Peer Buddy Program and have allowed us to be a part of their everyday lives. We are sure we have learned more from you than you have from us!

Fifth are the U.S. Department of Education, Office of Special Education and Rehabilitative Services (Grant Nos. HO23N10017 and H158Q960004) and the Tennessee Developmental Disabilities Council who funded us in providing technical assistance to the Peer Buddy Program, which has allowed so many students with extensive needs to participate in the everyday activities of high school life.

Sixth are the Peer Buddy project staff at Vanderbilt University who helped us seek, sort through, and organize researchers' and teachers' input—in particular, Paulo Alcantara, Melissa Brock, Greg Fischer, Joy Godshall, Mindy Harmer, Bridget Houser, Bogseon Hwang, Dan Killian, Jin-Ho Kim, and Frances Niarhos.

Seventh are Caleb Carter, artist, who illustrated *The Transition Handbook*, and Ada Hernandez, high school teacher, and Susan Hutchison, employment coordinator, who served as field reviewers.

Eighth is Paul Wehman, who so willingly and eloquently wrote the foreword to this text.

And, finally—and most important—are the editorial and production staff at Paul H. Brookes Publishing Company, who stuck with us throughout the production of this text: in particular, are Lisa Benson, Acquisitions Editor; Scott Beeler, Marketing Director, who saw promise in this text when it was nothing more than an idea; and Mary Olofsson, Senior Book Production Editor, who brought the project to fruition! For their hard work and support throughout the entire production process, we are forever grateful!

To my daughters, Brook and Meghan,
who have taught me what matters most in life (CH)

To my wife, Sharon,
my greatest support, finest teacher, and best friend (EWC)

The Transition Handbook

SECTION I

Introduction to
The Transition Handbook

Chapter 1

Why a Handbook
of Transition Strategies?

1-5   Summary

1-1   NEED FOR A MODEL OF SUPPORT THAT WORKS

Case Study 1.1.   Lester Anthony[1]

Lester Anthony, who was identified as having a disability in the ninth grade, is 16 years old and lives with his aunt, his younger brother, and his younger sister in a small apartment in a large urban housing project. An older brother and sister live elsewhere. Lester's mother, who has legal custody of him, has been in and out of jail for prostitution and selling drugs for as long as Lester can remember. His elementary school teachers remember Lester as affectionate, having a good sense of humor, quick to laugh and make jokes, and good at drawing his favorite sports figures. At school, Lester made passing grades and maintained good attendance until the seventh grade when his grades and attendance rapidly began to decline. During the eighth grade, Lester was suspended for 4 days for fighting with another student, 2 days for throwing rocks, and 1 day for verbally abusing a teacher. At that time, his aunt expressed concerns to Lester's teacher about her ability to cope with Lester, but no support was offered to her, to Lester, or to the rest of the family. During the next year, Lester was identified as having a learning disability and was placed in a resource room for English, math, and history classes. That same year, he missed 42 days of school and spent 5 days in a juvenile detention center for possession of drugs and disturbing the peace. Lester got a job in a large supermarket at the beginning of his sophomore year but was fired when he was caught by his work supervisor eating candy off a shelf while sitting on the floor. His resource room teacher believed that he would have been successful at work if he had had a job coach. During the first week of October of the same year, he slept through all his classes and received zeros. Lester has not been seen in school since.

Open the front section of any local newspaper or talk to any high school teacher or employer, and you are reminded that Lester's story, unfortunately, is not unusual. For many students, high school is not a positive experience leading to a successful transition to adult life. A promising career, satisfying personal relationships, a comfortable home, enjoyable leisure-time activities—the expectations many of us hold for adulthood—do not materialize for a sizable number of students who leave high school.

---

[1]From *Beyond high school: Transition from school to work,* by F.R. Rusch & J.G. Chadsey. © 1998. Adapted with permission of Wadsworth Publishing, a division of Thomson Learning. Fax 800 730-2215.

For many people, leaving high school can be a disappointment. Getting a job, attending college or trade school, or having satisfying social relationships may appear to be goals that will never be reached—even with a diploma in hand.

1.1.1 Life After High School

Despite growing attention in federal policy, research, and the media, for many students secondary education has not resulted in a successful transition to adulthood (Blackorby & Wagner, 1996). Unemployment, financial dependence, and lack of social relationships are the outcomes faced by many students when they leave high school. Three to five years after leaving school, fewer than 8% of young people with disabilities are reported to be fully employed or enrolled in postsecondary education, active socially, and living independently in the community (Wagner, 1995). Fewer than 10% of special education graduates are estimated to be living above the poverty level 3 years after graduation (Affleck, Edgar, Levine, & Kortering, 1990). These findings paint a dismal picture of adult outcomes for many students.

1.1.2 Transition Support Models

Some students need more support than typically is provided by a traditional secondary school curriculum to achieve the adult outcomes that many of us take for granted, such as a job, a car, or marriage. The importance of providing support for students as they make the transition from school to adult life has been advocated for since the mid-1980s (Halpern, 1985; Will, 1984). Support models that have received attention in the literature include Will's (1984) "bridges" model of school to employment proposed by the Office of Special Education and Rehabilitative Services (OSERS); Halpern's (1985) model of school to "community adjustment"; the Individuals with Disabilities Education Act (IDEA) of 1990 (PL 101-476), which mandates support for the transition from school to a range of postschool adult outcomes; and the 1994 School-to-Work Opportunities Act (PL 103-239), which addresses employment among all youth.

Support can make the difference in helping a student experience a successful transition from high school to adult life. Support can come from many sources: a friendly bus driver, an older brother, a teacher, an employer, or a best friend.

1.1.3   Purpose of a Transition Support Model

Although the scope of these models differs, each is designed to match the type and intensity of support to students' individual needs. The models are based on the assumption that students need varying amounts of support to fully participate in general education and the community during their transition from school to adult life (Rusch & Chadsey, 1998). For example, support strategies might include a co-worker giving a student a ride to work, a peer helping a student with limited use of her hands to eat lunch, or a vocational rehabilitation counselor assisting a student to develop a résumé. In *The Transition Handbook,* we define *support strategies* as any assistance or help provided directly to a student to promote a successful transition from school to adult life.

1.1.4   Lack of Research on Transition Support Strategies

There is little agreement, however, on recommended practices that support the transition from school to adult life (Greene & Albright, 1995). J.J. Stowitschek (personal communication, October 7, 1994) observed that "recent review articles have questioned what we know about what works in school-to-work transition, even after a decade of research, development, and demonstration." Kohler's (1993) review of recommended practices in transition suggested that there is little research support for current transition strategies. It is not surprising, then, that attending high school may not improve the adult outcomes of many secondary students receiving special education services.

1.1.5   A Research-Based and Teacher-Tested Support Model: *The Transition Handbook*

Research offers some insight into factors that may promote successful student outcomes, such as paid work experiences during high school, parent involvement, a network of family and friends, community-based instruction, and a good job match (Rusch & Chadsey, 1998). The field cannot ignore findings, however, that show that secondary education has not led to successful adulthood for many special education students. In an era of shrinking funding allocated for disability programs (Council for Exceptional Children, 1995), it is important to provide teachers with effective strategies to improve postschool outcomes for their students.

The Transition Handbook provides a model of support for secondary students that may improve their outcomes after high school. A unique feature of *The Transition Handbook* is that it contains only transition support strategies that are both research based *and* teacher tested. Although the type and intensity of support that students need to make a smooth transition to adult life will differ according to individual needs, such as a personal care attendant for a person with quadriplegia or a communication book for a student who is nonverbal, there are strategies appropriate for every student in *The Transition Handbook*.

1-2 OVERVIEW OF THE TRANSITION HANDBOOK

The Transition Handbook provides a new approach to the transition process: a focus on the *supports* a student needs to experience successful outcomes in adult life. This section provides an overview of the use of *The Transition Handbook*.

1.2.1 *Who* Should Use *The Transition Handbook?*

The Transition Handbook is intended for use by teachers-in-training, middle or high school teachers, students, parents, family members, friends, employers, job coaches, or services providers of students who need support in making the transition from school to adult life. These students include those with disabilities, such as physical impairments, intellectual disabilities, behavior disorders, autism, or sensory impairments. They also may include students at risk for school failure or school dropout, students who are from impoverished communities, or students who, for a variety of additional reasons, need support in the transition to postsecondary life. As acknowledged by the IDEA Amendments of 1997 (PL 105-17), these students also come from families who are increasingly ethnically and economically diverse and for whom English may not be the primary language.

1.2.2 *Why* Should You Use *The Transition Handbook?*

The Transition Handbook is designed to be used as a ready reference that teachers, parents, and others may consult when they are in need of strategies to support students in transition.

Members of a student's individualized education program (IEP) team (including the student!) will find it helpful to read *The Transition Handbook* before an IEP meeting to help them generate ideas for the student's goals and objectives and strategies for attaining them. It is hands-on, user friendly, and solution oriented. Practical examples, case studies, visual displays, and reproducible forms are provided to illustrate the use of more than 500 easy-to-use secondary transition strategies. Users do not need to read *The Transition Handbook* from cover to cover or use the strategies in the order in which they appear. Instead, *The Transition Handbook* is designed in a menu format from which teachers, in collaboration with others, may pick and choose strategies to use based on a student's individual support needs, choices, and preferences.

The Transition Handbook provides high school support strategies that teachers report they use in helping students make the transition to adult life. It's easy to find a strategy that will meet each student's individual needs.

1.2.3 *What Is The Transition Handbook?*

The Transition Handbook presents a wealth of secondary transition strategies that teachers and others may use to support students in the transition from school to adult life. The strategies come from an interactive process that bridges research and practice, which was conducted at Vanderbilt University in Nashville, Tennessee. They are based on a model of support that is the product of more than 5 years of model program development involving both researchers and teachers. These strategies are unique because they are both research based *and* drawn directly from teachers practicing in the field.

1.2.4 What's "New" About *The Transition Handbook?*

The Transition Handbook represents a new approach to the way we think about students with diverse abilities and students at risk of school failure. A concept that is just coming of age in the field is *educational supports,* which are services and assistance individually tailored to promote successful educational outcomes for students. Some students—those for whom *The Transition Handbook* is intended—may need more educational support than is offered by a traditional high school curriculum.

1-3 WHY A "HANDBOOK"?

A "handbook" implies a resource that is readily accessible and easy to use. The intent of *The Transition Handbook* is to be just that—a practical reference that is not just read once and put up on a shelf. Instead, our intent is to provide a resource that belongs on a desk or a workbench and can be consulted easily whenever a support strategy is needed.

Research findings may appear in forms that practitioners find difficult to have access to or to understand. If recommended strategies are to be adapted by the field, they must be packaged as products that are easy to find and easy to use.

1.3.1   The Research-to-Practice Gap

In addition to addressing high school students' support needs, *The Transition Handbook* addresses a critical area of need in secondary transition: the gap between what has been learned from research and what actually is practiced in the field (Sands, Adams, & Stout, 1995).

Persistent social problems and unfavorable postschool outcomes, such as lack of employment, are often cited as evidence that research findings are not being applied in the field. Research-based recommended practices, such as community-based instruction, have been found to be inconsistently implemented in secondary transition programs (Gallivan-Fenton, 1994).

Research findings, however, must be packaged in formats that are accessible to teachers, parents, and others (IDEA Amendments of 1997). For example, teachers are not likely to adopt practices that are found only in published materials that are difficult to find or understand. If researchers want effective transition support strategies to be integrated into practice, they must present them in ways that are acceptable and accessible to high school teachers. For their products to have credibility, researchers must also account for local school and community conditions, attitudes, and values (Lieberman, 1995).

1.3.2   Bridging the Gap: An Interactive Model of Program Development

A solution to the problem of integrating research and practice in secondary transition may be to involve teachers as interactive partners in program development. Instead of a "one-way" approach in which information flows from researchers to practitioners, an interactive approach to the research process involves teachers as contributing partners (Malouf & Schiller, 1995). An interactive model of program development calls for obtaining continual feedback from practitioners and incorporating this input into program planning, implementation, and evaluation.

To develop the transition support strategies found in *The Transition Handbook*, researchers asked teachers to identify practices they used in high school that work. The process was an interactive collaboration between teachers and researchers.

1.3.3 *The Transition Handbook:* An Interactive Model

The Transition Handbook is a unique resource because the transition support strategies it contains were developed through an interactive collaboration between teachers and researchers.

This process ensures that the strategies in *The Transition Handbook* are research based, field tested, and acceptable to teachers. The process also ensures that research findings in *The Transition Handbook* are presented in a user-friendly format that is easily accessible to teachers, parents, and others. By calling the resource a "handbook," we are emphasizing its everyday usefulness in the field.

The Transition Handbook is a result of a cooperative effort between researchers and teachers to develop and package strategies of secondary transition support derived from a research-based model. The next section briefly describes the interactive research-to-practice model that led to the development of *The Transition Handbook* (Hughes, Hwang, et al., 1997; Hughes & Kim, 1998; Hughes, Kim, et al., 1997).

1-4 DEVELOPING THE TRANSITION HANDBOOK

The development of *The Transition Handbook* was a 5-year process that involved both researchers and practitioners. The result is an array of transition support strategies that are both research based and field tested.

1.4.1 Identifying Research-Based Transition Support Strategies

The first step in the development of *The Transition Handbook* was to identify research-based transition support strategies and to arrange them as a proposed model of transition support. We conducted a comprehensive review of the transition literature, which yielded a total of 113 research articles that addressed transition support. As stated previously, in conducting our review, we defined *support strategies* as any assistance or help provided directly to a student to promote a successful transition from school to adult life. All support strategies that were shown to be effective in at least two research studies were included in a proposed model of transition support strategies.

1.4.2 Field-Testing the Strategies with Researchers

We then conducted a national survey to determine the acceptability of the proposed model of support strategies by the research community (Hughes, Hwang, et al., 1997). Each support strategy was defined, and examples were provided in a questionnaire. Researchers in the field were asked to rate the strategies and the model based on their importance to the transition process and to provide written comments. Findings showed that the model and all support strategies were highly valued by the research community. Evaluative comments were used to modify the model and strategies based on the researchers' input.

1.4.3 Field-Testing the Strategies with Teachers

To field-test the model and strategies among teachers, we listed the support strategies by the researchers' ratings and included them in a preliminary questionnaire accompanied by definitions and examples. Transition teachers from Nashville, Tennessee, were asked to review the questionnaire and provide their input. Based on their suggestions, we modified the strategies, definitions, and examples to make them more acceptable, accessible, and useful to practitioners. We also followed their suggestions for modifying our proposed support model and grouped the strategies under two main goals of our proposed support model: developing support in the environment and increasing students' competence. These goals are consistent with the research base in secondary transition and the overriding values in the field.

We then mailed the revised questionnaires to all secondary transition teachers identified in the state of Tennessee (Hughes, Kim, et al., 1997). We telephoned the directors of special education in each public school district to identify all teachers in their districts who provided secondary transition services. The identified teachers represented the entire state of Tennessee, including all urban and rural geographic areas. These teachers reported that they either taught in classrooms or served as itinerant or consulting transition teachers. They also reported that they taught students with intellectual disabilities, learning disabilities, multiple disabilities, serious emotional disturbance, autism, sensory impairments, orthopedic or health-related impairments, and language impairments.

Like the researchers, the teachers were asked to rate the support strategies and the model according to their importance to the transition from school to adult life. They were also asked to provide specific examples of how they implemented the strategies with their students. Results showed that the teachers judged the support strategies and the model to be extremely important to the transition process as well as acceptable to practitioners. Based on their feedback, the model of support was modified for a final time. The model that resulted, the Transition Support Model, is shown in Table 1.1. The teachers also listed a total of 592 ways that they implemented the support strategies in their transition programs.

1.4.4 Compiling the Strategies into *The Transition Handbook*

The Transition Support Model and the 592 support strategies that the teachers provided became the content of *The Transition Handbook*. After we received the teachers' responses, Vanderbilt research staff grouped the suggested support strategies into areas of student support based on the Transition Support Model. As we read through the teacher-generated strategies, the soundness, creativity, practicality, quality, and comprehensiveness of the teachers' suggestions stood out. The original research goal had been met by developing a model of student support, by identifying transition support strategies, and by testing their accept-

Table 1.1.   Transition support model

Developing support in the environment	Increasing students' competence
Promoting social acceptance	Identifying and promoting students' strengths
Increasing environmental support	Increasing students' self-determination
Increasing social support	Increasing students' choice and decision making
	Promoting students' social interaction

ability with a community of researchers and practitioners. We could not ignore, however, the obvious value of the array of research-based and field-tested transition support strategies that had been generated by the research process. We believed that we owed it to the practitioners who had so willingly shared their transition service "secrets" with us to compile their collective knowledge and make it available to all whose goal it is to support students in making the transition from school to adult life. That is how *The Transition Handbook* came to be developed!

1-5   SUMMARY

Our intent in writing *The Transition Handbook* is that it be solid and research based yet accessible to, fun for, and friendly to its users. Our primary audience is teachers, parents, service providers, and others interested in providing support to secondary students as they make the transition from school to adult life. Ultimately, however, our primary target is people like Lester Anthony in Case Study 1.1 who are not experiencing the outcomes we all value—a career, close relationships, enjoyment—when they leave high school.

Getting the right support for a student can make the difference between the prospect of disappointment or hopefulness when leaving high school. Our goal is that all high school students experience valued outcomes in their adult lives.

It is our hope that all students who need it will be served by a support plan like the one Lester receives (see Case Study 4.4 in Chapter 4), one that develops support in a student's environment and increases a student's individual competence, so that all students will experience productive, satisfying, and healthy adult outcomes.

REFERENCES

Affleck, J.Q., Edgar, E., Levine, P., & Kortering, L. (1990). Postschool status of students classified as mildly mentally retarded, learning disabled, or nonhandicapped: Does it get better with time? *Education and Training in Mental Retardation, 25*, 315–324.

Blackorby, J., & Wagner, M. (1996). Longitudinal postschool outcomes of youth with disabilities: Findings from the National Longitudinal Transition Study. *Exceptional Children, 62*, 399–413.

Council for Exceptional Children. (1995). CEC leads IDEA testimony at congressional hearings. *Today, 2*, 1–3, 15.

Gallivan-Fenton, A. (1994). "Their senior year": Family and service provider perspectives on the transition from school to adult life for young adults with disabilities. *Journal of The Association for Persons with Severe Handicaps, 19*, 11–23.

Greene, G., & Albright, L. (1995). "Best practices" in transition services: Do they exist? *Career Development for Exceptional Individuals, 18*, 1–2.

Halpern, A.S. (1985). Transition: A look at the foundations. *Exceptional Children, 51*, 479–502.

Hughes, C., Hwang, B., Kim, J., Killian, D.J., Harmer, M.L., & Alcantera, P. (1997). A preliminary validation of strategies that support the transition from school to adult life. *Career Development for Exceptional Individuals, 20*, 1–14.

Hughes, C., & Kim, J. (1998). Supporting the transition from school to adult life. In F.R. Rusch & J.G. Chadsey (Eds.), *Beyond high school: Transition from school to work* (pp. 367–382). Belmont, CA: Wadsworth.

Hughes, C., Kim, J., Hwang, B., Killian, D. J., Fischer, G.M., Brock, M.L., Godshall, J.C., & Houser, B. (1997). Practitioner-validated secondary transition support strategies. *Education and Training in Mental Retardation and Developmental Disabilities, 32*, 201–212.

Individuals with Disabilities Education Act (IDEA) of 1990, PL 101-476, 20 U.S.C. §§ 1400 *et seq.*

Individuals with Disabilities Education Act Amendments of 1997, PL 105-17, 20 U.S.C. §§ 1400 *et seq.*

Kohler, P.D. (1993). Best practices in transition: Substantiated or implied? *Career Development for Exceptional Individuals, 16*(2), 107–121.

Lieberman, A. (1995). Practices that support teacher development: Transforming conceptions of professional learning. *Phi Delta Kappan, 76*, 591–596.

Malouf, D.B., & Schiller E.P. (1995). Practice and research in special education. *Exceptional Children, 61*, 414–424.

Rusch, F.R., & Chadsey, J.G. (Eds.). (1998). *Beyond high school: Transition from school to work.* Belmont, CA: Wadsworth.

Sands, D.J., Adams, L., & Stout, D.M. (1995). A statewide exploration of the nature and use of curriculum in special education. *Exceptional Children, 62*, 68–83.

School-to-Work Opportunities Act of 1994, PL 103-239, 20 U.S.C. §§ 6101 *et seq.*

Wagner, M. (1995). *Transition from high school to employment and post-secondary education: Interdisciplinary implications for youths with mental retardation.* Paper presented at the 119th annual meeting of the American Association on Mental Retardation, San Francisco.

Will, M. (1984). *OSERS programming for the transition of youth with disabilities: Bridges from school to working life.* Washington, DC: Office of Special Education and Rehabilitation Services, U.S. Department of Education.

C h a p t e r   2

How to Use
The Transition Handbook

2-1 **What We Did**
2.1.1 Participating in an Interactive Research Process
2.1.2 Sharing the Support Strategies

2-2 **How We Organized *The Transition Handbook***
2.2.1 Choosing a Layout
2.2.2 Choosing an Organization
    2.2.2a Section I
    2.2.2b Section II
    2.2.2c Section III
    2.2.2d Section IV
    2.2.2e Appendix

2-3 **How You Can Use *The Transition Handbook***
2.3.1 Finding the "Right" Support Strategy
    2.3.1a Look at the Table of Contents
    2.3.1b Identify the Problem
    2.3.1c Look at Section II
    2.3.1d Look at Section III
    2.3.1e Try a Combination of Strategies
2.3.2 Finding Your Way Through Chapters 3–9

2-4 Getting Started

2-1 WHAT WE DID

Practitioners can learn from each other! Our goal in writing *The Transition Handbook* is to share with practitioners transition support strategies teachers use that work.

2.1.1 Participating in an Interactive Research Process

In Chapter 1, we recounted the 5-year interactive research process that we (Vanderbilt research staff) participated in with researchers and teachers. This process resulted in the Transition Support Model and 592 strategies, which transition teachers in Tennessee reported that they used to support high school students in making the transition from school to adult life. The interactive process ensured that the support strategies identified were both research based and field tested by practicing teachers.

The Transition Handbook makes it easy for users to have access to field-tested strategies that support students in transition. The format is designed to help users find the right strategies for each student's needs.

2.1.2 Sharing the Support Strategies

As we reviewed the almost 600 support strategies, we realized that we had collected an impressive array of teacher-generated knowledge and experience. The potential usefulness of the collected strategies to the secondary transition field seemed enormous! The strategies, however, existed within lengthy lists in the researchers' offices. True, tabulations and categories of the strategies had been published in professional journals and texts (see Hughes, Hwang, et al., 1997; Hughes & Kim, 1998; Hughes, Kim, et al., 1997). These publications, however, were not always easily accessible for teachers, parents, and others, and their contents were not always easy to understand. How "useful" were the collected strategies if practitioners could not readily find and use them to improve the often dismal adult outcomes of secondary students? We believed that it was our responsibility to serve the field by making the strategies available in a format that was both user friendly and practical.

2-2 HOW WE ORGANIZED *THE TRANSITION HANDBOOK*

We decided that the best way to share the transition support strategies that we had collected would be in the form of a hands-on, user-friendly, solution-oriented "handbook." We also determined that the layout of the handbook should add to the accessibility and appeal of the strategies.

2.2.1 Choosing a Layout

After we had made the decision to share widely the array of support strategies, we brainstormed with teachers to find the best layout and organization for *The Transition Handbook*. We knew that teachers didn't have time to read through pages and pages of text to find ideas to use with their students. Therefore, we decided to present the strategies in short "snippets" for teachers to glance through as they looked for solutions to particular problems. We also decided to include plenty of case studies and examples to show how the strategies could be applied in actual situations. Finally, we chose to illustrate *The Transition Handbook* with lots of photographs and drawings to make it appealing to the eye and fun to read and with humorous hand-drawn icons to guide readers in its use.

2.2.2 Choosing an Organization

We chose to organize *The Transition Handbook* according to the Transition Support Model, which had emerged from our interactive research process (see Table 1.1 in Chapter 1). The model contains two main goals: 1) developing support in the environment and 2) increasing students' competence. Seven areas of student support fall under these two goals and provide a theoretical framework for the teacher-suggested support strategies. The strategies are arranged in *The Transition Handbook* according to these areas of student support. *The Transition Handbook* is also organized into four main sections designed for easy access for readers.

   2.2.2a Section I   Section I presents introductory material for *The Transition Handbook* and contains two chapters. Chapter 1 describes the interactive research process from which the Transition Support Model and the support strategies were derived. Chapter 2 tells how *The Transition Handbook* is organized and how it should be used. Publications cited in these and the remaining chapters in *The Transition Handbook* are listed at the end of the chapter in which they are cited.

2.2.2b   *Section II*   Section II has three chapters and contains support strategies that relate to the first main goal of the Transition Support Model: developing support in the environment. Fortunately, a "deficit model" of student support, in which a student must be "fixed" in response to demands of the environment, is no longer accepted in education. This model is being replaced by a more "ecological" approach in which the environment is modified and naturally occurring support is maximized in response to the full array of an individual's needs, preferences, and choices. Our research shows that much support is available in most environments. In addition, acceptance of individual differences can be promoted in an everyday environment. The strategies in Section II allow teachers to "tap in" to and maximize support in an environment, as well as to build support and acceptance in environments in which they are lacking, in order to support students in the transition from school to adult life.

Chapter 3 presents strategies for promoting social acceptance, such as communicating an attitude of acceptance, promoting diversity awareness, and teaching skills that promote acceptance. Chapter 4 discusses strategies for increasing environmental support. These include gaining access to existing environmental support, developing environmental support plans, and modifying the environment. Chapter 5 contains strategies for increasing social support, such as communicating social support needs, developing social support plans, and gaining access to existing social support.

2.2.2c   *Section III*   Section III of *The Transition Handbook* contains four chapters that relate to the second main goal of the support model: increasing students' competence. When individuals are viewed as competent, they typically are accepted more readily into an environment. Being competent also allows people to have access to many benefits, such as job advancement, educational opportunities, and satisfying relationships. "Competence" is judged within the context of an environment. Being considered competent in one environmental context, such as consistently hitting home runs on a baseball team, does not mean that the same person would be considered competent in another environmental context, such as being a member of a spacecraft launching crew. Competence must be promoted, supported, accepted, and maintained within an environment. The strategies in Section III help teachers to build the competence of students within their everyday environments and to teach skills and arrange environments to support and maintain students' competence.

Chapter 6 provides support strategies for promoting students' strengths. These strategies include identifying and communicating students' strengths and needs and teaching students skills that need strengthening. Chapter 7 describes strategies for increasing students' self-determination, such as teaching self-determination skills and incorporating self-determination into daily life. Chapter 8 contains strategies for increasing students' choice and decision making, including increasing students' opportunities to choose, teaching choice making, and collaborating with others. Chapter 9 focuses on strategies that promote students' social interaction and includes increasing opportunities for social interaction and teaching social interaction skills.

2.2.2d Section IV Section IV contains one chapter, Chapter 10, which provides an epilogue to *The Transition Handbook*. Chapter 10 summarizes the purpose and content of *The Transition Handbook* and suggests future direction and action steps for readers.

2.2.2e Appendix The appendix to *The Transition Handbook* contains additional valuable materials for readers. Blank copies of the forms in *The Transition Handbook* are provided so that readers can reproduce and use to apply the strategies that they have learned. The Resources contain an extensive list of multiple sources outside of *The Transition Handbook,* including books, newsletters, World Wide Web sites, videotapes, and organizations. *The Transition Handbook* web site (www.transitionlink.com) is discussed on page 406. Readers can find out how to access a wealth of additional transition strategies and resources used by individuals across the country as well as submit their own strategies. The web site also includes extensive links to organizations and resources addressing the area of transition. The Index of Support Strategies is an alphabetical listing with page numbers of the many strategies found in *The Transition Handbook,* and the Index of Student Skills is a similar listing of the student skills and outcomes addressed in the strategies.

2-3 HOW YOU CAN USE *THE TRANSITION HANDBOOK*

The Transition Handbook is designed to be easy to use. To guide you in finding strategies that are appropriate for a particular situation, we offer the following suggestions.

2.3.1 Finding the "Right" Support Strategy

Let's say that you like the idea of using transition support strategies to help a student have a more successful transition from school to adult life. You probably already have in mind some students who are having some problems and could use some support. But how do you find the "right" support strategy to address a student's problem? Just follow these simple suggestions.

2.3.1a Look at the Table of Contents First, take a look at the complete Table of Contents, which begins on page v. All of the transition support strategies are found in Sections II and III and are arranged according to the Transition Support Model in Table 1.1 in Chapter 1. As you can see, Section II, which begins on page 27, is called Strategies for Developing Support in the Environment. This section contains Chapters 3–5, in which all of the strategies that address developing support in the environment are found. Section III, Strategies for Increasing Students' Competence, which begins on page 137 and contains Chapters 6–9, includes all of the strategies for increasing students' competence.

2.3.1b Identify the Problem Next, you need to identify the problem you're examining and then decide whether you will look in Section II or III. Is the problem you are dealing with one that you want to address by developing support in the environment for a student (Section II) or by increasing the student's competence (Section III)? For example, perhaps the problem you're thinking about has to do with one of your students, Beth, who works part time in the laundry department of a large hotel. Beth does her work well, which is operating

How do you find the right support strategy to address a
student's needs? Just follow the suggestions on pages
19–21 and you'll see how easy it is.

the dryer machine. She hums out loud much of the time, however, and talks to
herself. When she's around her co-workers, Beth tends to say the same things over
and over, such as talking about how her dog was run over. Beth has been working
at the same job for more than a year and is ready for something else. She would
like to move to the housekeeping department where the pay is a little better. Her
work supervisor, however, seems reluctant to promote Beth. You believe that it
has nothing to do with Beth's job performance because her evaluations are always
terrific. It's more likely that she just doesn't quite fit in socially at the hotel because
she talks to herself and because of her other atypical social behaviors. You've
noticed that Beth's co-workers seem to try to avoid her at break or "roll their eyes"
when Beth brings up her dog again. How can you make her work environment
more supportive of individual differences, such as Beth's, that don't affect job
performance?

2.3.1c   *Look at Section II*   You've decided that the problem is that Beth
doesn't fit in socially at her workplace, and you'd like to try to make that
environment more supportive. This means that you should turn to Section II and
find a strategy for developing support in the environment. Which chapter should
you look in? Because you're interested in determining whether Beth's work
environment can be more supportive of her social behavior, start with Chapter 3,
"Strategies that Promote Social Acceptance." When we take a look at the Table of
Contents for Chapter 3, on page 29, we find that the strategies that teachers
suggested for promoting social acceptance are divided into four main groups (3-1
to 3-4) and 10 subgroups (3.1.1 to 3.4.2). You decide that the problem would be
best addressed by Promoting Diversity Awareness (3-2). You would like the work
supervisor and co-workers at the hotel to be more aware of what a great job Beth
is doing at operating the dryer even though she may have some behaviors that are
different. You decide to turn to 3.2.2 on pages 47–50 to see what strategies are

suggested for Stressing Students' Strengths. There you find a suggested strategy for videotaping an employee while she's working and then showing the videotape to her work supervisor, pointing out how well the employee is doing. This sounds like a good idea because maybe Beth's supervisor doesn't even realize what a good worker she is. You decide to give that a try!

2.3.1d Look at Section III   You may decide, however, that if Beth appeared more competent in the hotel environment, she might fit in better. Then her work supervisor might be more likely to give her a promotion if he were to notice how good her production was on the dryer. You turn to Section III to find strategies for increasing students' competence. Because the problem is social, you turn to the Table of Contents for Chapter 9, "Strategies that Promote Social Interaction," on page 26. You look through the four main groups of the strategies listed and decide to look at 9-4, Teaching Social Interaction Skills. Maybe Beth could learn some new social interaction skills that would help her fit in better. You decide to turn to 9.4.3, Peer-Delivered Social Skills Programs, on pages 292–297. Maybe Beth's co-workers could help her learn to talk about different topics during break and not talk to herself so much while she works. You find a teacher-suggested strategy for having peers suggest different conversational topics to students and reinforce students for discussing them. You promise yourself to introduce the strategy with Beth and her co-workers as soon as possible.

2.3.1e Try a Combination of Strategies   You may want to try both approaches at the same time—developing support in the environment and increasing a student's competence. The support that's available in any environment relates to our competence there! You can decide how much time and effort you can put into providing support to address a particular student's problem and which approach or combination of approaches is more practical and more likely to yield positive outcomes for the student. You might find that using just one strategy works in supporting a student, such as starting a "peer buddy" program (3.3.2). Often, however, you will find that using more than one strategy in combination will produce more lasting results, such as collaborating with others to promote social interaction (9.3.2) or teaching students to monitor and reinforce their own social interaction (7.2.4).

2.3.2 Finding Your Way Through Chapters 3–9

Maybe you've decided that you're interested in a particular chapter and want to see what strategies are in it. But how do you find your way through it? How is the chapter organized? To make Chapters 3–9 (the ones with the strategies) easy to use, we've arranged them all according to the same format. Let's take a look at Chapter 3 as an example.

2.3.2a Overview   Turn to the first page of Chapter 3. As you can see, Chapter 3, like all of the chapters in Sections II and III, starts with an Overview. The Overview provides a background and conceptual framework for the chapter as well as a rationale for why the strategies that are in the chapter belong in a model of transition support. (Additional rationales are provided in boxes at the beginning of each subgroup of strategies in the chapter.) The Overview ends with a short paragraph that summarizes the organization of the chapter.

2.3.2b   *Photos and Drawings*   Below the Overview, you will see a photograph. Next to it is a short caption that summarizes the main ideas in the chapter and (we hope!) will inspire you to action in implementing some of the support strategies. If you page through *The Transition Handbook,* you will see that it is full of photographs and line drawings that illustrate the strategies and make it appealing to the eye and fun to read!

2.3.2c   *Case Studies*   The next section in each chapter is a case study. Take a look at Case Study 3.1, Kenneth Cartwright, on page 31. Kenneth's case study, like others in *The Transition Handbook,* presents the problem of a student in need of support. Kenneth's problem, in Chapter 3, shows what can happen when a student doesn't fit in socially at work. Solutions to Kenneth's problem are found in the strategies in Chapter 3. The case studies in Chapters 3–9 illustrate problems that are solved by the strategies and solutions contained in each of the chapters. The case studies serve to bring the strategies "to life" to help you see how you can apply them to your students' support needs.

2.3.2d   *Groups and Subgroups of Strategies*   After Case Study 3.1, you will see the heading Communicating an Attitude of Acceptance (3-1). Chapter 3 has 4 main groups and 10 subgroups of strategies. Where did these groups come from? In Chapter 1, you learned that all of the strategies in *The Transition Handbook* were derived from practicing transition teachers. We (Vanderbilt research staff) then placed the teachers' strategies into the framework of the Transition Support Model. The support strategies in each of Chapters 3–9 are arranged in groups according to that framework. Groups and subgroups are divided into strategies with similar types of student support. That's why you will see that Section 3-1 is divided into two subgroups of related strategies: Collaborating with Employers and Co-workers (3.1.1) and Collaborating with Students, Parents, Teachers, and Community Agencies (3.1.2). Each subgroup begins with a box that provides a rationale and conceptual basis for the strategies in the Transition Support Model. These rationale boxes build on the conceptual framework discussed in the Overview at the beginning of the chapter. You will also notice when you look through the Table of Contents that all of the groups of strategies are solution oriented rather than problem oriented. That's why you see such sections as Promoting Diversity Awareness (3-2) rather than The Problem of Diversity.

2.3.2e   *Starting Up, How to Do It, and Teacher-Proven Practices*   As you page through Chapter 3, you will see that the teacher-suggested strategies are displayed in short sections. These sections are entitled Starting Up, How to Do It, and Teacher-Proven Practices and are easily recognizable by their icons:

 # Starting Up:

How to Do It:

Teacher-Proven Practices:

The strategies are divided into sections within a chapter by similarity of their support methods. It is important to remember as you use *The Transition Handbook* that the strategies do not appear and do not have to be used in any particular order! Instead, they are displayed in the Starting Up, How to Do It, and Teacher-Proven Practices sections in a menu-type format like you'd find at a restaurant. At a restaurant, you may have entrées arranged in poultry, seafood, and vegetable sections on a menu, according to their main ingredient. Within each section of the menu, you may pick and choose whichever entrée you like. Strategies are arranged in *The Transition Handbook* in the same way. Similar support strategies are found in the same section—for example, Teacher-Proven Practices—and within that section you can choose whichever strategies appeal to you and offer a potential solution to a student's problem. You *do not* have to use the strategies in the order in which they appear.

2.3.2f *Teachers' Quotes*   All of the strategies in *The Transition Handbook* come from the 592 strategies that transition teachers reported they used to support students in the transition from high school to adult life. Most of these are found in *The Transition Handbook* in the Starting Up, How to Do It, and Teacher-Proven Practices sections. Some strategies that we think are especially good models are presented as teachers' quotes. For example, turn to page 36 in Section 3.1.2 of Chapter 3. Here you find the words of a teacher from Cookeville, Tennessee, supporting the view that teachers and community members should work together to increase the social acceptance of students with different abilities. We believe that teachers' quotes like this are helpful for showing you how actual teachers have used a strategy and for inspiring you to take action on your own, which is why we've included them!

2.3.2g *IDEA*   The Individuals with Disabilities Education Act (IDEA) Amendments of 1997 (PL 105-17) is the legislation that mandates transition from school to adult life in secondary education. The amendments are also guideposts for how to conduct a secondary transition program and how to be in compliance with the legislative intent of the law. To show you how using the support strategies in *The Transition Handbook* can help you to achieve the intent of IDEA and be in compliance with the law, we have included sections that refer directly to IDEA and are easy to spot by their icon:

For example, look at page 33 in Section 3.1.1 in Chapter 3. There you see the IDEA icon and a short summary of how the strategies in 3.1.1 tie in to the legislative requirements in the IDEA Amendments of 1997. The IDEA sections will help you to ensure that you are meeting the letter, and the spirit, of special education law when you implement the student support strategies in *The Transition Handbook.*

2.3.2h *Evaluating Outcomes*   Not only do you need to choose and use strategies that will support students in their transition to adult life, but you also need to evaluate the strategies as you use them to determine whether they actually are helping to achieve desired student outcomes. Forget about everything you might have heard—evaluating student outcomes does not need to be hard! We have included Evaluating Outcomes sections throughout Chapters 3–9 to show you how to evaluate. The Evaluating Outcomes sections are easy to find by their icon:

For example, look at page 39 in Section 3.1.2 in Chapter 3. There you find suggestions for collaborating with others to evaluate how well a student is fitting in and interacting with peers in an environment. Evaluating Outcomes sections also have sample forms to use as you evaluate student outcomes. Blank copies of the forms are found in the appendix for you to reproduce for free and use yourself!

2.3.2i *Cross-References*   Nothing in life exists in a vacuum! As you look through the Table of Contents of *The Transition Handbook,* you will see that strategies in one chapter may relate to those in another. How are you going to keep track of all of them? Relax! We've done all of the work for you. Look at page 35 in Section 3.1.1 of Chapter 3. In this section, you find strategies for collaborating with others to promote a student's social acceptance. Some of the strategies listed in this section relate to increasing students' social participation and social interaction, which are also addressed in other sections of *The Transition Handbook.*

But where? Don't panic! Just look at the Cross-Reference box on page 35. There you learn that related strategies are found in sections entitled Increasing Students' Social Participation (3-4), Increasing Students' Social Interactions (9-1), and Teaching Social Interaction Skills (9-4). You will find these helpful Cross-Reference boxes throughout *The Transition Handbook* to guide you to related strategies.

2-4   GETTING STARTED

Now you know how *The Transition Handbook* is organized, how to use it, and how to find the support strategies you're looking for. There's nothing stopping you now from providing support to your students who are having trouble making the transition to adult life. But how do you get started? What we've learned from the teachers who contributed their strategies to *The Transition Handbook* is that the best way to get started is to TAKE ACTION! And how do you do that? Remember Beth, whom we discussed in the How You Can Use *The Transition Handbook* section of this chapter? The first thing we did to start providing support to Beth in her transition process was to identify the problem. Then, we found a strategy, a solution, for this problem in *The Transition Handbook* and put it into action. And that's exactly what you can do—all of the strategies and resources you need are right here in this handbook!

REFERENCES

Hughes, C., Hwang, B., Kim, J., Killian, D.J., Harmer, M.L., & Alcantera, P. (1997). A preliminary validation of strategies that support the transition from school to adult life. *Career Development for Exceptional Individuals, 20,* 1–14.

Hughes, C., & Kim, J. (1998). Supporting the transition from school to adult life. In F.R. Rusch & J.G. Chadsey (Eds.), *Beyond high school: Transition from school to work* (pp. 367–382). Belmont, CA: Wadsworth.

Hughes, C., Kim, J., Hwang, B., Killian, D.J., Fischer, G.M., Brock, M.L., Godshall, J.C., & Houser, B. (1997). Practitioner-validated secondary transition support strategies. *Education and Training in Mental Retardation and Developmental Disabilities, 32,* 201–212.

Individuals with Disabilities Education Act (IDEA) Amendments of 1997, PL 105-17, 20 U.S.C. §§ 1400 *et seq.*

SECTION II

Strategies for Developing
Support in the Environment

C h a p t e r   3

Strategies that Promote Social Acceptance

OVERVIEW

Social integration and inclusion in the mainstream of life are primary goals of the transition movement. The Individuals with Disabilities Education Act (IDEA) Amendments of 1997 (PL 105-17), which affirm that *all* students should participate in the general education curriculum to the maximum extent possible, are intended to provide students with greater access to the general education curriculum to ensure more successful employment and independent living outcomes after graduation. Similarly, the Developmental Disabilities Act of 1984 (PL 98-527) stipulates that the focus of supported employment for workers with diverse abilities is integration with their co-workers without disabilities. In our view, *social integration* means fully participating in the interactions that occur within an environment to the same extent as do other people who are a part of that environment. By participating fully in the interactions in an environment, individuals gain access to myriad benefits, such as friendships, opportunities to learn, and personal satisfaction. Social integration occurs when individual differences are accepted and individual competencies are maximized and supported.

Not only is it critical that secondary transition instruction occur in the environments in which students will ultimately live their lives, such as in the community, in the home, and on the job, and that *all* students be included in school activities and classes alongside their general education peers, but it also is critical that students be socially accepted into these environments as full participants. Physical proximity—that is, simply being physically present in a environment—does not ensure that one is an active and equal participant in that environment. Teachers and others must take an active role to promote acceptance of students as equal members in employment environments, in general education classrooms, and in the community.

This chapter contains 4 main groups and 10 subgroups of strategies that teachers may use to promote social acceptance in an environment. It includes such strategies as communicating an attitude of acceptance, providing diversity awareness experiences, teaching skills and promoting attitudes that support acceptance, and increasing a student's participation in social activities.

Inclusion in the mainstream of life is a primary goal of transition. Unless people are socially accepted within an environment, they are not likely to be included as full, active participants.

Case Study 3.1   Kenneth Cartwright

Kenneth Cartwright is 18 years old and attends Pecan Valley High School. Kenneth is dependable, hard working, and easygoing. He also has a cognitive disability and extensive support needs; walks unassisted, although somewhat unsteadily; communicates with usually one or two words; and completes daily personal management tasks, such as shaving, with reminders and periodic help. At Pecan Valley, Kenneth spends his mornings in a life skills class and several career preparation classes. Kenneth eats lunch every day in the school cafeteria with general and special education students. Although Kenneth participates in many school activities with other students during the day, he has developed few friendships. Usually he sits alone in a class or walks by himself in the halls. When spoken to, Kenneth usually responds; however, he rarely starts a conversation.

In the afternoon, Kenneth participates in his school's transition employment-training program. Each day, he takes a bus from school to his part-time job at a large, nearby hotel. At the hotel, Kenneth works in the housekeeping department, where he collects used towels and sheets from the hotel rooms and transports them in a bin to the basement laundry facility. Kenneth is reliable at his job, remains on-task, and rarely misses picking up a sheet or towel from a hotel room. On the elevator or in the halls, however, Kenneth rarely speaks to hotel residents or co-workers. Some customers have actually complained to the hotel management about Kenneth because they feel uncomfortable when they meet him in the hall and he doesn't greet them. Kenneth's co-workers feel uncomfortable, too, and have started to avoid Kenneth because he doesn't hang out with them and joke during break and rarely seems to acknowledge their presence when they are working in the same area. Kenneth has been warned several times by his manager that in the hotel business it's important to be friendly, especially to customers. If Kenneth doesn't "shape up" in a hurry, his manager is afraid he may have to fire him. Otherwise, the hotel may start losing customers.

3-1   COMMUNICATING AN ATTITUDE OF ACCEPTANCE

3.1.1   Collaborating with Employers and Co-workers

When employers and co-workers feel that support, information, and assistance are available, they are more likely to be accepting of working with people who have differing abilities. Sometimes co-workers or customers are uncomfortable around employees with diverse abilities simply because they don't know them and don't know what to expect of them. Communicating an attitude of acceptance can help people overlook each other's differences and get to know each other.

Kenneth's lack of friends at school or possible job loss may not be recognized by those around him as a lack of acceptance in the environment. Communicating an attitude of acceptance may help others overlook Kenneth's differences, focus on his strengths, and accept him as an equal participant in everyday life.

Starting Up:

- Discuss the goals of a student's employment-training program at an employee meeting. For example, co-workers might not know that a student's goals are to make decisions independently and accept work-related criticism without getting defensive. Encourage employees to communicate any questions, concerns, or suggestions they may have about a student's program.

- Brainstorm with employers and co-workers ways they could interact with students to help students meet their goals. For example, rather than step in and do a task for a student when she is having difficulty, a co-worker could help the student problem-solve how to do the task independently. Doing so not only will help the student but also will reward the co-worker for having helped someone learn a new skill.

- Point out that along with a worker's differences, he has many strengths and ways to contribute to a job and a worksite. For example, although an employee's production rate may be slower than his co-workers', he makes up for it by never missing or being late to work. Another student may have such a positive attitude that working alongside him puts everyone on the job in a good mood. (See Communicating Students' Strengths and Needs, 6-3.)

- Talk with employees and supervisors regularly to promote understanding and open communication. Discuss any discrepancies between their perceptions of a student's performance and your perceptions. For example, a supervisor may believe that a young man is taking long breaks and is hardly ever at his desk in his office. However, as the teacher or job coach, you have been keeping track of the young man's hours and point out that he actually is at his desk more often than any other worker in the office.

Supporting a student throughout his or her transition from school to adult life may seem like a lot of work. But, don't worry—you don't have to do it alone! Remember, the IDEA Amendments of 1997 require that general educators participate in all decisions related to the individualized education program (IEP) process. And, beginning at age 16, or earlier if needed, transition services that will be provided by community agencies are to be included in the IEP. Transition is a collaborative process, not a solo process!

How to Do It:

- Don't hide! Let employers and co-workers know that you are available to discuss any questions or concerns that they may have about an employee. Have regular hours that you are available on the job, or give them your office or classroom telephone number or your pager number. Worksite personnel will feel more comfortable if they know you are readily available if they have a question, such as what to do if a student misses the bus or if a student gets sick.

- Get things out "on the table"! Before employment training begins for a student, openly discuss with employers and co-workers the expectations they have for each other on the job. It's hard for a new employee to fit in at a new worksite unless she knows what is expected. For example, if the policy at a downtown office is that employees go directly to the administrative assistant rather than to a co-worker when they run out of supplies, then that expectation should be made clear to everyone on the job.

- Remember to show your appreciation of employers who have been especially successful in hiring students and giving job promotions. School principals are always happy to hear of community support and are often willing to write letters of appreciation. Some teachers and employment specialists also have shown their appreciation by holding "Employer Appreciation Day" and publicly giving awards to top employers to thank them for their efforts and success. Invite members of the media, such as a local newspaper, to cover the event and make it a public occasion.

- Model an attitude of acceptance in the workplace, and build rapport with personnel at the worksite. Employers, co-workers, and customers will follow your lead. For example, you can show people at a bank how easy and fun it is to talk with a worker who uses a communication board. Or show them how you discuss sports events at a hardware shop with a worker who is blind, just like you would with anyone else. They will learn that they can do it, too.

Case Study 3.2   Kenneth Learns to Laugh

Rube Alweis, Kenneth's job coach, was concerned. Kenneth was one of his best workers, he liked Kenneth immensely, and he didn't want Kenneth to lose his job. In retrospect, maybe Kenneth's manager and co-workers hadn't been well prepared for accepting someone with Kenneth's differences into the work environment. Rube decided he had a job to do!

First, Rube arranged a meeting with the hotel manager and Kenneth's coworkers. During the meeting, Rube discussed the purpose of Kenneth's employment-training program and explained that it gave students like Kenneth a chance to learn work and social skills needed for successful long-term employment. Trying out different jobs gave transition students the opportunity to see

Communication is the key to building an attitude of acceptance in an environment. Underlying problems often can be solved by discussing them properly.

which jobs they liked best and which jobs were a good match with their particular skills, interests, and preferences.

Rube also mentioned that many students like Kenneth hadn't had much opportunity to work or interact with others in an employment situation, and, consequently, they hadn't learned what social interaction behaviors were typically expected in a workplace. Rube gave the hotel manager and Kenneth's co-workers the opportunity to voice their expectations of a hotel employee. They all agreed that they liked someone who smiled and said, "Good afternoon," in the halls; joked at break; and would make eye contact, wave, or smile when they worked together in the same area. Rube explained that if they modeled this same behavior with Kenneth, he would be more likely to meet their expectations. Rube also reminded them that Kenneth was one of the best laundry workers at the hotel, as evidenced by his work record, and that it would be advantageous to the hotel to keep him employed.

In closing the meeting, Rube reminded everyone that they could talk to him about any concerns they have about Kenneth. If any problems came up, Rube would be glad to meet with them to come up with a solution. Rube thanked everyone for supporting the employment-training program and for attending the meeting. He was glad he remembered to joke around with everyone and maintain a sense of humor during the meeting. Rube knew it was important to establish a rapport with the employees at Kenneth's worksite if he wanted Kenneth to be accepted.

Finally, Rube reminded himself to redouble his efforts to model an attitude of acceptance around Kenneth and around everyone at the worksite. By doing so, others would learn how easy it is to interact with people whose behavior might be a little different. So, when he passed Kenneth in the hall as he left the meeting, Rube yelled out, "Hey, Buddy!" put his "dukes" up, and pretended to go in for a shot with his fist at Kenneth's nose. Kenneth responded with a big grin and a "high-five." His co-workers looked in amazement—they had never even seen Kenneth smile! Before long, however, they, too, were taking "jabs" in the air at Kenneth in the break room and when passing him in the halls. Hearing Kenneth chuckle just made their day!

Cross-references: Increasing Students' Social Participation (3-4), Increasing Students' Social Interactions (9-1), and Teaching Social Interaction Skills (9-4)

3.1.2   Collaborating with Students, Parents, Teachers, and Community Agencies

Remember that you are a role model. Setting a positive example by interacting frequently yet casually with students with diverse abilities at your school will make it more likely that other students and teachers will accept these students and interact with them, too.

"Education is the key. The community must understand people with different abilities and how they and we can adapt so they can be accepted into society."
Teacher
Cookeville High School
Cookeville, Tennessee

Teacher-Proven Practices:

- Hold an introductory class on diverse abilities for peer buddies, teachers, and school staff. Discuss characteristics and behaviors that they are likely to encounter and how they should react. For example, it's helpful to know that a student with a learning disability may need help in organizing his daily assignments or that a student who uses a shunt to drain body fluids may need to be hospitalized occasionally as a result of infections caused by the shunt.

- Discuss with general education teachers and parents simple classroom modifications that are likely to help students with differing abilities fit in. For example, seating arrangements can be adapted for students with hearing or visual impairments, or quieter areas of the room can be set aside for those students who are easily distracted to work. (See Modifying the Environment, 4-5.)

- One "key" to successful inclusion of students into general education curricula and activities is to hold in-service sessions for school staff. Discuss the goals of high school transition programs and the benefits of including *all* students in the mainstream of school life. Remember, other school staff may not be aware of the purpose of secondary transition programs. (See Chapter 1 for reasons for providing secondary transition support.)

- Discuss with school staff the benefit to general education students of having students with diverse abilities in their clubs, activities, and classes. These benefits include an increase in self-esteem, acceptance of others, and the building of new friendships.

Special and general education teachers should decide—together with the students themselves and their parents or guardians—what the students' instructional objectives, program modifications, and behavioral supports will be when students are included in general education classes and activities. The IDEA Amendments of 1997 make it clear that general education teachers must be involved in these educational decisions.

Starting Up:

- At the beginning of the school year, have your students invite a group of general education teachers to a breakfast prepared and served by your students. At the breakfast, share information about your program, such as your goals and plans for the year, and give general education teachers a chance to get to know your students better. At the end of the year, host a "thank-you" breakfast for teachers and community people who have interacted with the students throughout the year.

- Try to ease into the process of building acceptance and support of new programs such as inclusion in your school. Include school personnel in decision making, such as where a classroom should be located or how to modify a class assignment. Other staff and administration members will be more likely to support and accept new ideas when they feel that they have ownership in and input into program development.

- Make yourself available to other staff members for information and assistance regarding students' needs and skills. Visit often the classrooms in which students are included. Talk with general education staff on a regular basis, or communicate often through the use of memos or checklists to promote an open line of communication. Discuss discrepancies between their perceptions of a student's performance and your perceptions. Don't wait for report card day to find out how a student is doing.

- Remember the importance of remaining visible to general education students. It's a good idea to get involved in school activities that involve all students, such as coaching a sports team or sponsoring a club.

It's a good time to brush up on those public relations skills!

Be alive—Don't hide!

Be around—Don't frown!

How to Do It:

- Speak at club and community events about the various community contributions of organizations that are made up of people with diverse abilities, such as People First and Self Advocates Becoming Empowered. Have social gatherings for community support personnel and parents. Getting to know each other informally helps to build a collaborative spirit.

Cross-reference: Organizations (see Resources in the appendix)

- Have small discussion groups with parents and community members to discuss communication, expectations, misunderstandings, levels of acceptance, and methods for promoting acceptance among *all* people. Include a variety of community members in transition and multidisciplinary team meetings to meet the full range of your students' needs. It's the law (PL 105-17).

- During all meetings with family, students, and community members, make sure that you first discuss a student's positive behaviors and academic, social, or other achievements, such as making the soccer team or being named

"Employee of the Month" at work. Then you can introduce areas that need support. Work toward having everyone agree on what it means to be socially accepted in an environment, and work together to provide the support needed to achieve these goals.

Cross-references: Communicating Environmental Support Needs (4-2) and Communicating Social Supports Needs (5-2)

Evaluating Outcomes:

Assessing Social Acceptance

It's easy to assess how fully a student is being accepted into an environment. Be observant, be a good listener, and keep written records. Here are some ways teachers have evaluated students' acceptance:

- Observe students interacting with general education peers outside the classroom, such as dancing together at a school dance, participating on the school track team, or "cruising" the mall together after school. Are students laughing and joking with their peers?

- Interview parents, employers, and fellow teachers occasionally to learn how well they think a student is fitting in within a particular environment. If they identify a problem, such as a student's sitting home all weekend without spending time with friends, then be sure to address it even if you don't agree or have not seen the problem at school. Continue to check with them to determine whether their perceptions change over time.

- Devise for employers, peer buddies, or general education teachers a quick checklist to fill out that addresses behaviors generally expected within an environment. The following is an example of a checklist that was used to evaluate the acceptance of a student's conversational interactions in a high school. (A blank, reproducible form can be found in the appendix.)

Behavior Checklist

Person completing checklist: __Arthur Luga__   **Date:** __October 28__

Student: __Anderson Blackwell__

	Strongly disagree	Mildly disagree	Don't feel strongly either way	Mildly agree	Strongly agree
The student has good conversational skills.	1	2	3	(4)	5
The student acts like most high school students when they eat lunch in a school cafeteria.	1	2	(3)	4	5
Most high school students would probably act like the student in this conversation.	1	(2)	3	4	5
The student's conversational behavior looks acceptable to me.	1	2	3	(4)	5
Most high school students would likely enjoy having a conversation with someone who acts like the student.	1	2	3	(4)	5
	1	2	3	4	5
	1	2	3	4	5

Comments: __The conversation was okay—I just wish that Anderson would talk about something else__

__besides the Cowboys!__

Form 3.1. Behavior Checklist. (From Hughes, C., Lorden, S.W., Scott, S.V., Hwang, B., Derer, K.R., Rodi, M.S., Pitkin, S.E., & Godshall, J.C. [1998]. Identification and validation of critical conversational social skills. *Journal of Applied Behavior Analysis, 31,* 438. Copyright © 1998 *Journal of Applied Behavior Analysis;* adapted by permission.)

Cross-reference: Peer Perception Questionnaire (Form 9-4) in Peer-Delivered Social Skills Programs (9.4.3)

Case Study 3.3   Communicating an Attitude of Acceptance: One Teacher's Story

"I do many things to communicate an attitude of acceptance in my high school. I teach a peer tutoring course to general education students that includes special education legislation, types and characteristics of disabilities, and instructional methods. The course is taught prior to any interaction with special education students. I also teach disability units in general education health classes and hold discussions with English classes when they are assigned to read books about people with disabilities. I have general education peers coach and train athletes in Unified Sports events. I also make announcements in school and community newspapers about current events or competitions taking place in my special education program.

"Prior to integrating my students into general education classes, I discuss expectations with the teachers and students in these classes. I also help raise community awareness and acceptance by providing instruction in the community using the grocery store, bank, etc. Community-based job-training sites allow my students' work to 'speak for itself.'

"This past year, I had more than 40 peer tutors involved in my special education transition program and had to turn down over 100 other students who wanted to be involved in the program. In addition, all my students, even those with very severe disabilities, are included in general education classes, eat lunch, and ride the school bus with their general education friends. My students also participate in many extracurricular activities, watch plays and ball games, and go to dances with their general education peers. I am very fortunate to be in an environment with tremendous support for and acceptance of my transition program."
Teacher
Karns High Schools
Knoxville, Tennessee

Case Study 3.4   Ms. Lewis's First Day

Ms. Lewis proudly entered King High School and quickly walked up the stairs to her very first classroom. The past 4 years of consuming textbook after textbook

"Talk with the individuals with whom a student will be interacting. A casual conversation can go a long way toward evaluating a level of acceptance and promoting an attitude of acceptance."
Teacher
Hunters Lane High School
Nashville, Tennessee

had finally paid off just 3 months ago when she received her teacher's certification in special education. Full of ideas and plans for her students, she began to think about the ways she would help them become important members in their school, workplace, and community. She knew that general class participation would be important, so she made a mental note to talk to several of the teachers on her wing. She remembered hearing about peer buddy programs in a college class and decided to speak with someone in administration about beginning one. And she marveled about the friends her students would make as she found ways to help them fit in with a peer group. What a great first year it was going to be!

The next day, Ms. Lewis discovered that King High School was not quite ready for such "radical" thinking. Mr. Feagan, the science teacher, expressed his "concern" that having a student who used a wheelchair in his lab might pose a safety risk. Mrs. Ross felt that the other students would end up losing out if she were expected to include students with disabilities in her social studies classes. And Coach Boyette excitedly explained that she already taught a separate physical education class for students with disabilities. The meeting with the administration was also puzzling. The principal said that the idea of a peer buddy program sounded tolerable, but she believed students would benefit more from experiences like being an office worker or library assistant. Anticipating that students would certainly be more receptive to her students, Ms. Lewis approached a group of adolescents in the lobby. Four of the students didn't realize King High School had any students with disabilities. The other two stated that they felt uncomfortable when the students did "weird things."

Frustrated and spent, Ms. Lewis went back to her classroom and sat down to reflect on the day. She thought about legislation such as the Americans with Disabilities Act (PL 101-336) and the IDEA Amendments of 1997 and realized that it takes much more than laws to change how people view individuals with diverse abilities. Moreover, she began to understand that negative attitudes aren't unique to just students but also can be present in both teachers and administrators. Pulling out a pen and a piece of paper, Ms. Lewis began to make a careful list of strategies that she believed would help promote diversity awareness at King High School, leading to the social acceptance of students with diverse abilities.

3-2   PROMOTING DIVERSITY AWARENESS

3.2.1   Providing Information About Students

Frequently, a lack of acceptance of students with differing abilities originates from a lack of information. By providing students, teachers, and community members with knowledge about the skills, strengths, and contributions of people with diverse abilities, we can help others create new opportunities and experiences that include *all* students equally.

Negative attitudes represent perhaps the most potent obstacle to the inclusion and acceptance of *all* students into the life of the school and community. The challenge of breaking down barriers of uncertainty and prejudice continues in every school. Fortunately, a number of avenues exist for helping others become more aware of the strengths, needs, unique characteristics, and issues that all students face.

The IDEA Amendments of 1997 stress that IEP teams are responsible for considering a student's cultural background and upbringing when developing an educational program. Teams should include members who are familiar with the student's culture, language, and family values. In addition, members should communicate to others ways of adapting instruction to meet a student's needs and educational goals.

"Before I joined the program, I really did not understand people with disabilities. I felt sorry for them. Now I know that each one has his or her limits and abilities. It's like becoming friends with anyone else."
Peer Buddy
McGavock High School
Nashville, Tennessee

Teacher-Proven Practices:

- Emphasize that all people—not just people with "disabilities"—have both strengths and limitations. For example, stress to an employer that a worker has perfect attendance and a great performance record, even if she has her own way of performing job tasks. Help others have realistic expectations of students who have different abilities.

- Remind employers and business owners about the advantages of hiring employees with diverse abilities. These include the benefits of enthusiastic, well-trained, reliable employees and employer tax incentives.

- Remember that students who interact with their peers with diverse abilities 1) are more accepting and less fearful of differences, 2) have an increased appreciation of diversity, and 3) possess a greater understanding of the beliefs and feelings that underlie others' behavior. Create opportunities for all students to interact. Work with other teachers to incorporate information related to differing abilities in existing units in classes such as social studies, civics, literature, teen living, and so forth.

- Before training begins at a worksite, as a job coach, hold an orientation meeting to answer questions and concerns from a student's prospective co-workers. Discuss the importance of co-worker relationships and social acceptance. Involve co-workers in role plays, and include the future new employee as much as possible.

Cross-reference: Communicating Students' Strengths and Needs (6-3)

Evaluating Outcomes:

Visual "Disability" Simulation

Objective: To provide a simulated "disability experience" for general education students and teachers. Be sure to allow participants the opportunity to observe how others in the school and community typically react to a person with a "disability."

Materials needed: Cane (orientation and mobility), blindfold

Setting: School and community environments (e.g., classroom, hallways)

Participants: Class of general education students

Procedures:

- Discuss/brainstorm with general education students the difficulties and dangers that people with low vision or blindness might face in moving about in familiar and unfamiliar environments.

- Have the students take turns being blindfolded. When a student is blindfolded, rearrange the environment so that objects are no longer placed in "natural" or expected places. Provide the student with a cane to use in "moving around" the new environment.

- Have the student walk to specific areas of the room or hall, such as from the door to a window, from the teacher's desk to a student's desk, or from the classroom to the cafeteria. (*Note:* Have a peer partner stay with the student to protect him from danger or injury.)

- After each student has had a turn, hold a discussion regarding how it felt to have a sensory loss. You may want to use the following questions to guide the class discussion:

  1. What dangers did you encounter in the environment when you were blindfolded?

  2. How could the environment have been modified to decrease the risk of injury?

  3. What types of environments (or objects in the environment) may make the area dangerous for people with visual impairments?

  4. How can assistance from a peer help a person who has low vision and is in a new environment?

Participating in a visual "disability" simulation can "open up the eyes" of peers of a student with low vision or blindness to the challenges presented by the environment.

Case Study 3.5   Getting the Word Out

Ms. Lewis was a little nervous as she entered the cafeteria for her first faculty in-service session. She had spent the past week trying to establish rapport with the general education teachers, particularly Mr. Boeing, an experienced teacher who was popular with many of the faculty. Knowing that teachers wouldn't be open to her students if they didn't know who she was, she tried to remain as visible as possible, hanging out in the faculty lounge and by the mailboxes and attending the first school football game and pep rally of the year. Ms. Lewis also spoke with the principal and convinced her not to hold separate in-service sessions for general and special education teachers. In addition, she asked if she could have some of the meeting time to introduce her fellow teachers to her special education program.

By lunchtime, the in-service session had been going on for nearly 3 hours. Looking around at the faces of the faculty, Ms. Lewis knew that one more lecture might not be well received. When the principal called her up, Ms. Lewis began her "pitch." Ms. Lewis, joined by Mr. Boeing, began by inviting the rest of the staff to take part in a disability simulation. Dressed in blindfolds, splints, and earplugs, teachers made their best attempts to navigate the school campus. Ms. Lewis chuckled as she witnessed the teachers gradually begin to understand the challenges presented by the environment. She explained to the teachers that the barriers at King High School weren't only physical but also attitudinal. She then shared with the group the numerous strengths that each of her students possessed and challenged the teachers to find ways of allowing the students to demonstrate those strengths in the general classroom environment.

Next, she talked excitedly about the benefits that general education students might receive: increased academic performance, more positive attitudes, improvements in self-concept, and new friendships. Dispelling the myth that teachers would have to focus much of their instructional time on the few students with diverse abilities, she shared with the teachers the instructional support she would be able to provide to them. Mr. Boeing then discussed some of the possibilities he saw for students in his classroom.

Back in her classroom, Ms. Lewis wondered whether the activity had been effective. She knew that having Mr. Boeing join her in speaking was a good idea as teachers appeared to appreciate hearing from a general educator. She knew that today was just a first step, but she hoped she had planted ideas in the heads of the faculty. Her next step would be to sow the idea in the heads of students.

"Before taking students to a worksite, such as a store, I talk with the employers about them and let the employer talk to the employees. Then I take the students to the worksite to meet the employer. Then I allow the employer to decide if he wants us to work in his store."

Teacher
Warren County High School
McMinnville, Tennessee

3.2.2 Stressing Students' Strengths

It's up to us! We have the responsibility to provide school and community members with information regarding the strengths and skills of students with differing abilities. Otherwise, they may never know because they are not likely to search for this information on their own. This is a great loss because by becoming aware of students' strengths, people are more likely to be accepting of differences and to have more realistic expectations of students who have different abilities.

"Promote your students' abilities to other employees. Display enthusiasm and professionalism toward your students. I have found that when I treat my students with respect and fairness, other employees observe this and will usually follow the same pattern."

Teacher
Whites Creek High School
Nashville, Tennessee

Starting Up:

- Point out to general education teachers, employers, and community members the positive aspects of a student's work and behavior. For example, a student with a physical disability may shake while she works but is a great problem solver and can work independently on tasks that require complex thinking skills.

- Help potential employers become aware of a student's skill repertoire and individual ways of performing job tasks by showing a video of the student's past job performance. For example, an employer might not know how good a student with a visual disability is at using a computer to type business reports.

- Give students a chance to demonstrate their competence by participating in a variety of events in the community. For example, as a member of a community theater group, a student could take tickets, pass out programs, or seat members of the audience as they arrive at the theater to watch a play.

Focusing on students' strengths is consistent with the philosophy and research supporting the IDEA Amendments of 1997. The amendments state that education is more effective when teachers hold high expectations for students. In addition, in developing the IEP, the IEP team is *required* by IDEA to consider students' strengths and to develop strategies for enhancing their education.

How to Do It:

- At regular meetings with work supervisors, stress the unique strengths of students, such as a positive attitude or taking initiative. When students are experiencing challenges, such as controlling their anger or increasing their accuracy on the job, discuss with the supervisor ways to modify the task or the environment to increase opportunities for success.

- Allow a student's work to speak for itself. Encourage teachers and work supervisors to observe the student successfully completing various tasks. Provide a video or photos of the student while working if teachers or supervisors cannot be present at the worksite. A picture really is worth a thousand words.

- By taking extra time to really get to know the students with whom you are working, you will be better prepared to convey their strengths that may not be readily apparent to employers at first glance. For example, an administrative assistant may notice that a student types much more slowly than the other secretaries in her office. You can point out, however, that the student makes considerably fewer errors than her co-workers and that all of the supervisors request that she type their reports whenever possible.

- Remember, a number of different qualities come together to form an excellent employee. Although a student may initially perform certain job tasks at a slower rate, he may have had perfect attendance at a previous job, worked marvelously with others, and conveyed a warm and positive attitude to customers. Articulate these strengths to potential employers.

Too often, teachers and professionals who work with students with diverse abilities may fail to stress students' strengths, instead focusing on their weaknesses and needs. This may contribute to students' having low self-esteem and little self-determination to excel inside or outside the classroom. In addition to sharing a student's strengths with school and community members, make certain that the students themselves hear your encouragement.

Cross-reference: "Strategies for Identifying and Promoting Students' Strengths" (Chapter 6)

Case Study 3.6   Letting the Community Know

Ms. Lewis's first semester as a teacher had been quite challenging, but she was extremely pleased with the progress she was beginning to see. Her fellow teachers and administrators had really gotten excited about the programs that she had proposed. Two general education teachers were already working with a number of students to put together a lunch buddy program. The ball had begun rolling! Ms. Lewis knew, however, that her students would need to be prepared for life in the community after graduation. In addition, the community would need to be prepared to receive these graduates.

As Ms. Lewis thought about the difficulties that students with diverse abilities frequently face in finding employment after high school, she realized that she would need to provide job-training opportunities before her students graduated. She created a simple flier that described her students and the types of services they could provide. After distributing it to more than 20 local businesses, she waited for the calls to pour in. The phone never rang!

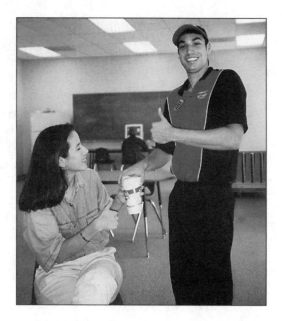

"Acknowledge the student's efforts toward a goal. Stress the issue that all individuals possess both strengths and limitations in varying mixtures and to different degrees."
Teacher
Melrose High School
Memphis, Tennessee

Ms. Lewis was baffled. Why weren't businesses knocking down her door to gain access to student volunteers? Why weren't they eager to have her students as trainees? In talking with other teachers, Ms. Lewis realized that it wasn't a lack of work that prevented employers from calling her but rather a lack of experience with her students. Whereas students and school staff had frequent opportunities to see students with differing abilities demonstrate their strengths and abilities, community members had fewer chances to be involved with these students. Undeterred, Ms. Lewis resolved to start out a little slower. She would begin by involving just one worksite in her community-based program for her students. Once established, she would use that as a springboard for involving other community businesses in her transition program.

3.2.3   Encouraging Community Involvement

For students with differing abilities, simply possessing the right set of job or daily living skills may not be enough to ensure their full participation in community life after high school. Opportunities for demonstrating and putting those skills to use must be made available. However, community members are often unaware of the need to create such opportunities. Introducing community members to students through visits and participation in transition programs will show the potential contributions these students can make to the community.

Teacher-Proven Practices:

- Encourage potential employers to visit already established community job-training sites. For example, in your own town, there may be a chain of drugstores or supermarkets that have been especially successful at hiring students from transition programs. Seeing the success of a business's job-training program might be an incentive for employers to consider one at their location.

- Remember that students who are currently attending high school will be a community's future employers and leaders. Be sure that students from general and special education classes have frequent opportunities to interact with each other and develop social relationships. Students will become better citizens in their communities as they learn from their interactions with each other.

- Invite community members to attend school programs and view the types of training you are providing. They may discover that your students are well trained in their particular area of business. Try developing informational programs about your students that can be delivered at various meetings attended by community members.

Regularly involving students in community functions and activities makes the task of promoting acceptance even easier. Having students take visible roles at public events allows community members to see the contributions of students with diverse abilities without having to come to the classroom. A student could serve as an usher at a city play, serve on a neighborhood cleanup committee, or work at the local Chamber of Commerce.

Starting Up:

- Make a list of potential participants who will be involved in ongoing public awareness activities. Include people such as family members, representatives of local business organizations that have successfully hired students, or local talk show hosts. Host a luncheon prepared by students during which you brainstorm with participants how to increase public awareness of your transition program.

- Make initial contacts with community members to inform them about public awareness programs through the use of introduction letters and local newspapers and radio and television stations.

- Solicit information from community leaders concerning the needs of local businesses. You may find that employee shortages exist in certain areas of the job market. By training your students to perform these much-needed services, you will increase the likelihood that they will find meaningful full-time employment upon graduation.

- Conduct regular information presentations with community members. A slide show or videotape can be a useful tool to communicate the goals and objectives of the training program and the skills of the students involved.

3.2.4   Using Technology and Media to Increase Public Support and Awareness

Technology and multimedia have become a way of life. Use a variety of new forms of communication, such as the World Wide Web, to help promote diversity awareness.

Case Study 3.7   Going Public

The students huddled anxiously around the television. The commercial break was almost over, which meant that they would be on next. Ms. Lewis watched the excitement from the back of the classroom, glad so many of her students would appear on the program. She was thankful for the television station's willingness to showcase her job-training program during the "Community Happenings" segment of the midday news. Although only a few minutes in length, the program would feature students working around town, brief interviews with employers, and an invitation for other businesses to participate in the program. Ms. Lewis was certain that this type of publicity would open up new opportunities for her students.

Television, newspapers, radio, and the World Wide Web are some of the media available to increase public support and awareness of students with diverse abilities. It's time to "spread the word!"

Teacher-Proven Practices:

- Many television and radio stations broadcast community calendars that highlight community programs and events. Call them well in advance so that they can include events that are taking place in your classroom.

- Talk to your local television or radio news station about doing a brief segment on your program. Many news stations broadcast human interest programs.

- Use the local newspaper to thank employers who have supported your program. Employers will appreciate the exposure, and other businesses may wish to join in.

- Solicit community support through articles in the school newspaper or parent newsletter. Parents are excellent resources for program ideas.

- Develop a World Wide Web site for your job-training program. Include clips of your students at work and in the community. Your students and their peer buddies can help you.

- Design for potential employers a brochure that includes photos of your students at work, a list of the jobs and services they can perform, and benefits for employers. Some employers may be surprised to find out what your students can offer them.

Using technology and media not only is an effective way to promote acceptance of your program but also is supported by the law. An intent of the IDEA Amendments of 1997 is to ensure that appropriate technology, media products, and activities are accessible to students, parents, and personnel and are integrated in the educational process. And, by using innovative technology and media, you are modeling technologically adept behavior.

The task of building community support for a school's transition program can be overwhelming for just one person. Fortunately, many avenues exist for getting the word out. Television, newspapers, radio, and the World Wide Web provide effective means of informing the public about the contributions that students with diverse abilities can make to the community.

Work, school, and community environments may not be accepting environments for individuals with diverse abilities. Individual differences may not be understood or appreciated. Fortunately, specific skills can be taught to students and others to increase the likelihood that such environments will become more accepting of diversity.

3-3 TEACHING SKILLS THAT SUPPORT ACCEPTANCE

3.3.1 Teaching Skills to Students

Without having work or social skills that are expected within an environment, students are more likely to feel isolated in their work or community environments, possibly lose their jobs, or perhaps not feel a part of their school environments. With careful planning, however, you can target those skills that are important to a student's acceptance in the workplace and community and among her peers at school.

How to Do It:

- Provide frequent opportunities for community-based employment training. Students can often learn expected skills easier by observing others perform them in the actual environment. For example, by observing a co-worker taking orders from customers at a restaurant or a supervisor doing the billing at a bank, a student can see expected behaviors in action. Then, he can try the behaviors and get corrective feedback, if needed.

- Teach accepted social-related work behaviors to students by modeling appropriate social interactions with co-workers. When you are in the community, model appropriate social interactions, such as greeting others and being friendly in stores, banks, and other businesses.

- Observe how co-workers request assistance at a worksite. Then, teach the student similar ways to request assistance, if needed, to complete a job task. For example, in some work environments, co-workers may ask each other for help. At other jobs, it may be more appropriate to ask a supervisor or administrative assistant.

- Teach students a range of skills that can be used across a variety of environments. Remember that social acceptance requires more than simply being able to "do a job." Be sure you also teach related skills, such as social interaction, independent living, and recreation/leisure skills, because there's a lot more to life than just work!

- Provide skill training in inclusive environments, such as general education classrooms, community programs, and worksites. Peers in these environments should be considered the accepted standard in terms of their dress code and social interaction skills.

Cross-references: Teaching Skills that Need Strengthening (6-4) and Teaching Social Interaction Skills (9-4)

Evaluating Outcomes:

Skill Training—Teaching Grooming

Hygiene skills, such as dressing and grooming, are critical to helping students meet expectations for personal appearance within any environment. Make sure when you teach these skills that they are consistent with those expected in an environment. For example, students should follow the dress code in their workplace or in the gym where they work out. It's also critical to have parents reinforce appropriate hygiene skills at home. The following is an example of how to teach one important self-care skill: grooming. A blank, reproducible form is included in the appendix.

1. Identify the target behavior (e.g., "Grooming and hygiene skills: Joe will shave his face before coming to school").

2. Determine the student's current level of functioning (e.g., "Joe is able and knows how to shave. He just seems to forget to do so on a regular basis").

3. Develop a plan for teaching the skill(s) (e.g., "Picture prompts and verbal reinforcement will be used in teaching the skill").

4. Monitor the student's progress in meeting the goal, and modify the plan as necessary (e.g., "Collect continuous data to make instructional decisions/changes when necessary").

An example data collection system follows. (For other data collection systems, see Observing and Collecting Data [6-1].)

Data Collection System

Student: Joe Wethers   **Date:** October   **Observer:** Ms. Lauderdale

Behavior: Joe will shave his face before coming to school.

Date	Yes or no	Comments
10/2	N	Said he didn't have razors—took him to store to purchase more
10/3	N	Joe said he forgot—gave him verbal reminders just before he left
10/4	Y	Great job!
10/5	—	Absent today
10/6	N	Said he forgot again! Gave him picture card to remind him
10/9	Y	Looked good! Joe was proud!
10/10	Y	
10/11	N	Said he ran out of time before his ride came
10/12	Y	Great job!
10/13	Y	Great job!

Y = Shaved before school   **N =** Did not shave before school

Form 3.2.   Data Collection System for teaching grooming.

3.3.2 Teaching Skills to Others

Teachers, students, employers, or community members may have had few opportunities to interact with students with diverse abilities. Often, people initially are unsure how to interact with people who they feel may be different from themselves. You can help by modeling appropriate interaction, increasing opportunities for interaction, and providing basic instruction in social interaction skills. By interacting with students with differing abilities, people will begin to see that *all* people are more alike than different.

"By teaching students in the community, the community begins to accept their diverse abilities and to work with them. The students in our high school have learned more about themselves by working with students with disabilities."
Teacher
Rutledge High School
Rutledge, Tennessee

Starting Up:

- Begin a peer buddy program that provides general education students an opportunity to learn new skills by working directly with their peers. Peer buddies report that they have learned much about themselves and how to interact with others by participating in these programs.

- Help other teaching staff plan an in-service session that informs community members and employers about interacting with people with diverse abilities. You may find that some of the participants volunteer to become involved with your students as mentors.

- Offer training and information regarding behavior support procedures to peers and parents of students with diverse abilities. For example, peer buddies may need to know what to do if a student presents challenging behavior, such as aggression, or how to encourage a student who is shy to hold his head up and talk.

Cross-reference: Peer-Delivered Social Skills Programs (9.4.3)

"'Peer tutoring, huh?' That was my first reaction to this class. The first day of school, I received my schedule and didn't know what the class was about. Of course, I had heard

Evaluating Outcomes:

Beginning a Peer Buddy Program

Peer buddy programs provide daily or weekly class times when participating students in general and special education may interact. By interacting and providing support, general education peers help students with diverse abilities become actively involved in the mainstream of high school life. Participating general education students, in turn, report that they are building new friendships and learning new social interaction skills. They also say that they have increased their appreciation of diversity, improved their communication skills, and improved their understanding of themselves and others. Pages 60–61 contain seven steps that have been used to develop the Metropolitan Nashville Peer Buddy Program in 11 Nashville, Tennessee, high schools. You can adapt them to start a program in your own high school. Remember to evaluate your progress by checking off each step and corresponding task as you go. (A blank, reproducible form is included in the appendix.)

about the class from former peer tutors but didn't know what to expect. Like many others, I had already made my assumptions about the class. Since that time, I have come to realize that these assumptions were incorrect. I thought that the Life Skills students would be helpless, but this is not the case. As the first couple of weeks went by, I began to see that many of the students were not much different from me. A lot of the students enjoy many of the same games and activities that I do, such as Bingo, UNO, Connect Four, and even basketball. As time has gone by, the majority, if not all, of the students and I have become good friends, especially the boys. I often begin basic conversations with them as with any other person on subjects or events that I feel we might have in common. Peer tutoring has been a wonderful experience for me. It has allowed me to make new friends who have slight differences, but with more similarities than you could imagine!"

Peer Buddy
Maplewood High School
Nashville, Tennessee

"Participating in a peer buddy program has been one of the most insightful experiences about life and about myself. I have learned that *every* student is unique, so you have to treat each person differently just as you would anybody else."

Peer Buddy
Glencliff High School
Nashville, Tennessee

Seven Steps to Starting a Peer Buddy Program

Step 1: Develop a one-credit course

☐ Incorporate into your school's curriculum a peer tutoring course that allows peer buddies to spend at least one period each day with their partners in special education.

☐ Begin building a base of support with the administration, guidance personnel, and teachers in your school for the inclusion of students receiving special education services in general education activities.

☐ Follow the established procedures of the local and state educational agencies when you apply for the new course offering.

☐ Include the course description in your school's schedule of classes.

Step 2: Recruit peer buddies

☐ Actively recruit peer buddies during the first year. After that, peer buddies will recruit for you.

☐ Include announcements, posters, articles in the school newspaper and PTA newsletter, videotapes on the school's closed-circuit television, and peer buddies speaking in school clubs and classes.

☐ Present information about the new program at a faculty meeting.

☐ Start slowly while you establish the course expectations.

Step 3: Screen and match students

☐ Have guidance counselors refer students who have interest, good attendance, and adequate grades.

☐ Arrange for students to interview with the special education teachers.

☐ Have students provide information regarding their past experience with students with diverse abilities and about clubs or activities that they are involved in and that their partners could join.

☐ Allow students to observe in the classroom to learn about the role of a peer buddy and whether they would be an appropriate match for the class.

Form 3.3.   Seven Steps to Starting a Peer Buddy Program. (From "They are my best friends": Peer buddies promote inclusion in high school, by Hughes, C., Guth, C., Hall, S., Presley, J., Dye, M., & Byers, C., *TEACHING Exceptional Children, 31,* 1999, [5], 32–37. Copyright 1999 by The Council for Exceptional Children. Adapted with permission.)

(continued)

Form 3.3. *(continued)*

Step 4: Teach peer buddies to use instructional strategies

☐ Model the use of prompting and reinforcement techniques.

☐ Conduct a peer buddy orientation that includes the concept of "people first," disability awareness, communication strategies, and suggested activities.

☐ Communicate teachers' expectations for the peer buddy course including attendance and grading policies.

☐ Provide suggestions for dealing with inappropriate behavior, setting limits, and modifying general education curricula.

Step 5: Evaluate the program

☐ Schedule observations and feedback sessions with peer buddies to address their questions or concerns.

☐ Provide feedback on their interaction skills, time management, use of positive reinforcement, and activities engaged in with their partners.

☐ Have peer buddies keep a daily journal of their activities and reflections, which should be reviewed weekly by the classroom teacher.

☐ Establish a Peer Buddy Club, which allows students to share experiences and ideas as well as gives the teacher an opportunity to offer ongoing training and feedback.

Step 6: Hold a Lunch Bunch

☐ Invite peer buddies to join students in special education for lunch in the cafeteria.

☐ Encourage the peer buddies to invite their general education friends to join the group, increasing social contacts for their partners.

☐ Remind general education students who, because of class conflicts, are unable to enroll in the course to join the Lunch Bunch.

Step 7: Establish an advisory board

☐ Develop an advisory board that includes students (peer buddies and partners), students' parents, participating general and special education teachers, administrators, and guidance counselors.

☐ Include community representatives to expand the Peer Buddy Program to community-based activities, such as work experiences.

☐ Meet at least once each semester to obtain insight and suggestions for evaluating and improving the program. Thank all members for their participation.

3-4   INCREASING STUDENTS' SOCIAL PARTICIPATION

3.4.1   At School

When students with varying abilities are isolated from each other, everybody loses! Students in general and special education alike lose the chance to develop social acceptance and appreciation of others. When students with diverse abilities have opportunities to interact frequently throughout the day and participate in *all* aspects of school and everyday life, we ensure that *all* students will lead more socially fulfilling lives.

How to Do It:

- Use as many supports as necessary to include students fully in general education classes. For example, have a student enroll in a culinary arts class with a peer buddy for social support. Without support, a student may be physically present but not socially included (see Chapter 5).

"Provide varied opportunities for students to be involved in the community—teaching social interaction, independent living, and recreation/leisure skills. This is the best way to increase their social acceptance and participation in everyday life."
Teacher
Greeneville High School
Greeneville, Tennessee

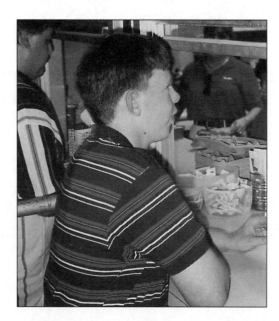

- Make sure that students with diverse abilities are involved in *all* school activities in which other students participate, such as assemblies, pep rallies, and field trips. Participating with a peer buddy can help students "mix" together socially rather than simply "tag along."

- Encourage students with differing abilities to become "peer tutors" in their skill areas. For example, a student may be especially knowledgeable about special effects in movies or an expert on the saxophone. Encourage students to participate in general education activities on the basis of their interests, skills, and preferences.

- Include peer buddies in off-campus community-based instruction, such as shopping at the mall or working. Doing so will embed social interaction opportunities for all students throughout the school day.

- Parents can provide information about hobbies or interests that are seen only by them. Encourage parents to get involved in promoting students' social participation with peers. Have parents provide transportation so that a student and peer buddy can attend games together. Doing so also allows parents to meet a student's friends.

Teacher-Proven Practices:

- Physically placing students in "mainstreamed" environments is not enough. A student may be in an integrated environment but have no social participation at all. Create opportunities, such as cooperative learning projects and peer buddy programs, that promote all students' active involvement in academic and social activities.

- Hold a discussion or question-and-answer session with general education peers about how they can increase their opportunities for social interaction with students with diverse abilities. For example, encourage general education students to help students with disabilities get involved on sports teams as a player, equipment manager, coach, or spectator.

- Give all students important, meaningful tasks to do in general education classrooms. Never just give a student "something to do." Find out your students' interests and strengths, such as public speaking or proofreading articles for the school newspaper, and encourage participation in those areas.

Cross-references: Increasing Students' Social Interactions (9-1), Promoting Peer Involvement (9-2), and Increasing Opportunities for Social Interaction (9-3)

3.4.2   At Work and in the Community

Promoting high levels of participation and involvement with co-workers increases an employee's chances of successful long-term employment and personal satisfaction, both on and off the job. Encourage and support students in becoming involved with other workers on the job and outside work, too.

"The brick masonry teacher took a student to work with him on his job after school. Now the student has a job and is earning over minimum wages!"

Teacher
Mitchell High School
Memphis, Tennessee

Full participation in school, at work, and in the community is the letter and the spirit of the law. Section 601 of the IDEA Amendments of 1997 states, "Disability is a natural part of the human experience and in no way diminishes the right of individuals to participate in or contribute to society. Improving educational results for children with disabilities is an essential element of our national policy of ensuring equality of opportunity, full participation, independent living, and economic self-sufficiency for individuals with disabilities."

Starting Up:

- Encourage students to attend company picnics and/or other work-related social activities. If they are hesitant, an interested co-worker could pick them up and accompany them to the event.

- Arrange for students to take breaks with their co-workers at work. You may need to prompt students to talk to their co-workers. Or try asking a willing co-worker to sit down at the same table with a student and start a conversation. Getting a game such as UNO going in the break room is another way to encourage social participation.

- Help students get involved in the community through participation in activities at community parks and recreation centers. Encourage parents to provide transportation and get peer buddies involved. You could even start an after-school program, such as swimming at the YMCA.

- Provide opportunities for students to sample as many worksites as possible before they graduate from high school. Remind them to consider the opportunities for social interaction that occur at a worksite when they make decisions about where to work after graduation.

How to Do It:

- Set up social opportunities during or after work hours to include *all* employees. For example, have basketball shoot-outs in a company's gym during lunch or an after-work social hour at a local pizza place.

- Include peers in *all* activities in which a student is involved throughout the day. For example, at work, integrate students into production teams with their co-workers. In the community, include peer buddies in a student's activities to model appropriate behaviors and provide support when learning new skills, such as using an automated teller machine.

Cross-reference: "Strategies that Promote Social Interaction" (Chapter 9)

Evaluating Outcomes:

Observing Students' Social Participation

How much are students *really* participating in social activities throughout the day? It's important to know because it may be that they are simply in proximity of their peers but not interacting socially with them. Here are some ways to evaluate how much students actually interact with each other in "inclusive environments":

- Observe a student's opportunity for and participation in community activities during a 1-month period using a simple tally sheet (see page 67). A blank, reproducible form can be found in the appendix.

- Keep a record of a student's attendance in a journalism, computer, or social studies class. Check with a peer buddy to determine the extent to which the student is participating in classroom activities and interacting with classmates.

- Ask a student to identify the social activities in which she participates outside school on a regular basis. Also, ask about which activities she would like to do but has not had the chance to do. Ask for parents' input as well.

- Use interest surveys and activity sampling to pinpoint students' interests. Then, on the basis of students' interests, arrange community and employment opportunities that allow students to work and interact with their general education peers, co-workers, and peers in the community.

Community Activity Participation Form

Student: Antonio London   **Month:** April

Activity	Monday	Tuesday	Wednesday	Thursday	Friday	Weekends	Total
Exercise at the YMCA		III				II	5
Church activities			III			IIII	7
Volunteer at nursing home				II			2
Softball league	III			I			4
Shopping at the mall					I	II	3
Movies with friends					II		2
Grocery shopping		IIII					4
Concerts/fairs				I	I	II	4
Other	I		I			II	4

Form 3.4.   Community Activities Form.

REFERENCES

American with Disabilities Act (ADA) of 1990, PL 101-336, 42 U.S.C. §§ 12101 *et seq.*

Developmental Disabilities Act of 1984, PL 98-527, 98 §§ 2662–2685.

Hughes, C., Guth, C., Hall, S., Presley, J., Dye, M., & Byers, C. (1999). Inclusion on the high school level: The Metropolitan Nashville Peer Buddy Program. *TEACHING Exceptional Children, 31*(5), 32–37.

Hughes, C., Lorden, S.W., Scott, S.V., Hwang, B., Derer, K.R., Rodi, M.S., Pitkin, S.E., & Godshall, J.C. (1998). Identification and validation of critical conversation sills. *Journal of Applied Behavior Analysis, 31,* 431–446.

Individuals with Disabilities Education Act Amendments of 1997, PL 105-17, 20 U.S.C. §§ 1400 *et seq.*

C h a p t e r   4

Strategies for Increasing Environmental Support

OVERVIEW

For many students, the success of their transition to adult life depends on the amount of environmental support they receive. Fortunately, most environments provide a variety of supports that exist naturally! When teachers, employment specialists, and others learn to identify this support, they can begin to match it to the needs of individual students. Whether it is a clock that signals breaktime, a sign that reminds employees to wash their hands, or aisle markers that tell a student where to find items in a drugstore, environmental supports help a student achieve greater independence on the job, in the classroom, and around the community. The first step in identifying environmental support is to visit a site and conduct an environmental survey of naturally occurring supports. Additional information gained through interviews with important others can be added to build a support plan for the student. Teachers, job coaches, and other service providers may also need to identify ways of modifying the environment to increase support, such as by propping a door open for wheelchair users or by providing shoes that do not require tying for individuals who have limited fine motor coordination. Environmental support may be promoted by increasing community awareness and interagency collaboration and by increasing access to services and resources. In doing so, we can provide students with a supportive environment that encourages rather than discourages their success!

This chapter contains 5 main groups and 10 subgroups of strategies that teachers may use to increase environmental support for a student. It includes such strategies as conducting site visits and observations, communicating environmental support needs, developing environmental support plans, gaining access to existing environmental support, and modifying the environment.

Environmental supports can be something as simple as a naturally occurring cue in a student's environment, such as a street sign or clock, that can be used to support her in initiating and completing an expected and desired behavior.

Case Study 4.1   Elisha Goes to College

Ms. Earndale's view:

Ms. Earndale had many dreams for her daughter—a paying job, a circle of friends, an apartment in the community—but college was definitely not one of them. Elisha had been an outgoing and active student while in high school, but college would be a different story. Elisha had always received such wonderful support from a constellation of people: classmates, peer buddies, general and special education teachers, and a variety of service providers. Where would her support come from in college? Besides, higher education was all about academics and intellectual pursuits. Wouldn't a student with physical and learning disabilities simply feel out of place?

Elisha's view:

If you were to ask Elisha, she would tell you that she absolutely loves her job! Working in the student union of the local community college allows her to earn money *and* hang out with her new friends, two of her favorite activities. Sitting in her wheelchair behind the coffee counter, she is famous for providing the best cup of java on campus! Still, Elisha wants more than anything to enroll in classes along with her friends. As with most new endeavors, many questions swirl around in Elisha's head: How would I find my classes? What should I do when I get there? Would the classrooms accommodate my wheelchair?

Rachel Miranda's view:

Rachel Miranda was so proud of how independent Elisha had become at her job at the community college after just 3 short months. As Elisha's transition teacher, Rachel had worked hard to find opportunities for Elisha to be successful in the community. So when Elisha mentioned that she would like to take classes along with the friends she had made at the college, Rachel thought it was a fantastic idea. As Rachel began to brainstorm ideas for including Elisha in community college courses, she focused her thoughts on ways of providing supports that were as typical as possible. She realized that having a special assistant in class would be awkward for Elisha. Besides, so many potential environmental supports were already available to Elisha. There were signs in the bookstore indicating which text to purchase for a class, maps that could guide Elisha around campus, and friends to help adapt assignments for her. In fact, if they tapped into many of the supports that were already available within the campus environment, they would have to add very few additional supports that would be atypical.

4-1   CONDUCTING SITE VISITS AND OBSERVATIONS

4.1.1   Conducting Environmental Assessments

For many students, an amazing world of opportunities opens up upon their graduation from high school. With careful planning and support, you

"Surveying the particular environment will help you identify what resources may be available to the student. Then, use these resources to help support a student."
Teacher
Maplewood High School
Nashville, Tennessee

can help ensure that these opportunities will be available to *all* students! Surveying those environments in which your students will live and work after graduation will help you identify supports that will help your students gain access to these opportunities.

Starting Up:

- Begin by visiting and observing each environment in which the student will participate. Be a detective; your job is to uncover all signs of support, such as friendly co-workers, as well as possible barriers requiring modification.

- Complete an environmental survey, such as the Job Analysis Survey (Form 4.1) that follows, to identify the demands of an environment and its potential supports (see pages 76–79). You can then check to see how well a student is doing in relation to these demands.

- Prioritize the demands required at a job, community site, or home, and place them in order of importance. Focus on the most critical demands first. For example, if it's important to be neat and clean on the job and a student's hygiene causes people to leave the room running, then you probably should focus on hygiene first!

- Ask parents, employers, and others about the unique requirements of a particular environment, many of which may not be apparent at first glance. It may turn out that you thought production rate was the most important consideration at a worksite, but instead accuracy really is most important.

"Finding time to visit worksites and community settings is difficult. Because I don't have time to visit all areas and write down my findings, I develop a checklist of environmental features that assistants or others can use to observe."

Teacher
Gallatin High School
Gallatin, Tennessee

Teacher-Proven Practices:

- Remember, you don't always have to develop environmental surveys on your own. In fact, a number of published assessments already exist that you may or may not need to modify. (Look in the Assessment section of the Resources in the appendix for more information.)

- Employment, residential, and recreational staff may be unaware of restricted accessibility that exists in their environments, such as narrow hallways or stairs. By sharing the results of your environmental survey, you may discover that many businesses or organizations are very willing to make modifications.

- While you are conducting a task analysis of a required skill, jot down potential sources of support for each step of the task. For example, a fast-food restaurant may have pictures of salad choices on a menu, or tables in a restaurant may be numbered.

Evaluating Outcomes:

Job Analysis Survey

Throughout high school, students with diverse abilities should be provided with opportunities to sample a variety of different job experiences. Once a potential worksite has been identified for a student, the next important task is to acquire information about the environmental, social, and task characteristics of the worksite. By identifying potential supports available in the work environment, we can increase our students' opportunities for independence and success on the job. Furthermore, by pinpointing these supports early, teachers and job coaches can incorporate them into on-the-job training from the beginning. The following steps should be followed when conducting a Job Analysis Survey using Form 4.1:

- Begin by identifying several potential worksites, taking into consideration factors such as distance from home or school, the number of students that the site can accommodate, the number and variety of jobs available, and the projected availability of such jobs after graduation.

- After identifying several initial training sites, select a site that differs from what your students have experienced previously in terms of the task, social, and environmental characteristics. This will allow students to have a wide variety of job experiences and enable them to find a job that matches both their preferences and their skills.

- Use the Job Analysis Survey (Form 4.1) to record information regarding the task, social, and environmental characteristics of the site and sources for support. (An example of a completed form can be found for Joseph, the man in Case Study 4.2.)

- Information for the Job Analysis Survey can be obtained from several sources. For example, managers or immediate supervisors can readily share job characteristics and expectations. Observing other employees performing the job can also provide important information. Finally, job coaches and teachers can perform the job themselves.

Case Study 4.2   Joseph Gets a Job

Joseph, a recent graduate of Woodcock High School, has been a student in the district's community-based transition classroom for a little more than 5 months. After sampling several jobs around the community, Joseph indicated that he had an interest in working at a local grocery store. He just seemed to get excited every time he went shopping or whenever he "faced cans" at his job-training site at the store. In preparation for job placement and training, Joseph's job coach, Emily, spent one morning talking with and observing employees work on a variety of tasks at Donaldson's Food & Drug Store. Next, she completed a Job Analysis Survey, noting many of the potential supports that would be available. Finally, she had the store manager look through the survey, filling in missing information. The process allowed her to identify clearly the store manager's expectations while identifying supports that would provide Joseph with a greater opportunity for success and independence. The next page contains a sample Job Analysis Survey Form. A blank, reproducible form can be found in the appendix.

Case Study 4.3   Finding Support in the Environment: One Teacher's Story

"When looking for sources of support for a student, you must check all environments: school, home, and work. At school, you must check that the classroom is located near other general education classes, the lunchroom, and break area. The home will require home visits. While you are visiting the home, find out what is important to the family. For example, our community is known as the 'Nursery Capital of the World.' If a student's family is in the nursery business, find out whether the family wants this for their child and whether this is what the child wants.

"Also, you must check to determine whether the home is accessible to the child. For example, one student requires an electric wheelchair at school for transportation, but the home is not accessible. In this case, get vocational rehabil-

Job Analysis Survey

Worksite: Donaldson's Food & Drug Store   **Date:** November 17

Basic Information

1. General job type or position: Stock person

2. Job tasks involved in the position: Examining shelves for empty slots, reading shelf tags, writing down low-count/missing items, locating items in storeroom, reading box labels, loading boxes on cart, cutting open boxes, matching items to shelf tags, stocking items on shelves, blocking shelves, breaking down boxes, and returning waste and materials to proper places

Three most time-consuming job tasks: Locating items in storeroom, loading boxes, stocking items

3. Worksite location and access to public transportation: Located on Reed St., in Millner Shopping Center (walking distance from the classroom). During the day, Joseph's job coach will transport him back and forth to the site 2 days per week. Joseph will also be able to use the public bus system. There is a bus stop in front of the store and within 1 mile of Joseph's home. As the distance between his home and the store is not large, a taxi would also be a financially reasonable option.

Task Characteristics

Job task requirements: Recognize areas in need of stocking, basic reading/writing abilities (or alternative way of recording low-count and missing items), means for reaching high shelves, understanding of storeroom organization, lifting boxes and placing them on cart, matching item numbers and names to shelf numbers/names, placing items on shelf in neat manner, reorganizing messy shelves, locating out-of-place items, breaking down boxes, cleaning up area, initiating work, and asking for help

General mobility requirements: Method for moving up and down aisles, method for reaching high shelves (through reaching or assistive device), method for reaching low shelves, ability to use arms and hands, method for lifting boxes of light to heavy weight and moving them to cart, method for pulling cart from storeroom to floor

Physical demands—gross motor: Bending down, reaching up, balancing, moving up and down aisles, lifting full and broken-down boxes, pushing boxes aside in storeroom, pulling all items simultaneously to front of shelf, opening large boxes, and pushing carts

Physical demands—fine motor: Using pencil/paper to record items, using a box cutter, opening boxes, placing items on/removing items from shelves (grasping), stacking items, shuffling items on shelves, and balancing on balls of feet

Length of work tasks: Stocking shelves is a continuous process. The length of time to finish isolated tasks varies depending on the items being stocked, the condition of the storeroom, and the day of the week (trucks deliver inventory on Tuesday and Thursday). For a given aisle, time required to

Form 4.1.   Job Analysis Survey for Donaldson's Food & Drug Store. (From Renzaglia, A., & Hutchins, M. [1995]. Materials developed for *A model for longitudinal vocational programming for students with moderate and severe disabilities.* Grant funded by the U.S. Department of Education, Office of Special Education and Rehabilitation Services; adapted by permission.)

identify missing items is about 8 minutes. Time required to locate and gather items for that aisle is about 15 minutes. Time required to stock those items is as much as 40 minutes. Cleanup takes 5 minutes.

Variability of daily job tasks: Although the routine is generally the same from day to day, the items to be stocked vary considerably each day. Certain items, however, must be restocked at least every day (milk, eggs, specials, etc.). Variability is highly determined by the section of the store to which the employee is assigned.

Problem-solving requirements: Worker must have ability to recognize which shelves need additional items, to determine how to shift items in storeroom to retrieve boxes on the bottom of stacks, to determine stocking pattern for individual shelves, and to decide what should be done with extra items that shelves can't accommodate; method for working quickly without damaging items; ability to stack boxes on cart without crushing them; and ability to creatively reorganize shelves in appropriate ways.

Production rate requirements: Worker must be able to work continuously on-task for the duration of the shift. Although variability makes it difficult to attach an exact number on production rate, the average worker completes approximately 20 boxes per hour. Employer's main concern is that empty shelves and specials are restocked immediately and that old stock is put out prior to new stock arriving.

Work product quality requirements: All items should be stocked until shelves are full, all shelves should be blocked (all items pulled forward so shelves appear full), all items must match shelf tags, all shelves should have a neat appearance and design, all materials should be returned upon completion, and storeroom should be kept neat and orderly.

Continuous working requirements: Worker will continuously stock shelves, except for during designated work breaks and trips to storeroom to reload pull-cart. Worker will continuously place items on shelf until each box is emptied.

Task-Related Characteristics

Co-worker presence/task-related contact: Except for brief interactions with other employees (particularly other stock persons), the worker will work alone. Other employees are almost always within sight or hearing distance and will frequently walk past the area in which the student is working. Most interaction with other stock persons occurs in the stockroom.

Nontask-related social contacts while working: Occasionally, another stock person will be working on the same aisle as the student, during which nontask-related interactions are appropriate (as long as it is not overly loud or of an inappropriate subject). Student will also have breaks during which he will likely interact with other store employees.

Social atmosphere of worksite: As the worker will be working the majority of the time on the floor of the store, he will be in the presence of scores of customers who are shopping and a few other employees as they work (often stock people and courtesy clerks).

(continued)

Form 4.1.   *(continued)*

Interactions with customers: Interactions with store customers are likely to be frequent. He will have to move out of the way of many customers and will probably be asked to help others locate particular items.

Supervisory contact: Initially, the job coach/trainer will work closely with the student, gradually fading his/her presence and checking in on student about every 10 to 15 minutes. His actual job supervisor will be another, more experienced stock person, who will check on his work approximately every 30 to 45 minutes initially.

Environmental Characteristics

Distraction level (noise/visual):   The noise and visual levels vary depending on time and day of the week. Busy times in the store can get extremely noisy and the aisles get especially crowded. However, most of the stocking is done at relatively quiet times of day with few distractions.

Comfort factors (temperature, space available, lighting, odor, sensory):
Temperature is comfortable throughout the store, except in the frozen foods, dairy, produce, and meat sections of the store. There is usually little work space available, as the aisles tend to be crowded with customers. Lighting is artificial but more than adequate. Odor factors are only an issue near the seafood and florist sections and when certain food containers break.

Equipment/tool use requirements: One pull-cart, box cutter, milk crate/stepladder, pad of paper, and pencil/pen

Natural Supports

Environmental support: Weekly and daily job schedules are posted above time clock, shelf tags tell employees where items are located and how many fit on a shelf, labels on boxes can be matched to shelf tags, storeroom is organized to match the store's aisles, pull-carts are available to avoid heavy lifting, milk crate/stepladders are available for reaching high locations, clocks are located throughout the store, city bus stop is located outside the store.

Supervisor and co-worker support: New employee training is typically carried out by co-workers, employees typically work in pairs when stocking particular aisles, co-workers often carpool to work together, supervisors are always on-site to provide assistance and answer questions, job tasks are flexible and supervisor is very willing to rearrange assignments, numerous opportunities for socialization exist (during break time, after work, employee softball team, etc.).

Job Task Analysis

	Approximate times	**Tasks performed**
1	10 seconds	Clock in.
2	30 seconds	Gather all necessary supplies (box cutter, notepad, pen).
3	2 minutes	Find and ask supervisor with which aisle to begin.
4	1 minute	Go to assigned aisle.
5	10 seconds	Look for first empty/near-empty shelf space on right side.
6	20 seconds	Read shelf label, locate item number, and record item number on notepad.
7	4 minutes	Repeat steps 5/6 until all empty/near-empty spaces on right are located.
8	4 minutes	Repeat steps 5/6 for all empty/near-empty spaces on left of aisle.
9	1 minute	Go to storeroom.
10	30 seconds	Bring pull-cart to area where needed items are stored.
11	1 minute	Locate box containing the first item on the list.
12	15 seconds	Place box on pull-cart.
13	15 minutes	Repeat steps 11/12 for each subsequent item on the list until pull cart is full.
14	2 minutes	Bring loaded pull-cart to assigned aisle.
15	15 seconds	Remove first box from cart and read item number.
16	1 minute	Match item number to shelf tag number.
17	15 seconds	Open the box.
18	2 minutes	Remove items and place them on the shelf.
19	1 minute	Block shelf area that has just been stocked.
20	15 seconds	Break down empty box.
21	40 minutes	Repeat steps 15–20 until all items on the pull-cart have been stocked.
22	2 minutes	Gather all empty boxes and place them on the pull-cart.
23	2 minutes	Bring pull-cart back to storeroom.
24	2 minutes	Dump cardboard in the trash area.
25	—	Repeat steps 10–24 until all items on the list have been stocked.
26	—	Repeat steps 3–24 until shift is completed.
27	10 seconds	Clock out.

_____Emily George_____   _____Leslie Erikson_____
Person completing the form   **Signature of employer or supervisor**

itation or the Department of Mental Retardation to build a ramp so that the chair can be used at home and in the community.

"The work situation must be safe for the student, too. For example, one student with pica (a condition that causes him to eat anything he sees!) eats out of the toilet. You could ask an employee to check the bathroom each day and clean and remove from the bathroom anything that might be harmful before the student uses the bathroom."
Teacher
Warren County High School
McMinnville, Tennessee

"I use observations that have been completed by school staff, employment personnel, and family members to identify support available in an environment. Also, I ask them to identify support needed and suggestions for modifying the environment."

Teacher
Riverside High School
Parsons, Tennessee

4.1.2 Observing Students' Performance

"To observe my students' performance, I get them involved in many school and community activities, such as clubs and activities. Then I observe them to find out how they get along and ways in which they participate."

Teacher
South Side High School
Memphis, Tennessee

"If a job task has several pieces and can be arranged on a table in front of the worker, watch to see how that individual performs the job. Then make changes, if needed, so the worker is not wasting time on each movement."

Itinerant Transition Teacher
Nashville Public Schools
Nashville, Tennessee

After identifying the demands and available supports at a particular job or community site, it is important to observe your students' behavior in those environments. The information you obtain will assist you in identifying the strengths, needs, and supports available to your students in order to build an effective support plan for them.

Rest assured! In completing an environmental assessment and work performance evaluation, you are in compliance with the requirements of the Individuals with Disabilities Education Act (IDEA) Amendments of 1997 (PL 105-17) for conducting a "functional vocational evaluation." This requirement means that you must evaluate a student's performance on the job in relation to the demands and environmental conditions of the worksite. Good job!

How to Do It:

- Use the Job Analysis Survey (Form 4.1) you completed as a checklist of skills to observe. The survey will guide you to identify a range of skills that are required on most jobs, such as fine and gross motor skills, problem-solving skills, ability to vary order of tasks, and getting along with co-workers or customers.

- Carefully record those areas in which students demonstrate skill strengths and areas in which students need support. For example, you may find out that a student can work continuously on required tasks without being distracted but "falls apart" when there are variations in task requirements. Breaking down a job into its specific requirements can help you identify exactly where a student's strengths and needs lie.

- Using observations completed by school staff, employers, and family members is an excellent way to supplement the information you gather. You can't be everywhere at once! Teach others what to look for in a student's performance, and learn to rely on their observations and perceptions in addition to the information you've gathered.

- As you watch a student, also note the different types of resources that are available, such as social support, environmental supports, or job modifications. If it turns out that the student is not "up to par" in some areas required by the job, you will already have identified potential sources of support that could be introduced to assist the student.

Cross-references: Observing Students' Interactions (5.1.2) and Observing Students' Performance (6.1.1)

Evaluating Outcomes:

Work Performance Evaluation

After completing the Job Analysis Survey (Form 4.1), the next step is to observe the student actually performing the specific job. The Work Performance Evaluation (Form 4.2) is used to summarize how the student performs under the various environmental, social, and task demands of the job in relation to available supports. Each step of the targeted job routine and features of the environment are recorded in the first of three columns. Next, indicate the student's performance level in relation to the job requirements. Finally, record the implications of the student's performance and potential supports available to the student that may enable him or her to complete the routine more independently and more successfully. Such supports can include those that are typically available to other employees (natural supports) or those that must be created or modified by the job coach.

The opposite page contains an example of a completed work performance evaluation for a student involved in community-based training at a grocery store. A blank, reproducible form is included in the appendix.

4-2 COMMUNICATING ENVIRONMENTAL SUPPORT NEEDS

Communicating with parents and important others is part of your job! The IDEA Amendments of 1997 require teachers to "assist parents to better understand the nature of their children's disabilities and their educational and developmental needs; to communicate with personnel responsible for pro-

Work Performance Evaluation

Student: **Joseph** Date: **10/30/99** Worksite: **Donaldson's Food & Drug Store** Evaluator: **Emily George**

Job task requirements	Performance	Implications
• Recognize areas needing stocking	• Joseph easily pointed out shelves that were clearly empty but had trouble with half empty shelves.	• Teach Joseph to understand all of the info on the shelf tag, especially the info that indicates number of items per box.
• Basic reading/writing abilities	• His reading/writing abilities are adequate. He relies too much on visual comparison for item placement rather than on reading labels.	• Provide Joseph with a written routine to help remind him to read labels and shelf tags prior to placing items.
• Means for reaching high shelves	• Joseph is of average height and can't reach the back of top shelves without help. When he tries, he knocks items over.	• Show Joseph how to safely use a milk crate or small step ladder to stock high items.
• Understand storeroom organization	• Because Joseph is still new, he doesn't yet understand the storeroom's organization.	• The storeroom is well-organized and easy to understand. It won't be hard for him to learn.
• Lift boxes/place them on carts	• He complains that boxes are too heavy but has no difficulty lifting them.	• Teach Joseph to lift only one box at a time and to use his safety belt.
• Match items to correct shelf tag	• Joseph says reading the tags is a waste of time when he can just match the items.	• Show Joseph how to evaluate the accuracy of his work.
• Place items on shelf neatly	• Joseph is extremely neat, but it affects his work rate.	• Show him how to balance quality with speed.
• Reorganize messy shelves	• Joseph likes "fixing up the shelves nice" and does an excellent job.	• Joseph seems to like organizing things!!!

General mobility requirements	Performance	Implications
• Method for moving up and down aisles	• Joseph can walk up and down the aisles.	• He can work long periods of time without getting tired.
• Method for reaching high shelves	• Joseph tried to reach shelves he clearly couldn't reach and knocked items over.	• Teach Joseph to use adaptive equipment such as ladders or milk crates.
• Method for reaching low shelves	• Joseph's back became extremely tired.	• Show him basic safety techniques.
• Method for lifting boxes and moving to cart	• Joseph complained about the heavy boxes.	• Avoid jobs requiring heavy lifting in future.
• Method for pulling carts from storeroom	• Joseph performs this job in the same way as other employees.	• Joseph said he liked to do jobs "like the other people do them." "Fitting in is really important to Joseph.

(continued)

Form 4.2. Work Performance Evaluation for Joseph. (From Renzaglia, A., & Hutchins, M. [1995]. Materials developed for *A model for longitudinal vocational programming for students with moderate and severe disabilities.* Grant funded by the U.S. Department of Education, Office of Special Education and Rehabilitation Services; adapted by permission.)

Physical demands—Gross motor	Performance	Implications
• *Bending down*	• His back got tired toward the end of the shift. He quickly gave up on bottom shelves.	• Future jobs requiring frequent bending over should be avoided.
• *Reaching up*	• No problems	
• *Balancing*	• No problems	
• *Moving up and down aisles*	• Joseph can walk up and down aisles on his own.	• It appears Joseph enjoys jobs where he can walk around. He dislikes stationary tasks.
• *Lifting full/broken-down boxes*	• When the distance required to lift a full box was short, Joseph complained very little.	• Help show Joseph how to unload his cart as he moves down the aisle, rather than having to transfer items from one end to the other.

Physical demands—Fine motor	Performance	Implications
• *Using paper/pencil to record items*	• Good writing skills	• To save time, show Joseph some shorthand.
• *Using a box cutter*	• Doesn't follow safety rules	• Emphasize safety rules at the workplace.
• *Opening boxes*	• No problems	• This skill will be useful for him at other jobs.
• *Placing/removing items on/from shelves*	• Joseph has excellent control and can work well in small areas.	• Future jobs requiring strong fine motor abilities should remain open for Joseph.
• *Stacking items*	• Able to stack food items up to four high	• Future jobs requiring strong fine motor abilities should remain open for Joseph.
• *Shuffling items on shelves*	• No problems	
• *Balancing on balls of feet*	• No problems	

Length of work tasks	Performance	Implications
• *Stocking shelves continuously*	• Joseph has a difficult time staying on task. He stocked about half a box on his own before finding something else he was interested in.	• Joseph doesn't perform well in highly distractible jobs. Also, the initial novelty of any job will likely result in difficulty for Joseph to stay on task.
• *Recording needed items*	• Joseph takes about twice as long to record items.	• Teach him time-saving techniques to improve his work pace.
• *Locating/gathering items in storeroom*	• Joseph was initially slow, but he is picking it up quickly.	• He learns quickly when things are organized.
• *Cleaning up*	• Joseph usually cleans up very quickly.	

84

Variability of daily job tasks	Performance	Implications
◆ Routine is generally the same day to day	◆ The routine of stocking is very predictable for Joseph. He is currently focusing on a small section of the store before moving on to other areas. Joseph enjoys the variety of patterns, items, and displays on which he gets to work.	◆ Less variability certainly makes Joseph work more quickly. However, he really seems to enjoy novel things and likes to ask questions about "unknowns." An ideal future job would definitely balance the predictability of routine with the novelty of variety.

Problem-solving requirements	Performance	Implications
◆ Recognizing shelves needing stocking ◆ Means for shifting boxes in storeroom ◆ Determining stocking patterns for shelves ◆ Deciding what to do with extra items ◆ Stacking boxes	◆ He easily pointed out clearly empty shelves but had trouble with half empty shelves. ◆ Joseph knocked several boxes over while trying to pull out the bottom box. ◆ He followed the established shelf patterns. ◆ Joseph asked a co-worker for help. ◆ No problems	◆ Teach him to read info on shelf tags that indicates the number of items a shelf holds. ◆ Show Joseph how to move boxes in safe and effective ways. ◆ Joseph does very well when he has a model. ◆ Joseph asks the same questions over and over and has some difficulty generalizing advice.

Production rate requirements	Performance	Implications
◆ Works continuously on-task for entire shift ◆ Average of 20 boxes per hour	◆ He had a very difficult time staying on task. He was constantly finding items he wanted to look at. He would stock about half of a box before stopping to look at something else. ◆ Initially, he was slow, but he is improving his pace with more experience.	◆ Joseph doesn't perform well in highly distractible jobs. ◆ The main concern is keeping Joseph on task. Jobs which require lots of independent work will require much initial supervision.

(continued)

Work product quality requirements	Performance	Implications
◆ Stock items until shelves are full ◆ Block shelves neatly ◆ All items match shelf tags ◆ All shelves have neat design/appearance ◆ All materials returned upon completion ◆ Storeroom kept neat and orderly	◆ No problems ◆ No problems ◆ Because he matches items, he often puts similar looking items in the wrong place. ◆ Joseph is extremely neat and careful to make sure the shelves look nice. ◆ Great job! ◆ Joseph makes very little mess in the storeroom.	◆ Teach Joseph to evaluate the quality of his work. ◆ It is actually someone else's job to keep this area clean.

Continuous working requirements	Performance	Implications
◆ Continuously stock shelves (except for breaks and trips to storeroom)	◆ As mentioned above, Joseph has a difficult time staying on task. He is very distracted by things and people around him.	◆ Joseph doesn't perform well on highly distractible job tasks. He is more likely to be successful at jobs with consistent, understandable routines.

Co-worker presence/task-related	Performance	Implications
◆ The job is primarily one in which the employee works alone.	◆ Joseph had a difficult time working alone when he was supposed to. Instead, he would go to other co-workers and bombard them with numerous questions.	◆ While asking for help is a good quality, knowing when not to is also important. Joseph may have trouble staying on-task in environments that involve working too closely with another employee. Moreover, Joseph tends to prevent other employees from doing their jobs effectively.

	Performance	Implications
Nontask-related social contacts ♦ Only occasional interactions with co-workers outside of breaks	♦ Joseph has had little opportunity to interact socially with other co-workers because he has had to return to the transition classroom upon completion of his work.	♦ Joseph says that the thing he enjoys most about work is talking to his co-workers. Future jobs that offer such opportunities would likely be enjoyed most by Joseph.
Social atmosphere of worksite ♦ Employee works in the presence of numerous customers	♦ The areas in which Joseph worked were constantly entered by customers and other employees. He greeted very few of them.	♦ Joseph needs to be taught appropriate ways to interact with customers (socially acceptable behavior) and may need help overcoming some of his shyness with them.
Interactions with customers ♦ Interactions with customers are quite frequent	♦ Numerous customers entered the area in which Joseph was working, but he initiated no conversations and offered few greetings.	♦ Again, Joseph needs to be taught appropriate ways to interact with customers (socially acceptable behavior) and may need help overcoming some of his shyness with them.

(continued)

Form 4.2. *(continued)*

Supervisory contact	Performance	Implications
• Supervisor checks in approximately every 30 to 45 minutes	• Joseph is quick to ask for assistance for every problem he encounters (big or small), often monopolizing the time of his supervisors.	• I suspect that more experience on the job will reduce the large number of questions Joseph has. He is well liked by his supervisor, and I would anticipate the same situation at future job sites.

Distraction level	Performance	Implications
• Noise levels • Visual distractions	• No problems • As mentioned before, Joseph was distracted by all of the food items that he had questions about. This keeps him off-task for a large percentage of time.	• Joseph might work better in a place with fewer visual distractions or when he is given opportunities prior to or after work to ask questions.

Comfort factors	Performance	Implications
• Temperature • Space available • Lighting • Odor / sensory	• No problems: Joseph is working in neither the frozen foods nor refrigerated sections. • Joseph tends to spread out a little more than his space will allow, making it difficult for customers to get around him. • No problems • No problems, except in the produce section.	• Teach Joseph to make better use of his workspace by organizing his materials more efficiently.

Equipment/tool use requirements	Performance	Implications
◆ Pull-cart	◆ No problems	◆ Supervisor will need to emphasize safety rules at the workplace.
◆ Box cutter	◆ Joseph had no problems using the cutter, but didn't adhere to safety rules.	◆ Show Joseph the benefits of certain adaptive equipment and the ways in which they can make his job easier.
◆ Milk crate/step ladder	◆ Able, but reluctant to use them.	
◆ Pad of paper/pen	◆ No problems	

Environmental support	Performance	Implications
◆ Job schedules	◆ Joseph picked up using schedule fairly quickly.	◆ Teach Joseph to use shelf tags to evaluate his work.
◆ Shelf tags	◆ Joseph is able to read them, but prefers not to use them.	
◆ Box labels	◆ No problems	◆ Provide specific instruction regarding how to use the equipment correctly.
◆ Stock room organization	◆ Joseph is learning to navigate the stockroom.	
◆ Pull-carts	◆ Joseph has some trouble stacking items.	◆ Provide instruction on reading time.
◆ Time clocks	◆ Joseph has difficulty reading the clocks.	

Supervisor and co-worker support	Performance	Implications
◆ Training carried out by co-workers	◆ Joseph really enjoyed his trainer—a college student around his age.	◆ In future jobs, Joseph would likely prefer to be trained by his co-workers rather than solely by a job coach.
◆ Co-worker carpool	◆ Joseph rides the community bus.	◆ Joseph would do well at jobs in which the supervisor is frequently present and willing to answer questions.
◆ Supervisor presence	◆ Joseph asks numerous questions of his supervisor throughout his shift.	
◆ Opportunities for socialization	◆ Joseph loves hanging out in the break room.	◆ Encourage frequent opportunities for Joseph to meet with co-workers.

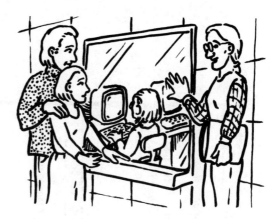

"I think it is important to take the time to explain to people about our purpose in helping students with the transition from school to the working world. We need to answer their questions and assist them in understanding our program."
Teacher
Pearl-Cohn High School
Nashville, Tennessee

viding special education, early intervention, and related services; and to obtain appropriate information about the range of options, programs, services, and resources available to assist children with disabilities and their families" (Section 682).

4.2.1 To Parents, Teachers, Community Agencies, and Others

By assessing both a student's performance and the demands of an environment, supports that are either available or needed will become much more evident. In preparation for building an individualized support plan, teachers must communicate with important others concerning ways of gaining access to and modifying those supports.

Starting Up:

- Talk with parents and teachers about the kinds of supports they are already providing to students. You may find out some ingenious and creative ideas, such as putting together socks of the same color in a drawer for a student with a visual impairment or having a student with a cognitive disability carry a photo of the bus stop nearest home when riding the bus. If necessary, suggest ways of strengthening or enhancing those supports.

- By ensuring that parents are active members of the assessment process from the beginning, you will increase the likelihood that they will be supportive of support plans developed by the individualized education program (IEP) team. Don't keep parents "in the dark" about your ideas; parent involvement is critical to a student support plan.

- Developing with parents and employers a support plan that can be carried out at home and work will ensure consistency in support in *all* of the environments in which a student is involved. When you let important others have input in what's included and feel some ownership of the plan, it's much more likely that the plan will be carried out!

- Let important others know what a student's needs are. For example, an employer may not know that a student with learning disabilities has difficulty prioritizing tasks and needs assistance in organizing his day. Suggest ways in which others can help make the student's experiences more successful and satisfying.

"In communicating with community members, the first priority should be to promote what the student with special needs can give to the community. Focus on the positive! As a result, positive change and support will follow."

Teacher
Cleveland High School
Cleveland, Tennessee

How to Do It:

- Encouraging all members of the student's IEP team— parents and family members, general education teachers, job coach, employer, physical therapist, and so forth—to provide input into the support plan will help ensure that a complete picture of the student's needs is created. You can't expect everyone to know everything about a student!

- Ask a student's general education peers for their ideas on modifying an environment to make it more accessible or supportive for the student. Their creative ideas may surprise you, such as a new style of backpack that helps a student organize her belongings or an easier way for a student to get from world history to commercial art class that avoids using the stairs.

- Regularly communicate a student's support needs to staff at vocational rehabilitation, the Department of Mental Retardation, and other community agencies that provide support to the student. Interagency collaboration is the key to addressing all of a student's support needs.

Cross-reference: Communicating Social Support Needs (5-2)

4.2.2 Interviewing Parents and Important Others

Interviewing individuals involved in the lives of students allows you to create a comprehensive picture of the supports that are currently available in these students' environments. Establishing open lines of communication with important others is imperative for acquiring critical information about support at the worksite, in the classroom, or in the community environment that is not available through direct observation.

Teacher-Proven Practices:

- Meeting with parents may be the only way to determine what they value and what their attitudes are regarding their child's future employment, social, and residential possibilities. Without knowing what parents think, you may be in danger of assuming that you always know what's best for a student.

"Establish lines of communication with persons significant to the student. Speak to parents, classroom teachers, students, co-workers, and employers to assess the levels of support that exist for the student."
Teacher
Hillcrest High School
Memphis, Tennessee

- Interviewing family members can help you determine a student's preferences, as well as the types of supports he or she is already provided at home. Families may have developed a communication system using pictures or symbols, which you could use at school or work, or they may have taught a student to use a timer and a checklist while completing his homework. You may also find out that the student really doesn't like pizza, which you had been trying to use as a reinforcer for getting his work done!

- Conversations with employers and community agencies can help others think about a student's support needs and potential solutions that they may not have been aware of. You may assume that an employer doesn't care about a student's need to take extra time when completing purchase orders, but it may be that the employer doesn't even know that this is a need of the student. Communication is the answer to many "problems"!

- Interviews may allow you to connect available resources to student needs in other environments. For example, adaptations that parents say they use for helping their child complete chores at home, such as an adapted broom or rake, could be used at a potential job-training site.

 When communicating with your students' families, you are likely to encounter many people who have different perspectives from yours, who have limited English proficiency, or who are from different cultural backgrounds. Recent findings indicate that by the year 2000, nearly one in three Americans will be African American, Hispanic, Asian American, or Native American (IDEA Amendments of 1997, Section 601). The IDEA Amendments of 1997 require you, as a teacher, to be responsive to the growing needs of an increasingly diverse society and a school population that is made up of a growing percentage of minority children and their families.

"In order to identify environmental support, you need to make a home visit. You must find out about family members' attitudes toward having the student work. Will they support it? If not, why not? Do they work? It may be that there is not anyone to help the student get up every morning to go to work—an alarm clock may be needed. The student may also need to learn to fix a simple breakfast.

"You must also visit the worksite to identify needed changes. For example, you may find there is a better place for the student to sit or stand to prevent potential problems from occurring. Moving a student's workstation so that it is not by a large window or door will help cut down on distractions if the student is easily distracted."

Transition Coordinator
Nashville Public Schools
Nashville, Tennessee

Cross-reference: Conducting a Home Inventory (Form 6.5) in Assessing Students' Strengths and Needs (6-2)

4-3   DEVELOPING ENVIRONMENTAL SUPPORT PLANS

Environmental support plans are the product of environmental assessments and communication with individuals who are important to the student. These plans give focus and direction to instruction in the community and on the job. At the same time, they assist a student in becoming as independent, successful, and happy as possible.

4.3.1   Developing Individual Environmental Support Plans

Support plans must be designed to address the individual characteristics of students and their work, home, or community environments. By recognizing that supports designed for one environment or individual may not be effective for another environment or individual, teachers and job coaches can devise plans that meet the unique needs of each student.

Starting Up:

- As with all instructional programs, environmental support plans must be based on an assessment of the individual and her unique needs, strengths, and preferences. Remember to ask the student what she thinks about her own support needs.

- All support plans should be a product of site visits, student observations, and interviews, as discussed previously in this chapter. Using the information you have derived from these sources, you can be assured that you are building a support plan that is specific to a student and her environments and that reflects the values and preferences of the student and her family.

- After identifying which supports are necessary, prioritize them in order of importance. Because you will not be able to address every need immediately, it's necessary to decide which are the most important needs. For example, if a young man is having toileting accidents in his auto tech class, you probably should address this before focusing on the legibility of his handwriting!

Cross-reference: Developing Individual Social Support Plans (5.3.1)

How to Do It:

- Environmental supports should be as similar as possible to those already present at a worksite. The more familiar the supports are, the fewer the differences that will exist between co-workers and students with varying abilities. For example, if co-workers are already using a "jig" to fold

"In setting up a support plan, I replicate practices within each environment so that all are similar—this helps to promote generalization. I send home a survey for parents to fill out, and I visit the home, group home, or other residential placement and the workplace. Then I plan programming and materials so that all aspects are as similar as possible. For example, the washing machine at school and in the school's training apartment is the same model, and the table settings at home and school are the same. At school, we use the same time cards and clocks as do many of the businesses in town."
Teacher
Karns High School
Knoxville, Tennessee

papers neatly, then why devise a new tool if this one also works for a student?

- Design support plans that include multiple environments, addressing a student's needs in school, at work, at home, and within the community. For example, if a student uses a wheelchair, then she will need accessible entrances, walkways, and hallways in all of these environments. Another student may have time management needs and will need to have environmental cues, such as watching to see when his co-workers return from break, established across all environments.

- Survey the student's immediate neighborhood to learn what resources are available, such as an accessible bus route, a book club that meets at a local bagel shop, or a nearby laundromat. Keep a record of what you find, take the student to visit the places, and provide telephone numbers, addresses, or a map to help the student use these resources.

Case Study 4.4   Lester Gets a Support Plan[1]

Lester Anthony was 13 years old and in the seventh grade when his language arts teacher, Ms. Raine, noticed that her usually lighthearted, amiable student seemed "down." Lester just did not seem like his usual joking, fun-loving self. A quick look at her record book showed that Lester's passing grades and good attendance had suddenly dropped. She knew she had a student who needed help!

At lunch break, Ms. Raine consulted with Lester's science, math, and physical education teachers, who all realized that they, too, had noticed a change in Lester's behavior. After school, Ms. Raine called Lester's home and was surprised to find out that Lester was now living with his aunt because his mother had recently been arrested and jailed again. The telephone call was followed up with a home visit, at which time Ms. Raine found out that Lester's Aunt Gladys was also caring for Lester's younger brother and sister. Aunt Gladys was very relieved to see Ms. Raine. She had been worried when Lester had become unruly at home, but she did not know what to do. He had always been so sweet and helpful with his brother and sister and had attended church and other activities with the family. Maybe it was caused by drugs, which were prevalent in the neighborhood, or

[1]From *Beyond high school: Transition from school to work,* by F.R. Rusch & J.G. Chadsey. © 1998. Adapted with permission of Wadsworth Publishing, a division of Thomson Learning. Fax 800 730-2215.

by the rough crowd he had started hanging out with. Ms. Raine and Aunt Gladys decided that Lester and she needed support.

Much happened within the next 3 months. A referral to special education resulted in a transition team meeting, which was attended by Lester and his aunt, his teachers, the special education consulting teacher, the school social worker, the school psychologist, and the school principal. At the meeting, Lester was identified as having a learning disability, and he and his aunt were told he could receive special education services. The team then worked together to build a support plan for Lester that would develop support in Lester's environment and help him develop his competence. The team continued to monitor and implement the plan throughout Lester's secondary school years. Lester graduated from high school at age 18 and began working in an auto body shop, a job that he had chosen himself. He now has many friends, enjoys sports, and attends church and social events regularly with his family. (See the Individual Support Plan on page 98. A blank, reproducible form is included in the appendix.)

4.3.2 Incorporating Environmental Supports into Instruction

If we're not careful, students may learn to depend on others for direction and assistance in the community and on the job. By incorporating environmental supports into instruction, teachers and job coaches can expect students to become more independent. In addition, using environmental supports during instruction will assist in the generalization of new skills, even in the teacher's absence.

Teacher-Proven Practices:

- In-school instruction should be similar to employees' on-the-job training. Adapt programs that already exist, such as a worksite orientation program. At work, support students in receiving the same training their co-workers receive, such as on the use of a computer or e-mail program.

- Students will be able to learn more easily if you use similar types of support in different environments and incorporate these into instruction. For example, if teachers at school use photographs to help a student learn new task sequences, then it would be a good idea to do the same at work. Inform parents, employers, and others what instructional supports are in use so that they can use them, too.

Individual Support Plan

Student: _Lester Anthony_   Date: November 6

Component	Action steps
1. Promote acceptance in the student's environment.	• The vocational rehabilitation counselor will meet with Lester's job supervisor to discuss Lester's job performance. Because Lester has difficulty remembering a sequence of tasks, his supervisor is becoming impatient with his performance. The counselor should explain the many work-related strengths Lester possesses. Together, the counselor and the supervisor can brainstorm ways of providing work adaptations that promote Lester's acceptance, such as a "to-do" list and daily schedule so that Lester can keep track of his job responsibilities.
2. Identify environmental support and provide needed changes within the environment.	• The school counselor will make a home visit to pinpoint sources of problems within Lester's neighborhood, identifying those times when Lester is likely to spend time with peers who are in trouble or using drugs. • Lester will attend the neighborhood Boys' and Girls' Club after school, rather than going home immediately. • Lester will become involved in school sports activities, such as track and basketball. • Assist Lester in changing his bus route so that he can attend sporting events.
3. Identify social supports from employers, co-workers, peers, and family.	• Match Lester with a male mentor through the "100 Black Men" mentoring program in the community. Mentor will meet with him throughout the week to assist Lester with homework assignments and provide social support. • Special education consulting teacher will help Lester with his school work in the general education classroom and will help his teachers adapt Lester's assignments. • School counselor will help Lester cope with the absence of his mother and will help Lester and his aunt improve their communication with each other. • Lester will get more involved in his church, including joining the church choir. • The vocational rehabilitation counselor will assist Lester in getting a job at a local supermarket, involving supervisors and co-workers during his training. • Lester will become involved in after-work activities with his fellow employees.

Form 4.3.   Individual Support Plan for Lester Anthony. (From *Beyond high school: Transition from school to work,* by F.R. Rusch & J.G. Chadsey. © 1998. Adapted with permission of Wadsworth Publishing, a division of Thomson Learning. Fax 800 730-2215.)

- It's a good idea to teach students methods they can use for adapting their environments, too. For example, if a young man with a physical impairment has trouble reaching across a table to use the copy machine at work, he could figure out how to rearrange the table. Such skills make the job easier and may result in greater independence on the job and around the community.

- Because responsibilities and expectations are likely to be changing constantly, reevaluation of an individual's support plan should also be ongoing. Also, a student's needs will change over time as she learns new skills and faces new situations and challenges, such as moving to a new neighborhood or applying for college.

Developing an individual environmental support plan is consistent with the requirements of PL 105-17 for the IEP. Specifically, the IEP must contain "a statement of the special education and related services and supplementary aids and services to be provided to the child, or on behalf of the child, and a statement of the program modifications or supports for school personnel that will be provided for the child" (Section 614). In addition, "beginning at age 14, and updated annually, a statement of the transition service components of the child's IEP that focuses on the child's courses of study (such as participation in advanced-placement courses or a vocational education program)" (Section 614) must be included in the IEP.

Cross-reference: Incorporating Social Supports into Instruction (5.3.2)

A variety of supports already exist in abundance throughout community, school, and work environments. Identifying and gaining access to these supports will result in more independence and acceptance of students with differing abilities.

4-4 GAINING ACCESS TO EXISTING ENVIRONMENTAL SUPPORTS

4.4.1 Gaining Access to Support Services

From the moment job training begins for a student, attention should be focused on fading the involvement of the job coach or teacher. To accomplish this, ongoing and natural supports should be used. Many individuals and agencies are available to provide this continued support. Using these services will allow a student to gain continued long-term success, independence, and acceptance on the job.

Starting Up:

- Many of the supports that students need are not directly related to their job performance but are critical to their successful employment and quality of life. Examples of services you may need to help students find are transportation, personal care, and a recreational program.

- Secure a listing of service providers available in the community. Often, supports are available from organizations that do not work solely with individuals with "disabilities." These can include Rotary, Elk, Moose, Civitan, and Optimist organizations; the YMCA; Big Brothers and Sisters; and Boys' and Girls' Clubs.

- Whenever possible, identify and use supports that are already available in the work environment. Doing so ensures that supports will be as similar as possible to those that all employees receive, such as an employee carpool, mentorship programs, or assistive devices such as carts and ladders.

Cross-reference: Gaining Access to Existing Social Support (5-4)

4.4.2 Establishing Interagency Collaboration

Ensuring the successful transition of a student from school to adult life often requires a large constellation of efforts. Fortunately, a number of organizations and agencies are designed to assist in this transition. The IDEA Amendments of 1997 require that collaboration between school and community agencies ensures that *all* of a student's transition needs are met. These collaborative relationships can be helpful resources when identifying and gaining access to environmental supports in community and employment environments.

Don't forget! Section 614 of PL 105-17 states that "beginning at age 14 (or younger, if determined appropriate by the IEP team), a statement of needed transition services for the child, including, when appropriate, a statement of the interagency responsibilities or any needed linkages," must be included in the student's IEP.

How to Do It:

- Assist community agencies in sharing information regarding the services they provide. You can help distribute brochures to families, schools, businesses, and community organizations; post information on a World Wide Web site; or compile information into a handbook.

- Involve agencies, such as vocational rehabilitation and other adult services, in the planning and implementation of students' support plans. If you expect these agencies to assist in the support process, you need to involve them "up front" in the planning process.

- Members of community agencies can be excellent resources when identifying the steps required to achieve certain employment outcomes, such as learning a new trade. Involve these people in the IEP meetings of students well before graduation.

- Vocational rehabilitation services may be a resource for acquiring funding for assistive devices used to support a student with diverse abilities in employment environments. Be sure to check whether a student is eligible for services; if the student is not eligible, then begin the referral process immediately.

Findings cited in Section 651 of the IDEA Amendments of 1997 indicate that "an effective educational system now and in the future must promote service integration, and the coordination of State and local education, social, health, mental health, and other services, in addressing the full range of student needs, particularly the needs of children with disabilities who require significant levels of support to maximize their participation in learning in school and in the community." In addition, the amendments state that "lasting change that is of benefit to all students, including those with disabilities, requires the involvement of State and local educational agencies, parents, individuals with disabilities and their families, teachers and other service providers, and other interested individuals and organizations in carrying out comprehensive strategies to improve educational results for children with disabilities" (Section 651).

4-5   MODIFYING THE ENVIRONMENT

4.5.1   Providing Needed Materials

Providing appropriate materials to employees with differing abilities can assist them in completing their job more efficiently and successfully in a manner similar to that of their co-workers. In the community and at home, such materials will assist a student in becoming a more active participant. Using materials that are typical of and valued in the natural environment will decrease the need for outside assistance, promoting the acceptance of the student.

Starting Up:

- The identification of appropriate materials should be determined by matching the requirements of the environment (from the Job Analysis Survey) to the supports needed by the student (from the Work Performance Evaluation). For example, if you determine that a student needs to do a lot of heavy lifting and bending on a job but doesn't have the physical strength, you may decide to place heavy materials on a table rather than on the floor to make the job easier.

IEPs for students must include a statement of the "supplementary aids and services to be provided to the child, or on behalf of the child, and a statement of the program modifications or supports for school personnel that will be provided for the child" (IDEA Amendments of 1997, Section 614). Such supports should be used to assist students in attaining their annual goals and in achieving greater involvement in general education and extracurricular activities.

- As you decide which materials to provide a student in work or community environments, keep a student's social needs in mind. Any modified materials should promote social interactions, not hinder them. If using a shopping cart to deliver mail in an office makes a student stand out and look "weird," then try for an adaptation that fits in better in the environment, such as a smaller pushcart.

- Many materials that are relatively inexpensive or "home-made" can act as effective adaptations. An electric stapler, a counting box, or a picture restaurant menu may be all that is necessary to allow a person increased independence. Don't spend a lot of money if you don't have to.

- Many companies provide common (or ingenious!) adaptive equipment and materials. Browsing through their catalogs can give you great ideas for making your own adaptations, or maybe you'd like to purchase some ready-made. Information about these materials can be found in the Technology and Augmentative Communication section of the Resources in the appendix.

Teacher-Proven Practices:

Teachers report that they have used the following environmental modifications:

- Provide desks at the right height. Have proper desks for people who are left-handed writers.

- If tables at a local restaurant are not high enough for wheelchairs to fit underneath, work with the restaurant owners and help them adapt the eating areas.

- Provide a switch to students with multiple disabilities so that they can listen to audiocassettes and watch videotapes. Learning how to use a switch to turn the audiocassettes and videotapes on or off can help them to control part of their environment.

- Use higher tables that accommodate students' wheelchairs to allow them to have access to computers.

- Provide wider spaces between office cubicles to accommodate students with physical impairments who may require assistance, such as those who use a cane or a wheelchair.

- Develop a nonstigmatizing jig or counting box so that students can count the correct number of items for packaging on the job, such as ceramic tiles or salt packages.

4.5.2   Making Environmental Modifications

The Americans with Disabilities Act (ADA) of 1990 (PL 101-336), in response to discrimination resulting from a "failure to make modifications to existing facilities and practices" (Section 12101), requires employers to

"We suggest that students in wheelchairs carry water bottles so they don't have to worry about drinking fountains they can't get to. We check with general education classroom teachers to discuss ways to modify the setting to adapt for students in wheelchairs. Sometimes they need assistance transferring to a regular chair; sometimes a specific table in the classroom can be used. Peers in the general education classroom are often very creative in adapting materials."
Teacher
Rutledge High School
Rutledge, Tennessee

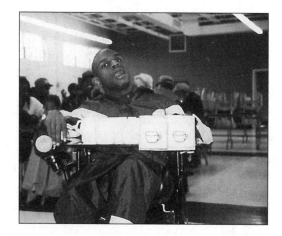

make "reasonable accommodations" for workers' needs. Environmental modifications typically have been used for a variety of reasons, including increasing an employee's work rate or quality. Environmental modification, however, can also be used to increase an employee's independence and acceptance on the job and to reduce the need for outside intervention.

Starting Up:

- All decisions to modify the environment should be made in partnership with the individual using the modifications and important others in the environment to promote acceptance of the modifications. For example, if you change the position of equipment in a computer repair shop to meet the needs of a student, this modification will also affect co-workers in the shop. If the changes make their job more difficult, this may be a problem for the entire repair shop crew.

- In addition to the student, involve co-workers in brainstorming ways to modify the environment. Because co-workers know the job, they are likely to have practical ideas about alternative ways to complete a task or shortcuts that will assist the student without compromising job performance.

- Ask people who are familiar with tools and hardware for help when devising environmental modifications. Ask a carpenter, a plumber, an electrician, or a mechanic for ideas on how to build jigs, ramps, switches, or other adaptive equipment to assist a student in daily living activities.

How to Do It:

- *Job carving* is one means of modifying a job to accommodate a worker's skills by devising alternative ways of completing job tasks at a workplace. However, be careful not to create new tasks that result in segregating a student from other employees.

- It may be easier to modify existing jobs than to attempt to create new jobs. Job modification can result in a student's performing tasks that are typical of those already present in the work environment, thereby promoting the acceptance of the student in the workplace.

- One reason that the ADA was crafted was to make employment or other environments more accessible to individuals with diverse abilities. A number of sources, including the Job Accommodation Network, provide free information about job accommodations to businesses and individuals with differing abilities. (See the Resources section in the appendix.)

Teacher-Proven Practices:

- If a student is having trouble gaining access to a building or room, contact some of the volunteer agencies in town. There are many organizations that will send volunteers to build a ramp.

- For students who have visual impairments or who are easily distracted, such as those with attention disorders, arrange their desks so that they are closer to the board and the front of the room. Have students with hearing impairments sit where they can see others' faces.

- Leave the door to your classroom open, if possible, for easy access to students. Students with visual impairments could sit close to the door so that they have fewer obstacles to meet in finding a seat and leaving the room.

"I noticed one of my students had difficulty picking up litter on a jobsite. I made him a stick with a nail in the end so he could 'spear' the litter and then put it in his trash bag."
Teacher
Hillsboro High School
Nashville, Tennessee

- Provide a homework area within a general education classroom where students could receive assistance from peers and not have to be separated from the rest of the class.

Making modifications to a student's environment is not just the sole responsibility of the special education teacher. Section 614 of the IDEA Amendments of 1997 states, "The regular education teacher of the child, as a member of the IEP Team, shall, to the extent appropriate, participate in the development of the IEP of the child, including the determination of appropriate positive behavioral interventions and strategies and the determination of supplementary aids and services, program modifications, and support for school personnel."

REFERENCES

Americans with Disabilities Act (ADA) of 1990, PL 101-336, 42 U.S.C. §§ 12101 *et seq.*

Hughes, C., & Kim, J. (1998). Supporting the transition from school to adult life. In F.R. Rusch & J.G. Chadsey (Eds.), *Beyond high school: Transition from school to work* (pp. 367–382). Belmont, CA: Wadsworth.

Individuals with Disabilities Education Act (IDEA) Amendments of 1997, PL 105-17, 20 U.S.C. §§ 1400 *et seq.*

Renzaglia, A., & Hutchins, M. (1995). Materials developed for *A model for longitudinal vocational programming for students with moderate and severe disabilities.* Grant funded by the U.S. Department of Education, Office of Special Education and Rehabilitation Services.

Chapter 5

Strategies for Increasing Social Support

OVERVIEW

As students advance through high school and approach graduation, their opportunities increase for jobs, community events, social organizations, apartment living, travel destinations, and relationships. With each new opportunity comes the challenge and excitement of learning about and adapting to new experiences. As students approach these transitions, the amount of social support that they receive influences the degree of success and satisfaction that they experience. Luckily, life is full of people! One of the greatest advantages of work, school, and community environments is that they are rich sources of social support. Opportunities to interact socially, engage in relationships, and receive social support abound in our everyday lives. And, when you think about it, we all are recipients and providers of a certain amount of social support, whether we are at home, at work, in school, or around the community.

Social support can manifest in a variety of ways. For example, students may need assistance with learning a new job or hobby, obtaining transportation, meeting new people, managing time, fulfilling responsibilities, finding housing, or solving problems. In addition, the intensity of social support needed differs from person to person. Whereas one student may need only an occasional reminder, another student may require ongoing assistance or encouragement. People's support needs also change over time.

Strategies that teachers can use to identify social support in an environment and match it to a student's needs are similar to those for identifying environmental support. A teacher needs to visit, observe, and analyze an environment as well as communicate and collaborate with important others. Social support may come from a variety of sources, such as friends of a student's brother or sister or someone who waits at the same bus stop to go to work. Sometimes students must learn skills to gain access to social support that exist in an environment; other times peers or co-workers need to learn to communicate with or offer assistance to a student.

This chapter contains four main groups and eight subgroups of strategies that teachers may use to increase social supports for a student. It includes such strategies as conducting site visits and observations, communicating social support needs, developing social support plans, gaining access to existing social support, and collaborating with others to provide support.

Using social support that occurs naturally in an environment, such as other employees on the job and fellow sports club members, instead of paid assistants will likely increase the amount of social interaction that a student experiences on the job and around the community.

Case Study 5.1   A Member of the Team

The arrival of spring signals the long-awaited beginning of softball season in the town of San Angelo. A visitor to the small community might wonder why so much fuss is made over just another game! Local businesses gather their employees together Tuesday and Friday nights to "slug it out" as company pride is either forged or broken on the softball diamond. In the stands, families and friends gather to cheer on Ed's Automotive, Cumberland Manufacturing, or any of the other company teams that have assembled that evening.

Despite the numerous spectators and athletes gathered around the fields this evening, Kelly Parlatour is focused on one player in particular, Scott Meijer. Kelly has been Scott's special education teacher throughout high school and remembers very clearly the first time he mentioned that he wanted to join the team. At the beginning of the past school year, Scott had not been involved in many community activities and had few relationships outside his immediate family. His mother was deceased, his father worked evenings, and his two brothers no longer lived at home. Yet as Scott described his hopes after graduation, it became clear that he desired close friendships and involvement in the community. Later that month, the IEP team met to help Scott plan his future.

Mr. Meijer talked with a family friend about getting Scott a job at Jacobson Electronics as a cashier. The vocational rehabilitation counselor arranged for Scott to be trained by another employee, although the counselor provided assistance when necessary. When Mr. Meijer expressed concern over Scott's getting to and from work, Kelly helped Scott find a co-worker who would be willing to drive him in exchange for splitting the cost of the gas. Scott loved his job immensely and developed some fantastic relationships with the people with whom he worked. It wasn't surprising, then, when Scott was asked to be the catcher for the company softball team.

Scott began preparing for the season early. He rode with a friend to the batting cages three times per week. At practice, a couple of the team's star players paired with Scott to teach him some basic fielding skills. And after practice, when the team went out for dinner, Scott was able to get to know his co-workers outside the store. On this particular evening as Kelly watched, Scott stood next to home plate, waving his bat in the air, eager to hit one "out of the park." Kelly's smile showed how proud she was of Scott and how grateful she was to all of the people who supported Scott in his goal to be "a member of the team."

5-1   CONDUCTING SITE VISITS AND OBSERVATIONS

5.1.1   Conducting Social Support Assessments

Often, assessment information is gathered only when a student is having difficulty fitting into a particular environment. In addition to providing information concerning how to address "difficult" behaviors in an environ-

The process of determining which social supports are available to a student in a particular environment should begin with visits to school, community, and worksites. Keep an open mind—support may be derived from unexpected sources!

ment, however, social support assessments can tell you the types of support that are helping to create a successful experience for the student.

Starting Up:

- Whether at work, in school, or around the community, begin by observing others in the environment to determine the types of support they are receiving, such as belonging to a "singles club," and the kind of social support they may be able to provide to a student, such as asking the student to join them at the next singles get-together.

- Getting input from other participants in the environments that you are observing has a twofold purpose. First, it can result in suggestions and ideas that you may not have thought of, such as asking a student whether he wants to join a hiking club. Second, it can help give ownership of a support plan to others.

- Don't assume that the types of support provided to one student in a community will necessarily be valued by the family or community of another student. In today's diverse society, it is especially important that teachers make home visits to determine the types of social supports that are available and valued by a student's family (see Conducting a Home Inventory [Form 6.5] in Using Informal Assessment Methods, 6.2.1).

How to Do It:

- As you visit the environments in which a student participates, note the people who live close by or come in contact with or work with the student, such as a student's favorite cousin or a friendly neighbor. These people represent potential sources of social support to the student.

- In work environments, a variety of co-worker supports are available. Although job-related support may be the most common, social supports that are not directly related to job performance are equally important. These can include providing emotional support, helping a student get along socially, answering questions, or getting a meal after work.

- Remember that students (and their environments) will change over time. When observing home, work, school, and community environments, identify sources of support that will be available to the student both now and in the future, such as long-time residents of a community or a well-established social club.

Cross-reference: Conducting Environmental Assessments (4.1.1)

In addition to being used to determine whether a child has a disability, assessment strategies should be used to determine the content of a student's IEP, as well as placement in the least restrictive environment. The Individuals with Disabilities Education Act (IDEA) Amendments of 1997 (PL 105-17) state that information provided by such assessments should include how a student will be involved in and progress through the general education curriculum. The individualized education program (IEP) team is required to work together to identify the social supports that will be available to a student to maximize general education involvement and to include these supports in a written statement in the IEP.

Evaluating Outcomes:

Identifying Social Support

Strategies that teachers can use to identify social support in an environment are similar to those for identifying environmental supports. The Natural Supports section of the Job Analysis Survey (see Form 4.1 in Conducting Environmental Assessments, 4.1.1) provides teachers with an assessment tool for developing a comprehensive picture of the social supports available at a given worksite. By observing other employees performing the job, interviewing supervisors and co-workers, and surveying the environment, teachers can isolate those sources of social support that enhance a student's job performance and promote his acceptance at work. The Job Analysis Survey can also be modified to identify supports in other environments. Tips for using the form include the following:

- Observe a student's everyday environments by "hanging out" and being visible without being a "pest." Ask a lot of questions because you might miss something or misinterpret someone's actions.

- As you complete the survey form, think about ways a co-worker or peer can support a student in adapting to the demands and environmental characteristics of an environment, such as taking notes for a student during a lecture. Ask for input from important others in the environment.

- Social supports, such as co-workers or employee assistance programs, that naturally occur in the environment generally are better accepted than supports introduced from outside a home, work, or community environment, such as paid employment specialists. Record in the Natural Supports section of the survey form those social supports that are typically occurring.

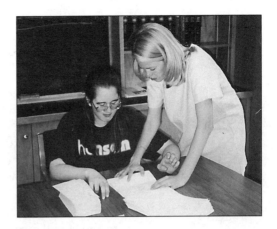

"I observe others who are involved in a
student's environments, noting any possible
ways they may be able to provide support. In
addition, I ask others about the types of
support they are able to provide."
Teacher
Pearl-Cohn High School
Nashville, Tennessee

5.1.2   Observing Students' Interactions

One of the most direct and accurate ways to identify social supports in a
student's everyday life is to observe the student as he or she interacts
with others in different environments. Note whether these interactions
enhance or impede the student's acceptance or competence in relation to
the demands of the environment. Because all students respond in unique
ways to the different demands of a particular environment, teachers
should note those areas in which individual students could benefit from
social support.

"I follow closely the interactions of students when they
are in community and general education settings. I
watch how they interact with others at school dances,
parties, or lunch or during recreational times. Casual
conversation with others can also give insight."
Teacher
Northside High School
Memphis, Tennessee

Teacher-Proven Practices:

- Use the job task analysis from the Job Analysis Survey on page 79 as a checklist of skills to observe. As the student performs each step, record the social supports, such as peers, that the student uses, as well as those supports that are available to but not used by the student, such as supervising or maintenance staff.

- Many students may need instruction on how to gain access to the social supports that are present in the environment. For instance, a student may need to be taught accepted ways of asking a co-worker for assistance. As you observe the student, indicate areas in which a student will need specific instruction (see Teaching Skills that Need Strengthening [6-4]; Teaching Social Interaction Skills [9-4]).

- As you observe students in their everyday environments, you may find that few social supports or opportunities for interaction are available. For example, a student enrolled in a community art class may be the only Spanish-speaking member of the group, or a worker employed as a night maintenance person may not have any co-workers on her shift. Jot down problem areas for which you will later brainstorm solutions with important others.

Cross-references: Observing Students' Performance (4.1.2 and 6.1.1)

Evaluating Outcomes:

How Natural Are a Student's Supports?

Providing a student with social support in the workplace or another environment is important in helping the student experience success and social acceptance. External supports, however, may unintentionally decrease natural supports and opportunities for social interaction available to the student. Natural supports may promote a student's acceptance and competence by providing assistance in ways that are routine and valued by others in the work environment. As you observe the students with whom you work in employment and other environments, ask yourself the following questions. Answering "yes" to the first four questions and "no" to the last three questions indicates that your students likely are receiving supports in a way that is both natural and non-stigmatizing.

1. Does the supervisor or manager spend as much time interacting with the student as with other employees?

2. Does the teacher or job coach keep a considerable distance from the student, except when providing direct instruction?

3. Do co-workers talk directly to the student instead of talking through the teacher or job coach?

4. Do teachers and job coaches direct co-worker questions away from themselves and toward the student?

5. Would other employees be embarrassed by the attention that the student receives from his teacher or job coach?

6. Has the teacher or job coach ever been mistaken for the student's mother or father?

7. If a minor crisis arises with the student, do other employees call for the teacher or job coach instead of the store manager or supervisor? (Jorgensen, 1992)

5-2   COMMUNICATING SOCIAL SUPPORT NEEDS

"Make all people involved in the student's life aware
of how they can provide support to the student.
Sometimes we take for granted that we all have
the same definition of support."
Teacher
Cleveland High School
Cleveland, Tennessee

5.2.1   To Parents, Teachers, Community Agencies, and Others

The active involvement of teachers, family members, and service
providers in pinpointing social support available to and needed by a student is critical to the effectiveness of any individual support plan. By solic-
iting the suggestions and input of others when identifying social support,
you can create a more comprehensive picture of a student's needs, as
well as communicate those needs to others in the student's environment.

Starting Up:

- Make businesses and organizations aware of the many
  types of social support they could provide to students,
  such as carpooling. Assure them that these supports can
  be used to benefit all employees.

- Bring together all individuals involved in a student's life
  to provide input into developing a complete picture of social support available to the student. It may be that important others will learn that supports successfully being

used in one area of a student's life, such as an interpreter or notetaker, may be introduced in another.

- Share with others the rationale for using social supports such as a peer buddy or Big Brother or Sister—not to make less work for educational assistants, teachers, or parents but to increase a student's social participation, friendships, and interdependence.

How to Do It:

- Ultimately, students and their families determine whether proposed social supports harmonize with their personal values, daily routines, and cultural expectations. Their views may be quite different from yours. Be certain to involve them throughout the planning process.

- People who interact with the student may have to be taught to provide social support. This may involve teaching a co-worker to modify job tasks, helping a classmate find ways of providing encouragement, or assisting a friend in teaching a new leisure skill.

- By keeping in frequent contact with family members, you can ensure that planned social supports are introduced across different areas of a student's life. Remember to provide support to parents, too, as you encourage them to involve their children in social activities in and out of school.

Cross-references: Collaborating with Students, Parents, Teachers, and Community Agencies (3.1.2); Communicating Environmental Support Needs (4-2); Communicating Students' Strengths and Needs (6-3); and Communicating with Parents, Teachers, and Others (8.2.1)

When teachers communicate with family members, employers, community members, fellow teachers, and important others, they multiply the number of strategies they have available to draw on in supporting a student. Providing social support for a student is a collaborative endeavor. The IDEA Amendments of 1997 require teachers to collaborate with other members of the IEP team to gain access to the experience, expertise, and support of others.

"I encourage lots of communication between myself and my students' families. That way I almost always know what parents' expectations are for their students and whether parents are pleased with their children's performance and social interaction at school. I also keep updated on work supervisors' observations of my students' job skills and social interactions at work."
Teacher
Hillsboro High School
Nashville, Tennessee

"I think that as part of the transition effort we should heavily involve the family of the individual in the planning process. Involvement with the employer should continue after the student has graduated."

Teacher
Treadwell High School
Memphis, Tennessee

"I would help people to understand the needs of the student and allow them to see how they can help students to have successful experiences."

Teacher
Cookeville High School
Cookeville, Tennessee

5.2.2 Collaborating with Students, Parents, and Important Others

Individuals in the environment in which a student is participating are often reluctant to interfere with the instruction or decisions of the student's teacher. These individuals generally are more willing to provide social support when they are given opportunities to participate in the planning process. By interviewing these individuals, teachers will allow others to share involvement in the student's program and gain important "inside" information regarding available social supports.

"Interview family members, employers, and co-workers to determine attitudes toward workers with disabilities. Identify key support personnel based on the interviews."

Teacher
Central High School
Ashland City, Tennessee

Starting Up:

- The real "authorities" on the social demands and social supports in a given environment are those individuals who are already successfully participating in that environment. Collaborate with these experts, including general education peers, co-workers, relatives, and community members, who know exactly what the social expectations are of a particular environment.

- Social supports can come in all shapes and sizes. Interviewing the student who will be the recipient of the supports will allow you to match the support preferences and needs of the student to the spectrum of supports available within the environment.

- Holding meetings with a student's family, friends, and co-workers can give you an opportunity to help them see how they can support the student. People may be surprised at the ways in which they can provide support. For example, an employer may help a new worker to better enjoy a baseball game they are attending together by explaining the rules of the game.

"An employer complained that one of my students wouldn't follow directions. He had told the student to sign his name on a time card but didn't realize that the student couldn't read. The student was too embarrassed to tell the employer. I discussed the problem with the employer, and together we figured out another system the student could use for filling out his time card."
Teacher
Nashville Public Schools
Nashville, Tennessee

The ability and freedom to make important life choices is valued by many people. The IDEA Amendments of 1997 recognize this fact and stress that the transition services provided to students be based on the individual student's needs, taking into account the student's preferences and interests. Allowing students to determine with which social supports they would be most comfortable and how they would prefer them to be delivered allows them to exercise that choice. Strategies for identifying a student's needs and preferences include interviewing her and important others.

Case Study 5.2   Living on My Own

Yvonne thought that it was about time that she got her own apartment. After all, living at home with seven brothers and sisters would be considered a challenge for even the toughest of people! Besides, she was 18 years old, had graduated from high school, and had just started job training as a library assistant. Yvonne had been enrolled in the district's 19- to 22-year-old community-based program for just more than 1 year, and her teacher, Mr. Carpenter, was working hard toward helping Yvonne realize her dreams of independence and involvement in the community. A new apartment seemed to be the next natural step.

Yvonne had a friend she had known in high school, Anna, who had recently lost a roommate and was looking for a replacement. Mr. Carpenter visited the apartment and spoke with Anna about the different expectations she had for her new roommate. Anna mentioned the types of chores that needed to be completed each week and the bills that had to be paid each month. In addition, she described her typical weekly routine, which included activities such as shopping, working, visiting with friends, going to church, and doing volunteer work. She indicated that she was eager to have a new roommate but was worried that her busy schedule might not allow her much time to help Yvonne with many of her physical needs. Mr. Carpenter reassured Anna that many people would be involved in supporting Yvonne and that she shouldn't worry that all of the responsibility would be on her.

Several weeks later (and aided by nine family members!), Yvonne moved into her new apartment. Even her classmates showed up to offer her help and congratulations. The excitement that everyone displayed was overwhelming. Mr. Carpenter and Ms. Malonee, a representative of a supported living agency, visited Yvonne once per week for the first month to observe how she adapted to her new living environment. They noted that Yvonne had already established supportive relationships with several of her neighbors and that she and Anna were getting along quite well. Anna, however, expressed concern that Yvonne was having trouble completing all of her chores, and Ms. Malonee observed that Yvonne was still not very involved in the community, despite her new residence.

Mr. Carpenter decided to gather together the individuals who were on Yvonne's planning team to discuss ways of providing support to Yvonne in her new environment. In addition, he hoped to develop a social support plan that would be carried out by the various members of the team. At the meeting, Yvonne began by explaining her vision for her life in the community. Next, several of her family members shared strategies they had used to support Yvonne when she was living at home. After Ms. Malonee explained the supports that her agency was willing to provide, Yvonne's work supervisor told the group that his company already had in place several programs that could address those same needs, including a carpool, a mentoring program, and a financial advisor who could meet with Yvonne. Before long, the blackboard was overflowing with more suggestions than Mr. Carpenter ever could have thought of himself. After arranging all of the supports into a plan for Yvonne, the group adjourned, excited to return in 1 month to reevaluate the effectiveness of the plan. Little did they know how much Yvonne would surprise them.

"In my program, employers provide input through an employer evaluation. Students are evaluated by general education teachers as to their integration and inclusion with their general education peers. Parents are involved by completing home inventories and in developing the IEP. Communication is ongoing through parent contacts throughout the year."

Teacher
Austin-East High School
Knoxville, Tennessee

5-3   DEVELOPING SOCIAL SUPPORT PLANS

Social support plans incorporate the information derived from site visits, observations of the student, and collaboration with important others in the student's life into a step-by-step blueprint for actively involving a student in everyday life in ways that are both productive and satisfying.

5.3.1   Developing Individual Social Support Plans

Often, there is a discrepancy between the supports available in a school, job, or community environment and the supports a student is receiving. The process of developing an individual social support plan involves gaining access to the supports available in an environment and matching them to the needs of the student.

Teacher-Proven Practices:

- Increased opportunities for social support frequently can result from making environmental modifications. For example, adjusting work schedules will permit co-workers to take a break together, rearranging a classroom lab will encourage two students to share a computer, and building a ramp will allow a student access to a church youth group.

- Help a student compile a "resource list" of social supports to turn to for assistance. The list could include peers in a general education class who could provide assistance on an assignment or in getting to the next class or include people who usually ride on the student's bus and who could inform him when his stop is coming up. Next, teach the student how and when to use such supports.

- Involving peers, family, employment staff, and community members as sources of social support, rather than just you alone as teacher or job coach, will ensure that those supports and efforts will continue long after high school when the student leaves the classroom or job-training site.

- Remember, it is both natural and desirable that students receive support from their friends and classmates, that employees receive support from their co-workers, and that community members receive support from neighbors or fellow businesspeople. Be sure to supplement, not replace, supports provided by the natural environment when you introduce additional supports.

All students should have the opportunity to learn and enjoy leisure activities with their peers both in and outside the classroom. Many students, however, will need support to assist them in taking full advantage of this opportunity. Students' IEPs must include a statement of the supports that will be provided for them to "be involved and progress in the general curriculum...and to participate in extracurricular and other nonacademic activities" (IDEA Amendments of 1997, Section 614).

"One of my students is very 'anti-social.' I called a meeting with the employer, co-workers, job coach, and parents and explained the skills I wanted to work on and told them the methods I had tried and what worked and what didn't. I asked for their ideas—others are often more willing to support me if they have input into the problem. For example, we wanted a student to learn to wave 'hello' when he entered a store. The employer and employees helped develop a plan. As a result, not only did they get to know the student and his family, but, to this day, when he enters the store, they will greet him openly and reach out to make his hand wave back if he does not respond independently."

Teacher
Warren County High School
McMinnville, Tennessee

How to Do It:

- As the team decides which supports will be used by the student, plan to use the least intrusive supports available in an environment, such as a family member or neighbor rather than a paid assistant. In a school environment, this might mean involving students before teachers, teachers before volunteers, and volunteers before specialists.

- Using natural social supports should have the effect of bringing individuals into contact with each other rather than isolating them. Make sure that the supports you provide don't result in a student's being unnecessarily "singled out." For example, a peer buddy as a support will blend in much better in a classroom than would an adult.

- All members of the IEP team, including community agencies, should be involved in the development of the student's social support plan. For example, the student's parents, employer, and supporting agencies should work together to help her experience success on the job.

Case Study 5.3   It's Great to Have Friends!

Yvonne's apartment wasn't the biggest or fanciest one in town. It didn't even have the nicest furnishings. But it was hers, and that made it the best! Anna and Yvonne had been roommates for just over 2 months, and already the two women were getting along extremely well. Yvonne's weeks were full of work and

"A female student works at a grocery store. She is allowed to lift only 15 pounds at a time. As a courtesy clerk, this can cause a problem with items such as dog food. She has informed her co-workers, and they know to help her when she asks. She also confides in a co-worker about her boyfriend."
Teacher
Central High School
Culleoka, Tennessee

community activities, which kept her busier than ever. Still, Yvonne occasionally found time to curl up on the living room couch and listen to her favorite CDs before Anna got home from work.

Soon, the planning team gathered together again to listen to Yvonne share how her second month had gone and to determine whether her support plan had been effective or needed fine-tuning. Yvonne described to her team the types of social supports she had received in different areas of her life.

Transportation supports: Because Yvonne didn't have a driver's license, getting around could have been difficult. However, a co-worker living in the next apartment complex drove her to and from work each day. Yvonne's brother picked her up for church each Sunday morning, and another church member drove her home when there was choir practice. Finally, Anna rode the bus with Yvonne to her community training program for the first couple of weeks until Yvonne had memorized the route. Just in case, Anna talked with the bus driver, asking him to remind Yvonne when she needed to get off.

Recreation/leisure supports: Yvonne met several friends through Anna at the apartment complex pool. Pretty soon, Yvonne had found companionship with three women with whom she went out to eat, shop, and dance. Her participation in the church choir also resulted in her meeting several additional friends. At the neighborhood yarn shop, she enrolled in a knitting class and was already knitting a scarf for her niece.

Employment supports: Yvonne went through the same job-training program as the other new employees, and Mr. Carpenter helped the library supervisor find ways to adapt some aspects of the training to meet Yvonne's needs. In addition, Yvonne was paired with a mentor, an experienced employee, who helped her adjust to the job and provided her with emotional support. Yvonne knew she could always call on Mr. Carpenter, but she quickly learned to turn to her co-workers or work supervisor first.

Personal supports: If Yvonne kept a messy apartment, Anna was even worse! The two decided to pay a housekeeper to visit their place twice per month for an "overhaul." In between, Anna showed Yvonne how to do some basic house cleaning and repairs. Yvonne met with a volunteer at the library to help her begin a budget. At the same time, Mr. Carpenter emphasized money management skills during community-based instruction.

Everyone was excited about the success that Yvonne was experiencing; the social supports they had planned for her were beginning to work. Yvonne was learning how rewarding living on her own could be and thanked everyone on her team for all of their assistance. Yvonne's family, teachers, and friends chuckled because they realized that they hadn't helped her in ways that were different or unusual. They hadn't even really gone too far out of their way to provide supports. But they did support her in her desire to be independent, and, to Yvonne, that made them the best!

Evaluating Outcomes:

Building and Evaluating a Social Support Plan

A student's transition goals and objectives as stated in the IEP are a good starting point for identifying the supports already provided to the student and for developing and evaluating a comprehensive support plan. By including the support plan in the IEP, teachers and providers are ensured that developing and evaluating supports is a team effort.

Several key components should be included in every support plan. These are the student's social support needs, the strategies used to address those needs, the person(s) responsible for carrying out the strategies, the anticipated outcomes, and the methods that will be used to evaluate those outcomes. Remember to address the student's social support needs in each environment in which he participates (or will participate). The next page includes a sample Individual Social Support Plan for a 20-year-old student named Alfred Otawba. A blank, reproducible form is included in the appendix.

Individual Social Support Plan

Student: __Alfred Otawba__   Age: __20__   Date: __September 8__

	Support needs	Support strategy	Person or agency responsible	Outcome	Target date	Evaluation method
Vocational needs	• Improved job performance at the bike shop	• Pair Alfred with another employee for continued job training.	• Vocational counselor will help co-worker adapt training. • Co-worker	• Alfred's job output will increase 20%.	11/15	• Co-worker will record the number of bikes Alfred builds each week
	• Accepting criticism from supervisors	• Job coach and co-workers will model expected behavior.	• Job coach • Adult service agency	• Alfred will say, "Thank you for the help," when given job feedback.	10/15	• Direct observation and student interviews
Community needs	• Transportation training, needs way to get to store, work, and various community activities	• Teacher/family will show how to use public transportation. • Friends provide rides. • Co-workers provide ride to worksite.	• Special education teacher • Parents • Peers • Co-workers	• Alfred will use public transportation to get to a desired location. • Alfred will contact and ride with a co-worker to his worksite.	11/15 10/15	• Log books and direct observation • Direct observation and communication with co-workers
Residential needs	• Planning meals that address Alfred's diet needs	• Nurse trains roommate to help Alfred plan meals that meet his diet needs.	• Nurse • Alfred's roommate	• With the assistance of a roommate, Alfred will plan weekly meals that meet his diet needs.	12/1	• Examine weekly menu of meals that Alfred plans.
	• Budgeting for monthly expenses	• Teacher will provide classroom instruction. • Parents will help Alfred.	• General and special education teachers • Parents	• Alfred will complete a monthly budget.	12/1	• Direct observation and communication with parents
School needs	• Involvement in an extracurricular activity	• Peer joins Alfred when attending extracurricular activity of his choice.	• Peers	• Alfred will participate in at least one extracurricular activity.	10/1	• Direct observation and conversation with peers
	• Increased class involvement during general education classes	• Peer can model behavior. • Teacher provides more chances for involvement.	• Peers • General education teacher • Educational assistant	• Alfred will increase his active involvement in class by 50%.	11/1	• Direct observation and conversation with teacher

Form 5.1.   Individual Social Support Plan for Alfred Otawba.

 As part of the plan to improve the educational and transitional services provided to students and their families, the IDEA Amendments of 1997 stress accountability for local educational agencies in improving the effectiveness and efficiency of service delivery, including developing strategies that promote accountability for results. In addition, community agencies participate in ensuring that students' support plans are carried out with successful outcomes. If these agencies fail to provide the transition supports described in a student's IEP, then the IEP team must reconvene to determine alternative strategies for meeting the student's IEP objectives.

Cross-references: Developing Individual Environmental Support Plans (4.3.1) and Establishing Interagency Collaboration (4.4.2)

"Encourage social interaction through a network of peer tutors at school and work. Assign peer tutors activities that carry over into the student's community and family life when possible."
Teacher
Riverdale High School
Murfreesboro, Tennessee

5.3.2 Incorporating Social Support into Instruction

Involvement in environments that are separate from the mainstream of everyday life can prevent or hinder the establishment of social supports for a student. When instruction occurs in integrated school, work, and community environments, the presence of same-age peers provides many opportunities for relationships and supports to develop. By incorporating these supports into instruction, teachers can increase students' opportunities for acceptance, success, and personal satisfaction.

Starting Up:

- Teach students first to request assistance from fellow class-mates, co-workers, or fellow sports team or club members before requesting it from you, the teacher, or job coach. Support from these individuals is more natural and easily available and is more likely to be present over the long term.

- Social interactions in the workplace can also lead to inter-actions and social support outside the job environment. Creating job tasks that are interdependent in nature will increase the opportunities that students have to interact on the job. In turn, co-workers who interact frequently on the job are more likely to spend time together after work and on the weekends.

- Include recreation and leisure training in a student's edu-cational program. Having skills that allow a student to participate in recreational activities with peers will pro-vide the student with opportunities to build friendships and become connected to social supports around the com-munity, such as at the YMCA, a singles club, or a women's (or men's) support group.

- Have peer buddies encourage and join students in partici-pating in school activities, such as assemblies, dances, sporting events, theater productions, and extracurricular clubs. Not only will the student enjoy it, but the peer bud-dies also will appreciate having developed new friend-ships and will feel better about themselves, too.

- Occasionally, students may need instruction on accepted social skills in a given environment. Teaching a student to initiate and respond in conversations with peers or dis-cuss more appropriate conversational topics can help a student develop his own social supports as well as make his interactions more enjoyable for everyone involved.

"Peers at school help a nonverbal student with multiple disabilities travel to and from the bus. The student uses Morse code with his eyes to communicate his needs."

Teacher
Lebanon High School
Lebanon, Tennessee

"Find a peer who has similar interests and make time for the two students to get together for fun and enjoyable activities outside school. Friendships will develop."

Teacher
Farragut High School
Knoxville, Tennessee

Cross-references: Incorporating Environmental Supports into Instruction (4.3.2) and Teaching Social Interaction Skills (9-4)

Remember to introduce similar social supports across all of the environments in which a student participates. Research shows that students are more likely to generalize their skills across similar instructional supports. For example, if a student has been taught to seek assistance by handing a peer a card at school, then teach her to use the same support in a store or on a bus.

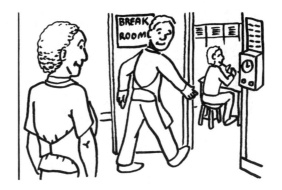

"A student who is doing job training at a hospital has learned to follow a work schedule by watching her co-workers. For example, when she sees the other employees go on break, she takes hers, too, without having to be prompted."
Teacher
Maryville High School
Maryville, Tennessee

5-4 GAINING ACCESS TO EXISTING SOCIAL SUPPORT

Identifying potential social supports in an environment is not enough. Teachers need to help students and important others learn how to gain access to this support. For example, families with limited English proficiency may not know how to find a mentoring program for their child, such as Big Brothers or Big Sisters. Or a student with learning disabilities may not know whether it is appropriate to ask for a time extension on a quiz. Learning to gain access to social supports is a skill we all need to develop—life is much easier with help along the way!

5.4.1 In the Community and at School

To become active and meaningful participants in community and school activities and environments, students need access to a variety of social supports. Try to find ways of using available social supports to increase the individual's success and acceptance. In doing so, students will benefit from participating in new experiences and developing new friendships.

"To help students access social supports, I encourage them to initiate conversation with their co-workers on topics such as their families, pets, clothes, transportation, etc. I also encourage co-workers to do the same. I make an effort to effect an air of openness at the jobsite."

Teacher
McGavock High School
Nashville, Tennessee

Teacher-Proven Practices:

Teachers and job coaches report having gained access to social support by doing the following:

- For a student who is having difficulty returning from break on time, a co-worker who shares the same break could prompt him or her to return to work.

- Peers from a student's school could volunteer to drop off the student at work on their way home if the student doesn't have a driver's license or a car.

- If a student has no independent means of transportation to and from work, a Plan for Achieving Self-Support (PASS) could be written to pay family members and co-workers to provide him or her with transportation.

- Delivery people at a pizza place or fast-food delivery service can drop off a fellow employee at home when they are out making deliveries.

- Students who work at community businesses can be encouraged to participate in company picnics and activities where social relationships and supports can be established.

- Students can volunteer to help with the lunch tray of a student with multiple disabilities. This is less stigmatizing to a student than having a teacher or educational assistant help.

Cross-references: Increasing Students' Social Interactions (9-1) and Increasing Opportunities for Social Interaction (9-3)

How to Do It:

- Link the student with a mentor at work to provide job training and orientation to the job (this is the way most people learn on the job).

- Invite community members and sponsors of a school-to-work program to attend a school or community activity such as a job fair or school carnival. You may be surprised to see how well they relate to your students when they are in a social environment.

- Don't leave participation in after-school and community activities to chance. Your students and their families may need a "nudge." Send home calendars of social events,

"I have planned social support for students, and often it is superficial and 'short-lived.' I have even made it a requirement of the peer-tutoring course I instruct. Friendships and social supports that are created by the student are far better, more stable, and usually nonsuperficial."
Teacher
Karns High School
Knoxville, Tennessee

such as community dances, and arrange for carpooling if they don't have a ride to an event.

"My students are allowed to use a pool at a jobsite at the end of each week. They swim with other club members and have made some new friends."

Teacher
Hillsboro High School
Nashville, Tennessee

5.4.2   Among Individuals

Social supports are *people*, and *people* are made up of many individuals. Put your public relations skills to work as you help the individuals who provide a student's social support learn to collaborate with each other. Doing so will demonstrate that the whole is more than the sum of its parts when it comes to working together to provide support for a student.

"During the open house at the beginning of the school year, the guidance office asked visitors to sign a notebook listing services they could provide to students. For example, some offered to give escorted tours of their businesses or to speak in class or at assemblies about career opportunities. Some offered interviews or job applications for practicing or actually applying for a job. These opportunities were open to the whole school, not just special education students."

Teacher
Fairley High School
Memphis, Tennessee

Teacher-Proven Practices:

- Make sure that *all* students participate in school functions, extracurricular activities, and school clubs so that they will fit in socially at school by sharing common experiences with their peers. Keep a tally sheet of students' activities (see Community Activity Participation Form [Form 3.4] in At Work and in the Community, 3.4.2).

- Find a peer who has similar interests as a student, and make time for them to get together for activities outside school. For example, students who like French could join the French club and go on club outings together, or students who like to volunteer could join the local Red Cross and do community volunteer activities together.

- Try to bring students into close contact with other employees on the worksite by arranging break time with and on-the-job training by co-workers. This will prevent having students simply be in proximity to their co-workers without talking or interacting with them.

Cross-references: Increasing Students' Social Interactions (9-1) and Increasing Opportunities for Social Interaction (9-3)

Evaluating Outcomes:

Evaluating Social Support Involvement

- Use the Work Performance Evaluation (see Form 4.2 in Observing Students' Performance 4.1.2) to compare the social support available in an environment and the extent to which a student is using the support. Pinpoint reasons why a student may not be using particular supports, such as Friday potlucks at work, and brainstorm how to get the student involved.

- Directly observe others in the environment as they interact with a student. People's expressions or the way they interact with a student can tell you a lot about how supportive their relationship is. Are they smiling and laughing with the student, or are they looking around and seeming distracted by and more interested in others? How is the student responding during the interactions?

- Schedule regular visits or conversations with people frequently involved with a student, such as a fellow member of the basketball team or chess club. Ask directly what sort of supports a student receives, or infer from their conversations how supportive an environment is.

- Interview the student. She may be the best judge of the supports that she is receiving. For example, she may report that peers in her general education classes are making fun of her. Check the student's judgment by direct observation. It may be that she is correct or that her peers are actually joking with her as they do with the rest of their friends. In either case, be sure to address the student's perceptions.

"Sometimes students at work get too much assistance from their co-workers. To give students opportunities to learn to complete their work more independently, we discuss with co-workers how to modify the task or environment. Often they are very helpful. Sometimes I use the same strategies with peers in class and in the school cafeteria."
Teacher
Rutledge High School
Rutledge, Tennessee

REFERENCES

Individuals with Disabilities Education Act Amendments of 1997, PL 105-17, 20 U.S.C. §§ 1400 *et seq.*

Jorgensen, C.M. (1992). Natural supports in inclusive schools: Curricular and teaching strategies. In J. Nisbet (Ed.), *Natural supports in school, at work, and in the community for people with severe disabilities* (pp. 179–215). Baltimore: Paul H. Brookes Publishing Co.

SECTION III

Strategies for Increasing Students' Competence

Chapter 6

Strategies for Identifying and Promoting Students' Strengths

OVERVIEW

Everyone possesses strengths in various areas: academics, sports, leadership, character, social relationships, or career performance. The Individuals with Disabilities Education Act (IDEA) Amendments of 1997 (PL 105-17) stress that students' individualized education programs (IEPs) emphasize students' strengths rather than weaknesses. The move from *deficit-based* educational programming reflects the belief that all students can and should be maximally included in everyday school, work, and community environments. As active participants in inclusive environments and provided with needed social and environmental supports, students gain the opportunity to expand their competence. As for all people, having the opportunity is the critical factor!

When individuals are viewed as competent, they typically are accepted more readily into an environment. Being competent also provides many benefits, such as job advancement, educational opportunities, and satisfying relationships. *Competence* is judged within the context of an environment. Being considered competent in one environment does not mean that the same person would be considered competent in another environment. Competence must also be promoted, supported, accepted, and maintained within an environment.

One of the first steps in building students' competence is to identify their individual strengths and the areas in which they need supports. Teachers can pinpoint these strengths by observing students' involvement in a variety of school, work, and community activities and by systematically recording and evaluating their observations. It is important to observe students in many different environments because people's strengths and needs vary according to the demands of an environment. Because observing students in different environments is both difficult and time consuming, teachers can use alternative assessments to gather information that is not accessible through direct observation. In addition, information can be obtained by collaborating with family members, peers, community members, co-workers, and other individuals who see the student regularly as well as by talking to the student herself. When a student's strengths and needs have been accurately identified, instruction should target those skills in a student's repertoire that need supports.

This chapter contains four main groups and eight subgroups of strategies that teachers may use to identify and promote students' strengths. It includes such strategies as observing performance and collecting data, assessing students' strengths and needs, communicating about students' strengths and needs, and teaching skills that need strengthening.

Case Study 6.1   A New Student at Washington High

Carlos Santanora was somewhat of a surprise. Autumn was already revealing itself in the leaves of the maple trees outside Washington High School, where students had been in classes for almost 2 months. Halfway through Mr. Kleeb's math lesson, Carlos hesitantly walked through the door, accompanied by his father and the school secretary. After asking his co-teacher to continue with the lesson, Mr. Kleeb, a consulting special education teacher, walked over and greeted his unexpected guests. Mr. Santanora shook hands and politely apologized for his "difficulty with English." He explained that he and his family had just moved to the United States after he had received a job promotion with a large computer company. The sudden move meant a new classroom, school, and country for Car-

Creating an accurate picture of a student's competence within a given context helps you identify ways to build on a student's strengths and areas of needed support. Be a good observer and a good listener!

los. Mr. Kleeb, knowing how apprehensive Carlos must have felt, assured him that he would do everything he could to assist him in his transition to his new environment. Mr. Santanora added that he knew little about the types of educational services Carlos had received at his old school but stated that he did hope his son would "make some new friends, pick up English, and learn to do more things on his own." With that, Mr. Santanora thanked Mr. Kleeb, hugged Carlos, and left for work. Mr. Kleeb stood at the door with a confused smile—glad to have a new student in his class but unsure of exactly where to begin with him. How long would it be before Carlos's files arrived from his former school? When (and if) they did arrive, would they provide Mr. Kleeb with helpful information about Carlos's educational program? What should he do in the meantime? Where should he begin?

6-1 OBSERVING PERFORMANCE AND COLLECTING DATA

6.1.1 Observing Students' Performance

The IDEA Amendments of 1997 stipulate that the local education agency (LEA) or state agency must conduct a full and individual initial evaluation before special education and related services can be provided to a student who is identified as eligible for services. In conducting the evaluation, the LEA must use a variety of assessment tools and strategies to gather relevant functional information, including behavioral factors, to assist in determining an appropriate educational program for the student.

Observing a student's performance within a given environment and systematically collecting data allow a teacher to target the specific strengths and needs of a student within the context and demands of a particular environment.

Many students' strengths will remain unidentified until students are given the opportunity to try new activities. When students participate across an entire spectrum of school, work, and community events, rather than only in those that typically are available to "students with disabilities," those untapped strengths can emerge. By observing a student as he participates in a new activity, teachers are able to identify those skill areas that need supports in order to increase a student's competence and participation.

Starting Up:

- Observe your students in the actual environments in which they will be participating. Artificial environments, such as simulated grocery stores, separate gym classes, or mock worksites, cannot accurately replicate the demands of the environment and do not give the student the opportunity to demonstrate strengths in related areas of behavior. Instead, observe a student's social skills while she is interacting with co-workers, or observe a student's problem-solving skills when materials with which to complete an assignment are missing.

- When involving students in new activities, remember that few people are proficient at skills they are trying for the very first time. Give students opportunities to practice new skills and routines, observing them periodically to see how their skills develop.

- In a work environment, task performance is only one of several areas that a teacher should observe. Other areas in which a student may demonstrate strengths include social relationships, self-care skills, communication abilities, and job-related skills such as punctuality or dependability.

- Incorporate students' preferences into the activities in which they are involved as you observe them. People are better at tasks they enjoy and select themselves (see Assessing Students' Choices and Preferences, 8.1.3).

Cross-references: Observing Students' Performance (4.1.2), Observing Students' Interactions (5.1.2), and Observing Students' Choices (8.1.1)

"I go to jobsites and observe students' social behavior and work skills. I make written notes on my observations and talk to the supervisor. I also observe students during their recreation and community activities and note their behavior."

Teacher
Farragut High School
Knoxville, Tennessee

Evaluating Outcomes:

How to Collect Data

Collecting information on a student's strengths and needs is critical to developing educational programs for all students. Knowing what information you want and having means to gather it are two different issues. After all, there are many ways to record data on any single student behavior. For example, let's say you want to identify a student's strengths and needs at a new job-training site. You could record the number of faucets she repairs (frequency), how many are fixed each hour (rate), how long each takes to repair (duration), how long it takes before she starts on her repairs (latency), the proportion of faucets she fixes correctly (percentage), and on and on. Whew! Figuring out which method to use will depend on two factors: 1) the target behavior, such as starting to work on the job, and 2) the information wanted, such as how long after punching a time card. The following section shows three types of observation systems that you can use to collect information about students' strengths and needs: event recording, interval recording, and task analysis.

Event Recording

How often does a student do something? Event recording can answer this question. You can either observe for example, the number of times a student sneezes in class or scores a basket in a game, or observe the outcome of a particular behavior later, such as the number of doughnuts baked or number of clothes folded correctly. The following example, Event Recording Datasheet, shows how to observe more than one behavior at a time. A blank, reproducible form is included in the appendix.

Interval Recording

What if a student performs a behavior for a long time, such as working without stopping or kicking the wall?

Event Recording Datasheet

Student: Emily Raptor   **Date:** March 25

Location: Lagner's Department Store   **Observer:** Ms. Roberts

Activity: Job training in the women's clothing section

	Time	Greeted others	Asked for assistance	Provided assistance	Items folded correctly	Items folded incorrectly
	9:00–9:15	III	II	II	ЖНГ II	I
	9:15–9:30	II	III	IIII	IIII	ЖНГ
	9:30–9:45	—	II	I	ЖНГ	—
	9:45–10:00	IIII	I	—	ЖНГ ЖНГ II	III
Total	1 hour	9	8	7	28	9

Comments: Emily greeted only employees she knew well and very few customers. She increased the number of items she folded correctly by almost 10 over her last effort. She seems to really enjoy working around her friend Jane.

Form 6.1.   Event Recording Datasheet for Emily Raptor.

You can use interval recording to estimate how long a student does something. By dividing an observation period into equal intervals (e.g., 10 seconds or more), you can identify those intervals in which a behavior occurs. The following is an example Interval Recording Datasheet observation form that can be adapted for use in work, school, home, or community environments. A blank, reproducible form is included in the appendix.

Interval Recording Datasheet

Students: Jeff and Andy

Date: April 12

Location: Charlemonte Bar & Grille

Observer: Mr. Gabel

Activity: Hosting during the lunch shift

Interval: minutes	On-task (Jeff)	On-task (Andy)	Socializing (Jeff)	Socializing (Andy)	Smiling (Jeff)	Smiling (Andy)
:10	✓	✓	—	—	✓	—
:20	—	✓	✓	—	✓	—
:30	—	✓	✓	—	✓	—
:40	—	—	✓	—	✓	—
:50	✓	✓	✓	—	✓	—
1:00	—	✓	✓	—	✓	—
1:10	—	✓	—	—	✓	—
1:20	✓	—	✓	✓	✓	✓
1:30	✓	✓	✓	—	✓	✓
1:40	—	✓	✓	—	✓	—
Total	4	8	8	1	10	2
% of intervals	40%	80%	80%	10%	100%	20%

✓ = Occurrence   — = Nonoccurrence

Comments: Andy worked almost constantly but didn't talk with any of the other employees or customers—he seemed a bit uncomfortable (few smiles). Jeff was a "social butterfly" but completed very little work.

Form 6.2   Interval Recording Datasheet for Jeff and Andy.

Task Analysis

Student: Marcus Anderson

Environment: Leitermann Corporation Employee Cafeteria

Goal: Marcus will complete every step independently on three consecutive trials by 4/12. Total score of 76.

Coding:
4 = Independent response
3 = Verbal prompt
2 = Gestural prompt
1 = Physical prompt

Steps		Trial 1	2	3	4	5	6	7	8	9	10
20	—	-	-	-	-	-	-	-			
19	Leave the lunch line	3	3	2	3	3	4	3			
18	Pick up lunch tray	1	1	2	2	2	4	4			
17	Sign credit card receipt	2	2	2	3	4	3	4			
16	Give cashier credit card	2	2	3	3	3	3	4			
15	Move to cashier station	1	1	2	2	3	3	3			
14	Place beverage on tray	2	2	3	2	2	3	3			
13	Locate preferred beverage	1	2	2	3	2	3	3			
12	Move to beverage station	2	3	3	3	3	3	3			
11	Repeat steps 9 & 10 (meat, veg., bread)	1	1	1	2	2	2	3			
10	Indicate preference	1	1	1	1	2	2	3			
9	Ask what food choices are available	1	1	1	1	2	4	3			
8	Move to food station	3	4	3	3	4	4	4			
7	Pick up napkin and place on tray	1	2	3	3	3	4	4			
6	Pick up spoon and place on tray	3	4	4	4	4	4	4			
5	Pick up knife and place on tray	2	3	4	3	4	4	4			
4	Pick up fork and place on tray	2	3	4	3	4	3	4			
3	Place lunch tray on rails	2	3	2	3	3	2	3			
2	Pick up lunch tray	1	1	2	2	2	4	3			
1	Enter beginning of lunch line	4	4	3	4	4	4	4			
	Total	35	43	47	50	56	63	66			
	Date	4/1	4/2	4/3	4/4	4/5	4/8	4/9			

Form 6.3.   Task Analysis for Marcus Anderson.

Task Analysis

Maybe you want to know what steps of an activity a student does well (or needs support to perform). By listing all of the steps of an activity in a task analysis, you can observe each step of a student's performance and whether support is needed. On page 146 is an example of a Task Analysis observation form that can be used in a variety of environments in which the student may be involved. A blank, reproducible form is included in the appendix.

How to Do It:

- Develop a checklist or inventory of skills and behaviors, such as social skills or study skills, that are important to successful participation in the target environment. As you observe the student, use the checklist as a guide for evaluating the student's performance.

- *Job sampling* (providing a student with a variety of employment-training experiences) allows you to observe students across a range of employment sites that represent both the students' career interests and the types of jobs actually available in the community. The Work Performance Evaluation (see Form 4.2 in Observing Students' Performance, 4.1.2) allows you to conduct a situational vocational assessment of a student's skills (see Job Sampling, 8.1.3).

- Remember, it is important to observe students in many different environments because people's strengths and needs vary according to the different demands of each environment. Visit students at home to observe their morning routine, at work to watch them interact with customers, or at the mall to survey their money skills.

- Be sure to observe students at many different worksites with varying degrees of "pressure." Jobs that require a high speed or production rate will affect individuals differently than those that require a slower pace. You may find that a student appears agitated, aggressive, or anxious in a high-pressure job, such as fry-cook in a fast-food restaurant. Try changing the student's job tasks to some with less pressure to determine whether his behavior relates to the job task or the worksite itself. Use this information to help determine job placement for the student.

"I have noticed the following behavior when students are comfortable and competent on a job. They will stop looking at me or the job coach for prompts and put all of their attention into the job."

Itinerant Transition Teacher
Nashville Public Schools
Nashville, Tennessee

Evaluating Outcomes:

Comparative Observations

Observing a student is one thing, but how do you know how well the student should be performing? How do you know what the "norm" is within a particular environment? For example, if you are interested in a student's rate of stacking computer disks at a warehouse, how do you know how fast the student should be going? A simple solution is to compare the student's performance with that of co-workers, students, or peers who are proficient in that environment. This allows for a standard by which to evaluate a student's performance as well as a goal to aim for in instructional programs. To compare a student's performance, just follow these four easy steps:

1. *Begin by identifying at least one peer in a particular environment who is proficient at performing the same routines, activities, or tasks as the student.* For example, you may choose to select another mechanic at a student's worksite, a teammate in her basketball league, a roommate from her apartment, a soprano from the community choir, or a classmate in school. If possible, identify several peers be-

cause people vary in their performance. *Example:* Mr. Roehler, James's special education teacher, noticed that James was very quiet at lunch. He hardly seemed to talk to anyone. Mr. Roehler wondered whether increasing conversational initiations should be one of James's IEP goals. However, he didn't know how much a typical high school student talked at lunch. He decided to do a comparative observation. He picked three general education peers who ate nearby in the same cafeteria as James and who frequently talked to their peers.

2.   *Observe the identified peers as they perform the target behavior, and record their performance.* Because everyone's behavior varies from day to day, remember to observe each peer's performance at least three to five times. Compile the information, compute the average performance, and then allow some flexibility to establish a range of performance that would be expected for the target behavior. *Example:* Mr. Roehler recorded the peers' performance over a 2-week period. It really wasn't difficult to do because he ate in the lunchroom every day anyway. James's peers initiated conversation at an average of three times per minute. Mr. Roehler decided to choose the range of two to four times per minute as a standard for James's initiating behavior.

3.   *Next, observe the student as he performs the same target behavior.* Remember to observe at least three to five times to establish an average and range for the student's performance. Then compare the student's performance with the range you established for the peers. Is there a big difference? If so, you may want to target the behavior for instruction and support. If not, the student may already be performing within the expectations of the environment. *Example:* As Mr. Roehler had suspected, there was a big difference between James's observed behavior and his peers' standard. In fact, it was worse than he had thought: During all five observations, James never initiated conversation once! Occasionally, he responded when spoken to, but that was all. It seemed that increasing initiations was a behavior that should be targeted in James's educational program.

4.   *Your job is not quite over.* Although you've been able to demonstrate through comparative observations

that there is (or is not) a difference in the student's performance and the established performance, you still need to find out whether important others in the environment agree with your findings. Even if your data show that there is a difference in performance, others may not believe that there is a problem (or vice versa). Be sure to ask others' opinions before initiating an instructional program; this will help you prioritize educational goals for a student. *Example:* Mr. Roehler discreetly asked James's peers in the lunchroom, his general education teachers, lunchroom staff, and James's parents whether they believed that James's lack of conversation during social times was a problem. They all agreed that it was! Everyone liked James, but, as one student put it, "He's like in a shell. He'll answer when I talk to him, but I really wish he'd joke around with me more and ask me about myself." Mr. Roehler was convinced: He would show his data to the IEP team and propose to include on James's IEP the goal to "increase conversational initiations."

"I make on-site observations of students at places where they go for recreation, school, work, and other activities. Then I compare what they do with others in those settings."

Teacher
East High School
Memphis, Tennessee

"To assess a student's skills and needs, first do the task yourself. Then have a general education peer do the task. Then have the student do the task him- or herself. Compare performance using a task analysis. This will point out the student's strengths and needs."

Teacher
Warren County High School
McMinnville, Tennessee

6.1.2 Collecting Data and Reviewing Students' Evaluations

According to the IDEA Amendments of 1997, the IEP team must review existing evaluation data as part of an initial evaluation of a student (if appropriate) and as part of any reevaluation. These data must include classroom-based assessments and observations, teachers' and related services providers'

observations, psychological reports, and evaluations and in-formation obtained from parents.

"A good checklist or logbook is helpful. I reverse how it's usually done by looking only for strengths or job match skills instead of problems. I list skills on the checklist that are needed for certain jobs. For example, is endurance most important or is work rate?"

Itinerant Transition Teacher
Nashville Public Schools
Nashville, Tennessee

Collecting data is critical in identifying strengths among your students. In addition to helping teachers target those aspects of a routine that students perform well, data gathered can be used as a basis for communicating with others about a student's skills. In fact, employers, parents, and important others may be pleasantly surprised when they see documentation that a student is actually performing certain tasks well.

Teacher-Proven Practices:

- Complete a task analysis of the activity or skill that you are observing the student performing, such as cooking breakfast. Recording the student's performance for each step of the task analysis will assist you in determining in which aspects of a routine a student is proficient and which areas may require future instruction and support (see Form 6.3 in Observing Students' Performance, 6.1.1).

- Data that are collected on only one occasion are not likely to be representative of a student's actual skills. Performance varies over time. Especially when a student is participating in a new environment, such as a new school or class, allow the student time to adapt while you take periodic data over time.

- As one person, you cannot be present in all of the environments in which a student participates throughout the day. Luckily, as stated in the IDEA Amendments of 1997, other individuals in the environment can assist with collecting data. For example, a co-worker could record the number of aisles stocked, a peer could note a student's progress on math problems, a baseball coach could keep track of a batting average, or a parent could indicate the time it takes to complete a chore.

- Go multimedia! Try videotaping or photographing a student at several points across time. The videotapes and photographs can be used to evaluate and document a student's progress over time. You can also use them for a teaching tool for the student or other students who are learning to perform the same or similar task.

- Collecting data provides you with a reference point against which to compare later improvements in student performance. In addition to academic and school-related areas, information should be recorded in work, community, and residential environments. Remember that students' performance varies according to the context of an environment.

Case Study 6.2   A Place to Begin

Mr. Kleeb had been teaching for several years and was used to having new students join late in the year. Usually, he would speak with their parents and former teachers, examine their IEPs, and look through their student files to determine where to begin. Carlos's situation, however, was different—no teachers to consult, no IEP, and no student records. Mr. Kleeb knew that he would have to begin by identifying Carlos's individual strengths and areas in which he needed support. Doing so would require observing Carlos's interactions in a variety of school, work, and community environments and carefully recording his findings.

Many of the students with whom Mr. Kleeb worked were already involved in activities throughout the school and community. Each week, he helped students learn important skills through purchasing food for the culinary arts class, depositing money in the bank for the athletic department, and buying school supplies for the central office. As Carlos participated in these activities, Mr. Kleeb used a task analysis to identify skills at which Carlos excelled and to determine where he might need additional supports. Mr. Kleeb discovered that although Carlos had never used (or seen) an automated teller machine, he knew exactly how to deposit and withdraw money from the bank. Moreover, he was familiar with how to purchase items at a store, and he even taught Mr. Kleeb the best way to pick out ripe fruit! Mr. Kleeb looked at more than just Carlos's participation in certain activities, however. He also watched for less visible strengths, such as how Carlos interacted with strangers, when he appeared confident or hesitant, how he dealt with unexpected problems, and to whom he turned for assistance.

Mr. Kleeb arranged for Carlos to gain some work experience at several community businesses. As a result, he was able to observe Carlos's performance across a variety of different job environments. Because two other students also worked at the same businesses, Mr. Kleeb asked a co-worker to evaluate Carlos's work skills against a checklist of skills he and the store manager had developed. Mr. Kleeb quickly discovered that Carlos loved working with people and was very successful at it. Before long, Carlos was working almost independently and had made several new friends.

Almost 1 month later, a worn package arrived in the mail, covered with foreign postage stamps. Mr. Kleeb, full of curiosity, opened the package and discovered a collection of documents from Carlos's former school. With a little help from a translator, Mr. Kleeb read through the entire contents of Carlos's educational program. Former teacher observations gave Mr. Kleeb some good ideas about some interests and activities Carlos might enjoy and do well at. However, he was surprised to discover that, in many ways, he didn't recognize the student described in those files: "Skill deficits in communication, functional academics, and social skills," "Emphasis placed on prevocational skills." The Carlos he had observed was an outgoing, excited student who demonstrated numerous strengths and talents. How could two people view a student so differently? Mr. Kleeb stepped back for a moment, glad that he had not relied solely on others' perceptions of Carlos but had observed and documented his strengths for himself.

"I use the student's psychological evaluation in combination with classroom behavioral observations to determine a student's need for additional supports. I also consider the observations of parents, co-workers, peers, and the students themselves."
Teacher
Hillcrest High School
Memphis, Tennessee

By the time students reach high school, they have benefited from the instruction and supports of many teachers and individuals. Their records are likely to contain a wealth of useful information regarding their experiences, performance, and strengths. Remember, you are required by the IDEA Amendments of 1997 to review current and existing evaluation data in determining a student's educational and related services needs, the IEP, and appropriate program modifications to allow the student to be involved in and progress in the general curriculum.

Evaluating Outcomes:

Evaluating Students' Data

- Communicate frequently with general education teachers regarding your students' grade reports rather than wait until the end of the grading period or semester. Doing so will keep you abreast of collaborating teachers' perceptions of students' work and will allow you to identify curriculum areas in which they are performing strongly or need supports or program modifications.

- Student files are frequently filled with past observations, teacher and parent interviews, assessment results, and former IEPs. Combine this information with current evaluations to identify students' areas of competence and needed supports.

- Keep track of your students' daily school and work attendance and behavior. This information can help you identify days that tend to be problematic for a student. Then adapt the daily schedule to accommodate the student's needs. For example, a student is consistently sleepy and late to school on Mondays because she visits her stepmother on the weekends. Try to have community-based instruction for the student in the afternoon on Mondays, and start the day at a slower pace.

"At his job-training site, a student was gathering aluminum cans for recycling. By observation, we noticed that he would drain the cans in the trash can properly, but sometimes he would take trash out of the garbage to keep for himself: large bags, papers, and plastic 2-liter bottles. After instructing him not to remove trash from the cans, we periodically would pair him with another student to monitor his behavior."

Teacher
Pearl-Cohn High School
Nashville, Tennessee

6-2 ASSESSING STUDENTS' STRENGTHS AND NEEDS

Appropriate assessment is essential to the development of an IEP for any student. The IDEA Amendments of 1997 provide guidelines for using assessments when developing programs for a student. The IEP team must "use a variety of assessment tools and strategies to gather relevant functional and developmental information, including information provided by the parent,…not use any single procedure as the sole criterion,… [and] use technically sound instruments that may assess the relative contribution of cognitive and behavioral factors, in addition to physical or developmental factors" (Section 614) when determining whether a student has a disability and the content of his or her IEP.

6.2.1 Using Informal Assessment Methods

"I use a home–community activities inventory that has a checklist of tasks and is filled out at every IEP meeting with the parent. I use systematic data collection to determine steps on a task analysis that cause difficulty. I use student profiles to facilitate information sharing with the vocational rehabilitation counselor and general education teacher feedback forms for information on integrated classrooms. To assess vocational training, I use employer evaluations."

Teacher
Karns High School
Knoxville, Tennessee

Informal assessment has many advantages. It allows you to assess a student's skills within the context of the environment in which the behavior is expected to be performed. Rather than assess a student on a generic set of skills, such as "job readiness," which may have no relevance in the immediate environment, you can assess only those skills that are needed in your students' everyday lives. Let's say that one of your students has trouble ordering her favorite meal, a grilled chicken sandwich, at the local fast-food restaurant. You don't need to assess every restaurant skill that she has—only the skills she needs to order her sandwich. Informal assessment lets you focus on only those skills that count in a particular student's daily life.

Evaluating Outcomes:

Behavioral Checklist

Behavioral checklists help you focus on behaviors of interest. They can be teacher-made or commercially prepared. Teacher-made checklists have the advantage of reflecting only the skills that are important in a student's environment. Commercially prepared checklists are ready-made and save you time. In either case, information can be obtained quickly by either observation or interviews. On the next page, there is an example of a form that can be used to evaluate an employee's social skills on the job. A blank, reproducible form of the Employee Social Skills Checklist is included in the appendix. Different forms can be devised for other behaviors.

Starting Up:

- When assessing a student's strengths, involve as many people who work with the student as possible. This will provide you with information that you don't have the time or opportunity to gather. Also, incorporating the perspectives of others into your evaluation will help eliminate any bias that may occur when only one person completes a student's assessment.

- Try contact "logs" for maintaining communication between yourself and others who work with a student and for keeping up ongoing assessments across different environments. *Here's how:* Ask parents, general education teachers, employers, and others to record information about a student's performance in a spiral notebook, planner, or calendar (whichever a student prefers) that accompanies the student and is exchanged among all parties. You'll be better informed about your students and important others in their lives.

Employee Social Skills Checklist

Student: _Lyndon Shakespeare_   **Interview/observation date:** _3/22_

Work environment: _Computer Universe on Blanco Road_

Skill	Always	Sometimes	Never	N/A	Comments
➢ Does the student greet co-workers when arriving to or leaving work?	☑	☐	☐	☐	Lyndon especially likes greeting Karen!
➢ Is the student punctual and on time?	☑	☐	☐	☐	
➢ Does the student look approachable (e.g., smiling, well-groomed)?	☐	☑	☐	☐	Sometimes Lyndon needs to be reminded to tuck in his shirt.
➢ Is the student polite (e.g., jokes, uses social amenities)?	☑	☐	☐	☐	Extremely courteous!
➢ Does the student greet/interact with customers in an acceptable way?	☑	☐	☐	☐	
➢ Does the student greet/interact with co-workers in an acceptable way?	☑	☐	☐	☐	
➢ Is the student meeting expected work performance goals?	☐	☑	☐	☐	Lyndon often gets so wrapped up in talking with others that he doesn't finish his work.
➢ Does the student turn to co-workers for assistance when needed?	☐	☑	☐	☐	
➢ Does the student give and receive directions/instructions well?	☐	☑	☐	☐	Lyndon can get upset when his supervisor gives him work feedback.
➢ Does the student give and receive praise/criticism well?	☐	☑	☐	☐	
➢ Does the student get along well with his or her peers?	☑	☐	☐	☐	
➢ Does the student seem to fit in with a social group at work?	☑	☐	☐	☐	Lyndon has several great friends at work!
➢ Does the student spend break or lunch with co-workers?	☑	☐	☐	☐	Sometimes he tries to go on break with co-workers even when it isn't his turn.
➢ Does the student interact with co-workers outside work?	☑	☐	☐	☐	

Form 6.4.   Employee Social Skills Checklist for Lyndon Shakespeare.

- During school, work, and recreational activities, pair a student with a peer who can evaluate the student's performance on important tasks. This will allow you an opportunity to work with other students and provide you with a peer's perspective on a student's strengths. For example, if a student's goal is to increase positive self-statements, then have a peer keep a simple tally of occurrences.

- Don't overlook one of the best sources of information regarding students' strengths: the students themselves! You may find that they have more insight into their own performance than you think. Give students regular opportunities to evaluate their own performance and to suggest areas of supports.

"Pretesting, oral reading, and chalkboard activities provide much information about students' strengths and needs. Discreetly questioning students privately one-to-one helps clarify puzzling cases in which students are having problems."

Teacher
Fairley High School
Memphis, Tennessee

Teacher-Proven Practices:

- The Work Performance Evaluation (Form 4.2) in Observing Students' Performance, 4.1.2, is an informal vocational assessment that can be modified to reflect the skills required in your students' actual work environments. Save yourself some work: Keep a log of the forms you develop so that you can reuse them in the same environment with different students.

- *Remember:* You can't follow your students around all day (nor would you want to) to find out how they're doing. Give yourself a break. Collaborate with others such as parents and employers to develop a checklist of important student competencies. Let others use the checklist across different environments as a guide for assessing students' strengths and needs. Get together at a brown bag luncheon and compare outcomes while you socialize.

- Ongoing assessment is the key to effective instruction and support. You need to keep on top of your students' progress. Practice may result in a student's mastering a skill that was once difficult, whereas changes in jobs, people, or activities may result in a student's being challenged in an environment that was formerly routine. Expect and adjust for change in performance.

Evaluating Outcomes:

Conducting a Home Inventory

Perhaps more than anyone, parents know their children best. Moreover, individuals who live with the student on a day-to-day basis (e.g., parents, siblings, relatives, support staff, roommates) are in a position to observe strengths and needs that cannot be witnessed by a teacher in school and work environments. Asking these individuals to help a student complete home inventories of a student's activities and involvement can assist teachers in developing instructional programs and opportunities that meet a student's needs. They also allow parents an opportunity to express their preferences and personal values. For example, some parents may believe that women belong "only in the home." The home inventory gives you a chance to discuss the advantages of community-based transition programs *and* be responsive to parents' viewpoints.

The next page contains a sample Home Inventory Form. (Blank, reproducible forms are included in the appendix.)

"Provide job sampling—observe students in various job settings. Do interest surveys with students. Informal testing and checklists can also provide additional information on students' strengths and needs."

Teacher
Whites Creek High School
Whites Creek, Tennessee

Home Inventory Form

Personal Information

Student: __Jared Hutchinson__   Age: __20__   Interview date: __September 24__

Where do you live? ___ House __✓__ Apartment   How long have you lived there? __11 months__

Who lives with you? __two roommates (Michael and Samuel)__

Do you have relatives who live near you? __yes__   Who? __brother, parent, aunt, & uncle__

Likes and Dislikes

	What do you like?	What do you dislike?
Foods (snacks, treats, special diet)	Fast food—Burger Hut, McRey's	Seafood
	Popcorn	Dairy products (allergic)
	Chinese food—egg rolls, fried rice	
Activities (hobbies, sports, places, events)	Working in workshop with father	Bowling
	Wichicumba Redbirds baseball games	
	Computer games/World Wide Web	
	Watching movies	
Work (jobs, chores, volunteer events)	Working at Sheare's Hardware	Cleaning jobs—mopping, bathrooms, etc.
	Landscaping, working in the garden	Working alone
	Volunteer with Habitat for Humanity	
	Anything outdoors!	

Concerns

Are there issues that keep you from enjoying community events?
(e.g., toileting accidents, hitting others, loud screaming)

What issues?	Where do they occur?	What is the result?
Afraid to take bus alone	Downtown	Stay home, miss the Redbirds
Get angry at work	At the hardware store	Yell at Mr. Sheare

Form 6.5.   Home Inventory Form for Jared Hutchinson. (From Allen, W.T. [1988]. *Read my lips: It's choice*....St. Paul, MN: Governor's Council on Developmental Disabilities, Department of Administration; adapted by permission of Allen, Shea & Associates.)

Your Community

A "map" of your community will help develop a picture of where neighbors live, work, and play. Make sure to fill this out completely.

Streets

Which streets in your neighborhood do you use frequently?	How do you use them?			Are there...	
	Walk	Car	Bus	Signals	Crosswalks
Neese Drive	✓				
Nolensville Boulevard	✓			✓	✓
Twin Oaks Parkway		✓		✓	✓
Antioch Drive	✓				✓

Family & Friends

Whom do you visit?	How far away?		How do you get there?			How often do you visit?			
	1–5 blocks	5+ blocks	Walk	Car	Bus	Daily	Each week	Each month	Other
Mom and Dad		✓		✓			✓		
Brother	✓		✓						3Xwk
Aunt and Uncle		✓		✓				✓	
Friend (Richard)	✓		✓			✓			
Friend (Hank)		✓		✓			✓		

Community Activities

Where do you go?	How do you get there?			When?		How often do you go?			
	Walk	Car	Bus	Week-day	Week-end	Daily	Each week	Each month	Other
Redbirds games			✓		✓			✓	
Church		✓		✓	✓		✓		
McLane's grocery store		✓		✓			✓		
Work (Sheare's Hardware)	✓			✓		✓			
Hobby shop and computer store	✓			✓	✓		✓		
Library		✓		✓	✓			✓	
Movies		✓			✓		✓		
Volunteer activities		✓			✓			✓	

(continued)

Form 6.5.   *(continued)*

Strengths and Training Needs

Here is an opportunity to talk about what you like to do, the talents that you have, and which supports might help you become more independent in the community!

Circle area: (Community)   Recreation/Leisure   Home   Work   Other

Strengths

What activities do you do?	What is involved in that activity?
Go to the community library on Nolensville Blvd.	Find books using computer, read mags., socialize
Barber shop	Get haircut, pay, & tip; talk w/barbers, read mags.
McLane's grocery store	Find ride, buy groceries with roommate
Crestwood Outlet Megamall	Find ride, get money from ATM, find bargains!
Video rental store (in convenience store)	Walk to store, browse and choose movie, pay
Dentist's and doctor's offices	Wait & read mags., tell doctor problem, pay bill
Superplex movie theater	Find ride, purchase tickets/snacks, talk after
Various restaurants	Walk/find ride, order from menu, eat, pay bill, talk

Training Needs

What things would you like to learn to do?	What things get in the way?
Sometimes go places alone (grocery store, mall)	Don't know how to use the bus or call a cab
Go to the YMCA	Don't know how to get membership or what is there
Attend more Redbirds baseball games	Lack of money, don't always have a ride
Go to the dance club with friends	Never danced before, don't know what is there

Potential supports: Instruction can focus on travel training. Family member or roommates could take Jared to the YMCA one evening to show him the courses and equipment they offer. Help arrange for Jared to work a few extra hours and/or find where Jared can get discount game tickets—see if co-worker might want to join him.

What do we know . . .

. . . about your community? Jared lives near several busy streets, which he walks down. He gets rides to several of his relative's homes and walks to others. He is very active in the community, getting rides to activities throughout the week.

. . . about your likes and dislikes? Jared loves eating out, especially at fast-food restaurants. Allergic to dairy products! Loves computers, baseball, movies, and woodworking. Likes working with others outdoors and working with tools. Doesn't like bowling or jobs that require cleaning.

. . . about your strengths? Jared is already very involved in many community activities and enjoys trying new experiences. He gets along well with others and seeks help when he needs it.

What things have you decided you would like to work on with us?

Community	• Travel training, including riding the bus and taxi
	• Learning how to write checks and use debit card
	• Trying some new activities (dance club, YMCA, etc.)
	•
Recreation/leisure	• Getting involved in some community classes, such as woodworking and cooking
	• Joining a community or work baseball/softball team
	• Learning how to develop an exercise program
	•
Home	• Budgeting for monthly expenses
	• Getting along with my roommates (conflict resolution)
	• Making certain meals and snacks
	• Programming my VCR
Work	• Getting faster at the work I do (improving productivity)
	• Making more friends at work
	• Getting a promotion
	•
Other	• Learning how to stand up for myself (self-advocacy skills)
	•
	•
	•

6.2.2 Using Formal Assessment Methods

We are becoming an increasingly more diverse society. As the ethnic and cultural profile of our country changes, IEP teams must ensure that their assessments address the diversity of their students. The IDEA Amendments of 1997 require that materials used to assess students be "selected and administered so as not to be discriminatory on a racial or cultural basis; and [be] provided and administered in the child's native language or other mode of communication, unless it is clearly not feasible to do so" (Section 614).

"I assess a student's competence in at least two ways: By evaluating their progress on academic and vocational goals in their IEPs and by measuring their performance on a variety of standardized tests."
Teacher
Treadwell High School
Memphis, Tennessee

Most of the assessment that is appropriate for high school transition students is *informal* and is often teacher-designed and specific to a particular work, school, or community environment. For example, a teacher may develop a checklist for monitoring a student's reaction to anger-provoking situations. *Formal,* or standardized, assessment can augment the information derived from informal assessments to aid in developing educational programs, evaluating student progress, and determining eligibility for programs. Formal assessment provides information about a student in relation to a standardized norm, typically nationally or statewide. For example, a student's language development could be compared with that of a national sample of general education students.

Starting Up:

- Although you should never rely solely on commercially prepared assessment instruments, developmental scales and adaptive behavior tests can provide valuable insight into a student's strengths and needs.

- Keep in mind that you are trying to get as much information as you can about a student's strengths and support needs. This means that you will need to use a variety of formal and informal assessments, each of which reveals different types of information about a student. Your job is putting it all together!

- Formal assessments typically provide less information about a particular student in the context of a particular environment than informal assessments. Formal assessments do have advantages, however. For example, they can save you time because they are already prepared. Also, by following the directions, an educational aide or other assistant may be able to administer some assessments that do not require a professional evaluator.

- Standardized tests are just that—standardized. Consequently, the results of a standardized assessment, such as an adaptive behavior scale, usually can be easily communicated to and interpreted by other professionals. Communicating information about a student makes collaboration among providers easier.

Formal assessments that teachers have found helpful for secondary students include the AAMR Adaptive Behavior Scales, the BRIGANCE® Life Skills Inventory, the Quality of Life Questionnaire, and the Woodcock Reading Mastery Test. More information about these and other formal assessments is in the appendix.

The IDEA Amendments of 1997 state that students with disabilities are to be included in general state- and districtwide assessment programs, with accommodations, where necessary. Accommodations provided for students should directly address their individual needs. For example, you could change the environment in which a student takes the assessment; vary the format of the test; allow a student to respond in a different way, such as speaking rather than writing; extend the amount of time a student has to complete the test; or provide an alternative assessment.

6-3 COMMUNICATING STUDENTS' STRENGTHS AND NEEDS

 Communication with parents must be ongoing! According to the IDEA Amendments of 1997, IEPs must include statements of how teams will measure student progress on annual goals and how the students' parents "will be regularly informed (by such means as periodic report cards), at least as often as parents are informed of the nondisabled children's progress" (Section 614). By informing parents of their child's strengths and needs, teachers encourage parents' involvement in students' educational programs.

"If a student were working as a courtesy clerk at a grocery store, I would talk with her co-workers. Most cashiers started out as courtesy clerks and would be able to monitor the student's progress the most."

Teacher
Central High School
Culleoka, Tennessee

6.3.1 Collaborating with Parents, Teachers, and Others

Student information obtained through observation and assessment has only limited use if you keep it to yourself! The next step is to share that information. Remember, teaching should be a team effort. Collaborate with parents, fellow teachers, and important others to develop educational programs that are based on shared information from all parties involved.

"Talk to any general education classroom teachers that the student may have. Ask them to describe to you the problems that they see with the student. Then, incorporate teaching solutions or ways to deal with the problems while the student is in the resource class."

Teacher
McEwen High School
McEwen, Tennessee

Starting Up:

- Collecting student data is not an "end" in itself—the purpose of data is to communicate information. Share your data with important others in a student's life. You may find that a parent is less interested in his daughter's improvement in telling time and more impressed with her increase in social interaction.

- Collaborate with employers and community leaders when developing checklists of skills that you think are critical in their environments. You may find that what you thought was a "survival skill" in an environment may be considered irrelevant by important others in that environment.

- Be specific when you communicate student information gathered through observation and assessment. "Jason does pretty well at work!" is not as helpful to an employer as "Jason independently performs the first nine steps of his cleaning task but needs partial assistance for the final two steps."

- Grading a student should be a collaborative process between the special education and general education teachers. Provide guidelines to the general education teacher on how to modify her grading policy for a student. You can use the form on the next page to suggest a modified grading system for students in general education classrooms. Change the form as you like to reflect skills specified in a student's IEP. (A blank, reproducible form is included in the appendix.)

"Involvement of important others in the selection and learning process of activities ensures that they are relevant to the student and those around him or her."

Teacher
Volunteer High School
Jonesborough, Tennessee

Developing a student's IEP on the basis of information specifying a student's strengths and areas of need is a collaborative team effort. The IDEA Amendments of 1997 stipulate who should be included on the IEP team. Team members include the student's parents, at least one general education teacher and one special education teacher, a representative of the

Modified Grading System for Students in General Education Classrooms

Grading period (circle one): 1 ② 3 4 5 6

Student: _Shonda Amendelian_

General education teacher: _Ms. Levy_   Course title: _Government_

Suggested modifications: _Shonda benefits when class instructions and assignments are written out and kept in her sight. She gets along well with her peers and works especially well with a partner who can provide her with support._

Objectives	Date											Average
	8/11	8/14	8/19	8/21	8/25	8/27	9/1	9/4	9/8	9/10	9/16	
On time	P	I	P	I	I	I	P	I	I	I	I	97
Has materials	P	P	P	I	I	P	I	I	I	I	P	95
Sits in assigned seat	S	P	I	I	I	I	I	I	I	I	I	97
Follows directions	U	U	S	P	P	S	P	I	P	I	I	87
Asks for help appropriately	P	P	P	I	I	I	I	P	I	P	I	95
Interacts with peers appropriately	I	P	I	I	I	I	I	I	I	I	I	99
Follows classroom rules	U	S	S	S	U	P	S	P	P	S	P	81
Completes tasks as instructed	S	S	S	S	P	S	S	P	S	P	P	84
Has positive attitude	I	I	I	I	I	I	I	I	I	I	I	100
Completes modified assignments	P	P	P	S	S	S	P	P	P	S	P	87

Suggested Codes:
I = 100 Meets objective independently
P = 90   Needs a prompt to meet objective
S = 80   Requires several prompts to meet objective
U = 70   Unable to meet objective

Scoring: You may assign either a letter grade or a numerical grade.

Directions: Each time you grade the class members on assigned work or tests, you may choose to grade this student on the above modified criteria, if appropriate. Please return this sheet to me at the end of the grading period. Thank you!

Form 6.6. Modified Grading System for Students in General Education Classrooms for Shonda Amendelian.

LEA, an individual who can interpret the instructional implication of evaluation results, other individuals at the discretion of the parents or LEA, and the student, if appropriate.

Cross-references: Collaborating with Employers and Co-workers (3.1.1); Interviewing Parents and Important Others (4.2.2); Collaborating with Students, Parents, and Important Others (5.2.2); and Communicating with Parents, Teachers, and Others (8.2.1)

"Communication between the people who supervise, assist, and care for the student should be ongoing. Identify what areas the student needs help in, and implement how to get needed changes made."
Teacher
Cookeville High School
Cookeville, Tennessee

Teacher-Proven Practices:

Hints from teachers for collaborating with others include the following:

- Develop written profiles of the students with whom you work to share with vocational counselors and potential employers and co-workers.

- Ask parents what chores their child does well at home and what areas need more work.

- Ask parents to complete an inventory of their child's independent skills at home and in the community.

- Consult weekly with the student's job supervisor. Include identified problem areas in instructional and support programs.

- Keep a checklist of expected student behaviors and have teachers, co-workers, and peers fill it out. Share it with the student when needed.

"I assess students' strengths and needs through formal testing and by observing throughout the day. I also ask other teachers for frequent feedback on a student to assure me that I am not biased in my observations."

Teacher
Huntington High School
Huntington, Tennessee

6.3.2 Interviewing Students and Others

Don't expect too much of yourself! By observing and assessing a student, you will have compiled important information about a student's strengths—pat yourself on the back! But as only one person, you will never have direct access to everything you need to know about a student. Sometimes you have to ask for information. Employers, parents, students, and others usually are very willing to be interviewed by you; after all, they're interested in a student's competence too!

"I talk with parents to see what the student's chores are at home. In planning with parents, additional chores can be given, and even enhanced, with in-school jobs."

Teacher
LaVergne High School
Shelbyville, Tennessee

Teacher-Proven Practices:

- Interview individuals who regularly interact with the student but who aren't typically consulted during IEP team meetings or assessments. Cafeteria workers, bus drivers, store owners, neighbors, and teammates all can provide information about a student's strengths and support needs.

- Look for ways that work, school, and community activities can be modified so that areas of need can become areas of strength for a student. Interview teachers, work supervisors, peers, and community members to determine how flexible a particular job or activity is and ideas for modifying it (see Chapters 4 and 5).

- Assessment and observation don't tell all. By meeting one-to-one with important others who spend time with a student, you can learn their perspective on the strengths they think a student has. What you thought was a liability may be viewed by others as an asset.

- The best source of information about a student's strengths may be the student herself! Take time to interview your students regularly. You may be surprised to find out how much insight they have into their own strengths and needs. Use alternative modes of communication with students who are nonverbal (see Assessing Preferences Using Alternative Communication in Assessing Students' Choices and Preferences, 8.1.3).

"I help students achieve competence by asking important others what skills are important, and then I find means of supporting these skills in order to raise the individual's level of independence."

Teacher
Volunteer High School
Jonesborough, Tennessee

 The importance of collaboration is made explicit in the law. The IDEA Amendments of 1997 state that research and practice have demonstrated that an effective educational system must "promote service integration, and the coordination of State and local education, social, health, mental health, and other services, in addressing the full range of student needs, particularly the needs of children with disabilities who require significant levels of support to maximize their participation and learning in school and the community" (Section 651).

"I believe that satisfaction from others is very important to students [with disabilities] just as with anybody. Often, their self-esteem is very low, and they need all the support they can get. All of my students attend their IEP meetings so they can hear me discuss with their family all of their academic and vocational accomplishments."

Teacher
Pearl-Cohn High School
Nashville, Tennessee

6-4 TEACHING SKILLS THAT NEED STRENGTHENING

The IDEA Amendments of 1997 state that the federal government has an ongoing obligation to support programs that enable students to acquire the skills that will empower them to lead productive and independent adult lives. In addition, teachers are required to assist students in developing the competence that is needed for participation in school and postschool environments (e.g., postsecondary education, vocational training, employment environments, independent living, community environments). As a result, transition services must include "instruction, related services, community experiences, the development of employment and other postschool adult living objectives, and, when appropriate, acquisition of daily living skills" (Section 602).

Case Study 6.3 Another Success!

Autumn was quickly giving way to winter, and Carlos was gradually feeling at home at Washington High. Juggling his time among classes, job training, and responsibilities at home, Carlos kept himself quite busy. Mr. Kleeb was also proud of the success that Carlos was finding and continued to search for ways to help him demonstrate the many strengths he possessed. As a result, Carlos was quite happy in his new environment.

Mr. Kleeb knew, however, that the amount of acceptance and involvement Carlos had in school, work, and community environments would be influenced by how competent he appeared in those environments. Using informal assessment methods would help to determine which of Carlos's skills might need additional supports and instruction. With the help of a translator, Mr. Kleeb adapted a home inventory for Carlos and his father to complete in their primary language, Spanish. Carlos and his father together decided that Carlos would benefit from instruction in daily living skills such as budgeting, doing laundry, and cleaning the house and through greater involvement in community activities. Mr. Kleeb was grateful for their input and decided to talk with other team members to get their input.

Mr. Kleeb spoke with several general education teachers and discovered that each expressed similar concerns regarding Carlos's social involvement in their classes. Although Carlos had made some friends at work, he appeared to be uncomfortable when interacting with his same-age peers. A conversation with an educational assistant confirmed that social skills instruction would be an important goal. Mr. Kleeb decided to interview a peer of Carlos's, who frequently worked with him in cooperative learning groups. The peer suggested that Carlos might fit in better if he learned to participate in some recreation and leisure activities that were popular in the area, such as snowmobiling and ice hockey. At the same time, his peers could learn some of the activities that Carlos enjoyed, such as soccer.

Conversations with those individuals who were involved in Carlos's education provided a multitude of suggestions. Mr. Kleeb gathered the team together to prioritize educational goals and determine who should carry out instruction and how. Presenting the results of his observations, assessments, and conversations, Mr. Kleeb helped others see which new skills would need to be taught and encouraged others to identify ways of incorporating these new skills into daily activities. In doing so, each team member was helping Carlos become more competent and better accepted.

Providing students with environmental and social supports can help a student attain competence and success on the job, in school, at home, and around the community. In addition, students can build their competence by learning new skills. When teachers have identified student skills that need strengthening, they should focus instruction on developing competence in these areas.

"When the teacher allows student leadership in the classroom paired with responsibility for tasks, competence is developed. Role-playing allows students to see themselves as others see them."

Teacher
Fairley High School
Memphis, Tennessee

6.4.1 Teaching New Skills

"By developing a task analysis of activities we are teaching, we are able to determine what steps of a routine are learned, what still needs to be taught, and when progress is being made."

Itinerant Transition Teacher
Nashville Public Schools
Nashville, Tennessee

The information gathered from observing students, conducting assessments, and collaborating with important others should guide the selection of new skills to be taught to students. Teachers should prioritize these skills on the basis of input from parents, students, and others on the IEP team.

"I talk to the general education teachers that students have. I ask them to tell me problems that they see with the students. Then I incorporate teaching solutions or ways to deal with these problems into instruction."

Teacher
McEwen High School
McEwen, Tennessee

Starting Up:

- By examining the data you collected when observing and assessing the student in school, work, home, and community environments, you can begin to target those skills that need strengthening. Your data will also serve as a performance standard by which you can evaluate the success of instruction.

- Enroll students in courses that address their areas of need. Vocational courses at the high school and community college levels can teach students valuable employment skills. General education English and math classes can teach communication skills. Community education courses in recreation and leisure activities can help students develop hobbies and social skills that lead to increased competence and new friendships.

- A variety of teaching techniques can be used to teach new skills to students, such as prompts and positive reinforcement. Selection of a teaching method should be based on the student's needs, the skill being taught, and the acceptability of the technique within an environment. For example, although time-out may be effective in some situations, the acceptability of this technique at work or in the community is questionable.

- Available to teachers are many resources that describe state-of-the-art teaching techniques. Consult the appendix for a list of suggested texts, manuals, and videotapes. Share with your colleagues the resources and techniques that work.

"Through observations of students during daily activities, I develop one-to-one relationships with the students in order to discuss appropriate and inappropriate behavior and activities. Through role-playing and 'rap' sessions, I let the student see what skills are needed to become a better citizen who will be accepted by the community."
Teacher
Raleigh Egypt High School
Memphis, Tennessee

6.4.2 Incorporating New Skills into Daily Life

Simply learning how to perform a new skill doesn't guarantee that a student will use the skill. Teachers should provide students with frequent opportunities to practice skills to assist them in becoming more fluent. Also, students should have the opportunity to practice a new skill across a variety of environments, tasks, and people.

"If I observe a weakness that a student might have, we will repeat and practice that task on the job. Also, if needed, I will set up the same (or similar) tasks at school for them to practice and work on."

Teacher
Pearl-Cohn High School
Nashville, Tennessee

How to Do It:

- Talk with students' supervisors, parents, and community leaders to determine which skills that are critical in other environments need to be reinforced by practice in the classroom.

- Practice makes perfect! Giving students frequent opportunities to practice new skills throughout the day and in different environments will ensure that those skills are mastered more quickly and performed when needed.

- Find ways of increasing students' involvement in extracurricular and community activities. The more students are able to participate in such activities, the more opportunities they will have to practice important skills and demonstrate competence to their peers.

Cross-references: Incorporating Self-Determination into Daily Living (7-3), Teaching and Increasing Students' Choice and Decision Making (8-3), and Increasing Students' Social Interactions (9-1)

"I stress the importance of and have many discussions with students about responsibility, good manners, positive attitudes, and work performance."

Teacher
Pearl-Cohn High School
Nashville, Tennessee

The IDEA Amendments of 1997 emphasize the involvement of all students in general education and other integrated programs. Specifically, they call for annual goals that enable a student to be involved in and progress in the general curriculum and to participate in extracurricular and other nonacademic activities. As teachers identify areas in which students are being challenged, they should look for ways of incorporating skill instruction into the existing curriculum. This allows students to learn skills from watching their peers and to practice those same skills in the actual environment.

"General education teachers can incorporate vocational objectives into their English or math curriculum. Copies of the academic objectives (scope and sequence) should be available to special education teachers so that they can assist in teaching math and language skills to better prepare students for success."
Teacher
Treadwell High School
Memphis, Tennessee

Teacher-Proven Practices:

- Incorporate student preferences and interests into skill instruction. Discuss interests with verbal students, or use trial-and-error experiences with new activities with students who are nonverbal (see Assessing Students' Choices and Preferences, 8.1.3).

- Remember that for a new skill to be maintained it must be reinforced. For example, if you are teaching a student to use a vending machine, it is critical that the student complete the whole activity and get the reinforcer: the candy bar or can of soda. People don't continue to put money in vending machines unless they get something for it.

- As you design a task analysis of a job, consider modifying steps that will allow the student to learn and maintain a new skill more easily. Don't make learning a new task harder than it needs to be. For example, color-coding automotive tools can help a student select the appropriate one for a job.

- Teach skills that are functional within the student's environment. Generic skills, such as sorting, are not likely to be maintained unless they are functional, useful, and reinforced within the everyday environments in which a student participates. For example, if a student is taught to order from a table at a sit-down restaurant but orders only take-out from a drive-thru, then ordering from a table is not likely to be maintained.

"I give students opportunities to try new activities. Often, this involves encouraging students to take courses in music, art, typing, computers, or other areas that the student has never been exposed to."
Teacher
South Side High School
Memphis, Tennessee

REFERENCES

Allen, W.T. (1988). *Read my lips: It's choice*....St. Paul, MN: Governor's Council on Developmental Disabilities.

Individuals with Disabilities Education Act Amendments of 1997, PL 105-17, 20 U.S.C. § 1400 *et seq.*

C h a p t e r   7

Strategies for Teaching Self-Determination

OVERVIEW

As a teacher, parent, or service provider of students with diverse abilities today, you probably already know that self-determination has become a "buzzword." Put simply, *self-determination* means that people speak up for themselves and make and act on their own lifestyle choices, pretty much like everybody else hopes to and, to some extent, probably does.

The focus on self-determination dates to the normalization movement of the 1970s (Nirje, 1972). The idea behind self-determination is that important others take into account a person's choices, preferences, and aspirations so that the person can experience the respect to which any human being is entitled. The skills that promote self-determination include self-management, self-advocacy, choice making, problem solving, decision making, and goal setting. Legislation that backs up self-determination includes the Individuals with Disabilities Education Act (IDEA) Amendments of 1997 (PL 105-17) and the Rehabilitation Act Amendments of 1992 (PL 102-569), which require incorporating self-determination into educational and rehabilitation programs.

Self-determination calls for a change in our thinking and our behavior. In the past, we may have been taught to speak and make decisions for students. Major lifestyle decisions were made for students, often without considering their interests or preferences. Now, we are learning to step back, listen, and get out of the way. At the same time, we are learning how to teach people skills so that they can speak up and act for themselves instead of teaching them to depend entirely on us. We are also learning to provide support so that students can manage their daily lives, be responsible for their own behavior, make decisions, and act on their decisions.

This chapter contains three main groups and eight subgroups of strategies that teachers may use for teaching self-determination skills to students. It includes such strategies as promoting students' self-determination, teaching self-management and self-determination skills, and incorporating self-determination and self-management into daily living.

Making choices, expressing preferences, and advocating for ourselves are rights that many of us may take for granted. Many students, however, have not had the opportunity to exercise these rights or develop these skills. Self-determination teaches students how to put the "self" into their educational programs!

Case Study 7.1   Speakin' Up

Beverly Duncan doesn't remember much about school until her sophomore year in high school. That's the year they started a People First chapter at McIntyre High. Beverly had been in a special class for students with "moderate and severe disabilities" for most of her school career, and her sophomore year was no exception. Although she had had excellent supervision and care during those years, each day was pretty much like all of the rest. The daily schedule was set by her classroom teachers and usually consisted of alternating patterns of group or individual activities. Before Beverly began any activity, the materials she needed were already in place, whether it was a self-care skill, such as buttoning a shirt, or an art project such as making a Valentine's Day card. Beverly spent most of her time in her own classroom except when she went with her entire class to the gym, to the lunchroom, or outside for recess. It had been this way for years—all the way through elementary and middle schools, and now even high school. If she had ever once been asked what she wanted to do, Beverly sure couldn't remember it.

On September 17 of her sophomore year, something different happened. Ms. Deal, Beverly's life skills teacher, announced that a new school club would be meeting that day and that the class was welcome to join. Sure enough, during club period, two people whom Beverly had never seen before came into class and began talking. Ms. Deal introduced them as Skip Driscoll and Wanda Reid, members of the local chapter of People First. Skip and Wanda explained that, if the students were interested, People First would help them start a club right in their own school. By joining the club, the students could begin to learn how to set goals for themselves, make decisions about their own lives, and speak up for themselves. Ms. Deal added that she would like to work with the club members and begin to include their choices and goals in their daily schedules. She also said that she was glad that the People First members were helping. For a long time, Ms. Deal had wanted to help her students speak up and act on their own decisions; she just didn't think she knew how to do it.

Right then and there, Beverly signed up for the very first McIntyre High chapter of People First. She anxiously awaited every other Wednesday, when clubs met during second period. And something new gradually began to happen to Beverly! She began to realize that she had a right to "dream" about what she wanted to be in her life and what she wanted to do to make that dream come true. Another thing that the club meetings helped Beverly do was to get to know herself better—what she liked and didn't like, with whom she wanted to spend time, and what she wanted to do. She began to explore different careers by attending job fairs on campus, trying out different jobs at school such as working in the office or in the school child care center, and sampling different jobs through McIntyre's job-training program. Beverly also decided to try out new hairstyles by visiting the cosmetology department at school, and she became interested in fashion, shopping for her own clothes for the first time with friends at the mall. In getting to know herself, Beverly started to let other people know her, too. For the first time, you could hear Beverly "speaking up" for herself—on the bus if someone tried to take her seat, at home if she wanted to try something new without her mother's help, and at school when she was asked which class she would like to sign up for or which job she would like to try next semester. (See the Organizations section of the Resources in the appendix for how to contact People First.)

7-1   PROMOTING STUDENTS' SELF-DETERMINATION

"Self-determination is...

- Having a choice
- Knowing more about ourselves
- Dreams and goals and going after it
- Being in control
- Making your own decisions
- Spending money our way"

Southern Collaborative of Self-Advocates
People First of Tennessee, Georgia, and Alabama
Murfreesboro, Tennessee

7.1.1   Educating Students About Self-Determination

Sometimes the first person you must convince about self-determination is the student. After many years of having few opportunities to make choices or decisions and to act on those choices, students are likely to have learned to "let someone else do it," even when doing so might go against their own preferences or interests. Letting students and others know that self-determination is every person's right and responsibility is often an important first step.

"I give my students as much independence as possible so that they can make their own choices and experience the consequence of these choices—at work, at school, and in social situations. I let them experience the consequence of a poor choice, too—like when selecting the wrong item from a vending machine."
Itinerant Transition Teacher
Nashville Public Schools
Nashville, Tennessee

The IDEA Amendments of 1997 clearly support students' self-determination. The amendments require that students be involved in the development of their individualized education programs (IEPs) as members of their own IEP teams and that they attend their IEP meetings as active participants. The amendments also state that students' educational programs must be based on their preferences and interests. One year before students reach the age of majority, they must also be informed of their rights that will transfer to them when reaching their majority. These requirements put considerable responsibility on students. To fulfill these requirements, we must support students in learning new self-determination skills.

Starting Up:

- Discuss with students the importance of setting their own goals. Give them opportunities to set their own educational goals, and include these goals in their daily activities. Then teach students to monitor their performance so that they can determine whether they've met their goals. For example, a student may want to learn to apply her make-up by herself. By checking her appearance each day, she can feel good about choosing her own goal and acting to reach that goal. And, in doing so, she is learning about self-determination, even if she has never heard of the word!

- At the beginning of the day, ask students to tell or list their activities planned for the day. Also, have them discuss the responsibilities that go with these activities. Being self-determined means being aware of the consequences of one's actions and taking responsibility for those consequences. For example, students may list an art project or shopping for clothes as one of their activities for the day. They must also be aware of the consequences of these activities, that is, either cleaning up after the art project or paying for clothes they choose at the mall.

- Talking to students about the importance of maintaining control of their emotions goes a long way toward educating them about self-determination. Students who feel they can control their own emotional outbursts, such as anger or hurt, will feel more in control of their environment. Involving students in a social skills self-management program may teach them about the benefits of self-determination.

Cross-references: Teaching Self-Management and Self-Determination Skills (7-2) and Teaching Social Interaction Skills (9-4)

"I teach a unit on self-determination and self-management skills. I point out to students reasons why people should exercise self-management skills in the workplace and school environment, and I teach them to monitor their own behavior."

Teacher
Cumberland County High School
Crossville, Tennessee

"Allow students to experience the consequences of their actions. In everything they do, students must learn to be responsible for their own actions and understand why they are responsible."

Teacher
Sheffield High School
Memphis, Tennessee

Teacher-Proven Practices:

- Give students the responsibility of managing their personal daily schedule, and let them manage their own time. Allow them to learn the consequences of their behavior, such as being late to class or forgetting to prepare for class. Let them experience the success of getting to their job-training sites on time and completing their job tasks on time.

- Being self-determined means knowing how to prioritize activities in your life. Help students learn to prioritize by making lists, such as a list of things that must be done to achieve a goal (e.g., passing a driver's test) or a list of steps for preparing for an IEP meeting. Picture lists can be used with students who don't read or write.

- Controlling one's behavior may be easier in some environments than in others. Just think about yourself—do you find it hard to read when the television is blaring or when others are talking? Suggest an alternative time or place for students who are having trouble controlling their behavior, such as moving to a quiet area at the worksite for someone who is becoming agitated by others or taking a job at a noisy industrial site for a worker who has difficulty controlling her own loud, distracting sounds.

"Reminding students of the consequences of their behavior helps them to manage their own behavior. I tell students a rule such as 'wait until you go outside after the bell to tap or make a beat' and then 'make your decision to stop your behavior or miss your computer time' if the behavior persists. They self-manage their own behavior."

Teacher
Fairley High School
Memphis, Tennessee

"I teach students about self-determination by using behavior management techniques that link rewards and consequences to behaviors. I use a behavioral contract when necessary. I also teach them about problem solving and provide feedback to them about their strengths and needs."

Teacher
Hillcrest High School
Memphis, Tennessee

7.1.2   Collaborating with Peers, Parents, and Others

"We want to be seen as leading the way to a better future for all people with disabilities. We want to be seen as people who advocate for transportation, housing, jobs, education, health care, and other issues. We want to be seen as active, productive, and contributing citizens in the community."

Southern Collaborative of Self-Advocates
People First of Tennessee, Georgia, and Alabama
Murfreesboro, Tennessee

Self-determination is as much about changing our behavior as it is about changing our students' behavior. It's time to let students learn to make their own decisions and choices, learn from their own successes and mistakes, and try new experiences when the opportunity comes along. It's time for us to learn how to *support* students in making and acting on their own decisions, rather than making those decisions for them.

"One of my biggest obstacles in the area of self-determination is usually the family! Independence is a scary thing for everyone, especially for parents. I've found that including the family in the very first stages of developing self-management strategies is vital."
Teacher
Hunters Lane High School
Nashville, Tennessee

How to Do It:

- Collaborating with others who interact with the student is critical to ensuring that self-determination skills are used by a student in different environments. Talk with family members, co-workers, community members, general education teachers, school staff, and others to identify ways in which they can support a student's self-determination skills, such as letting them choose a preferred way of doing a task or decide which bus route to take home from the job.

- It's a good idea to include peers in discussions about self-determination. Peers can provide examples of self-determination in their own lives, such as saying "no" to drugs or telling a date that his behavior is inappropriate. Peers can also model appropriate use of self-determination skills for students.

- Peers can help teach self-determination skills. Many times a student will be more likely to take a suggestion from a peer than from you. For example, a peer may suggest to a student that she would look much prettier if she would brush her hair and keep it pulled back away from her face, and the peer may remind her to practice her grooming each day. If you were to make such a suggestion, the student might feel angry or hurt. When her peer does so, however, she may pay attention and start taking responsibility for her own appearance.

- Have parents assign specific tasks at home so that students can learn responsibility. Teach students to monitor their behavior on their tasks and keep a record of their performance in a folder that they take to school. Remember to have parents check the students' work, too, to see whether they agree with the students' self-report.

Cross-references: Communicating an Attitude of Acceptance (3-1); Communicating Environmental Support Needs (4-2); Communicating Social Support Needs (5-2); Communicating Students' Strengths and Needs (6-3); and Communicating with Parents, Teachers, and Others (8.2.1)

"I involve students in role-playing situations with their peers that are typical of 'real life.' I then let them decide how they will manage themselves in those situations. Role-playing with their peers helps them see what the consequences of their actions would be."
Teacher
Ridgeway High School
Memphis, Tennessee

"Support from home is extremely important in this area. Ask parents to use a checklist of a student's duties taped to the refrigerator at home. At school use picture cues or tape record sequences of events."
Teacher
Hillsboro High School
Nashville, Tennessee

7-2   TEACHING SELF-MANAGEMENT AND SELF-DETERMINATION SKILLS

The goal of self-determination for all students is clearly embedded in the IDEA Amendments of 1997. The amendments state that the federal government has an ongoing obligation to support programs, projects, and activities that help students acquire skills that will *empower* them to lead productive and independent adult lives. The amendments also state that "an essential element of our national policy [is] ensuring equality of opportunity, full participation, independent living, and economic self-sufficiency for individuals with disabilities" (Section 601). Educational personnel are required to ensure that students "have the skills and knowledge...to be prepared to lead productive, independent, adult lives, to the maximum extent possible" (Section 601).

How do students learn to become more self-determined? How do they learn to set goals, work to achieve these goals, advocate for themselves, make decisions, and solve problems? One way is to learn to use self-management skills to control, guide, and direct their own behavior. Self-management strategies include such skills as self-instruction, picture prompts, self-monitoring, and self-reinforcement. Using self-management strategies, students can learn that, to a large degree, they are the ones who are in control of their own lives.

"Steps to Self-Determination

- Build a circle of friends
- Share the dream
- Make an individual budget
- Pick out who will give supports
- Connect with and give back to the community"

Southern Collaborative of Self-Advocates
People First of Tennessee, Georgia, and Alabama
Murfreesboro, Tennessee

Teaching students to use self-management strategies can make life easier for you! When students learn to manage their own behavior, they become less dependent on your help and assistance. You will discover that you have more time to spend on other activities or with other students.

Case Study 7.2   Not Just a "Piece of Cake!"

Everyone knows that Badecoli's Italian Restaurant & Pub is where politicians and local celebrities go for a good meal. That's why Hsin Tu was so glad to have gotten a job there; besides that, they were famous for having the best "Sheer Indulgence Chocolate Cake" in town! In high school, Hsin had put together a strong résumé, having had many job experiences at businesses in his community. His transition teacher had worked with him on his interviewing skills, and he had gotten his new job just 1 month ago. He was excited about working as a prep cook during four lunch shifts each week.

Throughout high school, Hsin's teacher worked closely with him at different worksites. Whenever Hsin had questions or needed assistance, his teacher was always right there to help him. Hsin always knew what to do, when to do it, and what the consequences would be because his teacher told him. As it turned out, working at Badecoli's was a much different experience for Hsin.

Although he had received employee training at Badecoli's, his transition teacher, Ms. Carlin, had expected Hsin to be much more independent on the job. Although Hsin did fine during training, his performance slipped drastically as soon as Ms. Carlin was no longer standing next to him during each shift. Hsin really didn't know what to do without her! After all, no one had ever taught him to work on his own. Everything would go along all right until he had to make a decision for himself, like the time he ran out of tomatoes for the salad or when the food chopper broke and he was in the middle of cooking apples. As the days went on, Hsin was running into more and more difficulty at work. It wasn't such a "piece of cake" after all! In fact, Hsin didn't even like to go to work anymore. Before long, Ms. Carlin got a call from Hsin's supervisor, asking her to stop by to talk about Hsin's job performance.

7.2.1 Teaching Self-Management

We all use self-management strategies in different areas of our lives—a grocery list on our refrigerator, a to-do list in our daily planner, a recipe for cooking dinner, or a note pinned to a tote bag. The same strategies can be taught to students to help them decrease their dependence on others and increase their independence and self-determination on the job, in school, at home, and around the community.

You may have noticed that some people are better "self-managers" than others are! Some people always seem to know where their keys are, get to their appointments on time, and never run out of gas. How do they do it? They probably have good self-management skills. But don't worry if your students (or you!) don't. Self-management, like any other skill, can be taught!

Starting Up:

- With so many self-management strategies available, identifying which one is most appropriate for a student can be challenging. For example, if a young man is forgetting to greet customers at his job in a pharmacy, should you teach him to self-instruct, self-monitor, or use picture prompts? The Teaching and Evaluating Self-Management form on the next page lists seven steps you can use to decide which strategy will work best in a particular case. (A blank, reproducible form can be found in the appendix. See pages 193–197 for how to use this form.)

- A self-management strategy should match the strengths, needs, preferences, and interests of the students using it. As with all educational programming, individualize your instruction for each student. Students will be more likely to learn a new skill, such as self-management, if they feel they will get something out of it. For example, if a student knows she will keep her job only if she continues to come to work on time, she will be more likely to use a self-management technique such as setting her alarm clock each day.

- Be a good model of self-management for your students. By showing them ways you use self-management strategies in your own life, they can see how to do it as well as the advantages of being a self-managed person. If your room or office is always a mess and you are always trying to find things, your students may learn to be the same way. However, if they see that you always put things in their place and consequently always know where everything is, they are likely to learn the advantages of maintaining order at home, work, and school.

Teacher-Proven Practices:

- Teach students to use self-management strategies as you would teach them to do anything else. Use learning principles such as modeling, corrective feedback, opportunities to practice, prompting, and reinforcement. Begin to with-

Teaching and Evaluating Self-Management

Student: Hsin Tu   **Environment:** Badecoli's Restaurant & Pub

1. **Identify the problem:**

   Co-workers report that Hsin is leaving important ingredients off of food dishes and that he is taking too long to fill food orders.

2. **Verify the problem:**

   Observed Hsin during a lunch shift (1 hour) and compared his performance with that of his co-workers. He is making 3x as many errors and taking 3x as long to complete tasks.

3. **Determine acceptability:**

   Supervisor is worried about Hsin's accuracy and speed, but his primary concern is with accuracy.

4. **Identify natural supports in the environment:**

   The restaurant has large training pictures of each step of the food preparation process, and the pictures are the same ones that co-workers use. Also, two other employees work side by side with Hsin and could assist him.

5. **Select a self-management strategy:**

   Use picture prompts in the form of the training pictures.

6. **Teach self-management skills:**

   Teach Hsin to perform each step by following the picture prompts using modeling, prompts, corrective feedback, and reinforcement. Fade instruction by moving from verbal reminders to gestural reminders to no prompts at all.

7. **Evaluate student's performance:**

   Observed Hsin several weeks later—his speed and accuracy match that of his co-workers. Both wait staff and cook staff agree that Hsin's job performance is acceptable.

Form 7.1.   Teaching and Evaluating Self-Management form for Hsin Tu. (From "Utilizing self-management to teach independence on the job," by Lagomarcino, T.R., Hughes, C., & Rusch, F.R., *Education and Training in Mental Retardation, 24,* 142. Copyright 1989 by The Council for Exceptional Children. Adapted with permission.)

draw your assistance as students learn to use the self-management strategies on their own.

- Learning to self-manage means learning new skills for students. Give them lots of feedback and praise as they learn. Learning a new skill can be hard work. Remember, your students may have been depending on you for a long time to act for them. Now they have to act for themselves. If you meet with resistance at first, don't give up. They, and you, will be much happier as they grow more independent.

- Students communicate in many different ways. When teaching students to manage their own behavior, you may need to use many forms of communication. A student who is nonverbal or is a nonreader may benefit from using picture cards to self-manage. For readers, a written list carried in their wallets or backpacks may work. Be flexible and creative. Adapt self-management strategies to your students' own forms of communication.

- When students are first learning to manage their own behavior, you may want to use a reward system in which students earn points for independent performance. As students become better in using their self-management strategies, they can learn to deliver their own points or rewards by using self-reinforcement, such as buying a soft drink after completing a work shift.

Cross-reference: Teaching Skills that Need Strengthening (6-4)

"We teach a step-by-step process for the completion of a task. Audiovisual materials like picture cards are used in accordance with the situation. Repetition is also extremely important to my students—'one time only' is quickly forgotten."
Teacher
Raleigh Egypt High School
Memphis, Tennessee

Evaluating Outcomes:

Teaching and Evaluating Self-Management

Teaching self-management to students sounds good, but how do you do it? What do you do with a student who just can't seem to get up in the morning to get to school or a student who can't seem to control her anger and "mouths-off" to her boss at work all the time? Or what about the student who doesn't shave, use deodorant, or brush his teeth most of the time and offends his peers just by his odor? With so many different problems and students, where do you start? You'll find that teaching self-management is not hard if you follow these steps.[1] Use Form 7.1 (Teaching and Evaluating Self-Management) on page 191 to guide you:

1.   *Identify the problem.* Begin by gathering information about a student's performance in an environment, such as at the baseball park, on the job, or on the bus to work. Do people in that environment believe that a student's performance needs to be improved in some way? The first step in teaching self-management is to find out whether people think there is a problem. You can do this by asking them questions or by having them fill out an informal assessment. Be sure to ask a variety of people in an environment, such as co-workers, employers, teachers, family members, peers, or community members. Also, remember to ask the student herself!

Cross-references: Assessing Students' Strengths and Needs (6-2) and Communicating Students' Strengths and Needs (6-3)

Example: Hsin Tu's supervisor at Badecoli's Italian Restaurant & Pub had already received three complaints about

---

[1]From "Utilizing self-management to teach independence on the job," by Lagomarcino, T.R., Hughes, C., & Rusch, F.R., *Education and Training in Mental Retardation, 24,* 139–148. Copyright 1989 by The Council for Exceptional Children. Adapted with permission.

Hsin from customers' suggestion cards when he first mentioned to Ms. Carlin that Hsin was having a problem. Hsin was forgetting to include some important ingredients, such as the house dressing on salads or herb garnishes on appetizers. Besides that, three waitresses had complained about how long it was taking Hsin to get food orders to them during the lunch rush. And, just as important, Hsin himself told his supervisor that he was "getting confused" by all of the orders and didn't know which ones to start on first, especially when the restaurant was crowded.

2.   *Verify the problem.* Different people in an environment may evaluate a student's performance differently. It's important to check whether a problem identified by a person really is a problem. You can do this by observing a student's performance and then comparing it with the performance of a peer or a co-worker. If the student's performance is very different from that of a peer who is successful in that environment, there may indeed be a problem. Discuss your findings with others (including the student) to decide whether the problem is big enough to do something about it.

Cross-reference: Comparative Observations in Observing Students' Performance (6.1.1)

Example: Ms. Carlin decided to observe Hsin for an hour during one lunch shift. Because there were two prep cooks in addition to Hsin, Ms. Carlin compared his performance with that of his co-workers. She recorded the time it took to make each salad and how many errors each employee made (which she determined by talking to the wait staff). She discovered that Hsin was working at about one third the rate of his co-workers and that errors occurred approximately three times as often. Besides that, she noticed that every time Hsin filled a salad order, he made it in a different way.

3.   *Determine acceptability.* What should a student's behavior look like? How much should it resemble the behavior of others in an environment? The answer will vary

from environment to environment. Collaborate with supervisors, teachers, co-workers, peers, community leaders, and others, as well as the student, to discuss what performance level is acceptable in an environment and what behaviors are practical to expect. Learn to negotiate expectations with others.

Example: Ms. Carlin sat down with Hsin's supervisor to discuss her observations. The supervisor stated that although he hoped Hsin would learn to work faster, the most important requirement was that Hsin make the salads correctly. In the meantime, he would allow Hsin's co-workers to take responsibility for making sure all of Hsin's salad orders were completed on time.

4. *Identify natural supports in the environment.* Often, already present in an environment are supports that can prompt students to begin, continue, or end an activity on their own. For example, bus schedules may be listed at a bus stop, bells may signal the beginning and ending of class or work shift, or textbooks may contain a list of questions for self-study. Students can learn to use these naturally occurring supports and reinforcers to guide their behavior as they learn to self-manage.

> **Cross-references:** Job Analysis Survey (Form 4.1) in Conducting Environmental Assessments (4.1.1) and Conducting Social Support Assessments (5.1.1)

Example: Ms. Carlin used the Job Analysis Survey she had completed when placing Hsin at Badecoli's to determine what supports in the environment could help Hsin complete his job accurately and independently. She discovered that the restaurant had training pictures that could be hung above the salad prep area. The pictures provided a visual task analysis of the required steps used for making each type of salad.

5. *Select a self-management strategy.* Three questions should be asked when deciding which self-management strategy to teach a student. First, there are several

self-management strategies from which to choose, such as self-instruction, permanent (picture) prompts, self-monitoring, and self-reinforcing (see 7.2.2, 7.2.3, and 7.2.4). Which of these strategies matches the requirements of the environment? For example, if a job requires an employee to move around, picture prompts that are permanently placed in an environment may not be the best choice. Second, is the procedure acceptable by others in the environment? If the environment is very quiet, such as a library, then teaching a student to self-instruct aloud would not be a good idea. Third, which strategy does the student prefer? If students are to become responsible for their own behaviors, then they should be involved in selecting how they will manage their behavior.

Example: Ms. Carlin decided that picture prompts would help Hsin manage his own work behavior. They were already available and matched what Hsin needed to know to do his job of salad preparation correctly. Besides that, the pictures were the same ones other employees used during their training and, therefore, would be acceptable to his co-workers. Fortunately, Hsin thought the pictures were "cool," and he was willing to give them a try.

6.   *Teach self-management skills.* There are three steps to teaching self-management. First, identify the steps of the target behavior, such as shaving or using an automatic teller machine, and the self-management strategy (e.g., self-monitoring, self-instructing). Second, teach each step of the target behavior and self-management strategy using appropriate instructional techniques, such as prompting, modeling, and providing feedback. Third, start withdrawing your assistance gradually as soon as possible. For example, start standing farther away from the student or visit the workplace less often. After all, independence is one goal of self-management.

Cross-reference: Teaching Skills that Need Strengthening (6-4)

Example: Ms. Carlin decided that the easiest way to identify the steps of making salads was to make them herself as she followed each step on the training pictures that she had placed on the wall. As she did so, she checked off each picture as she performed each step. She then taught Hsin to do the same, using modeling, prompts, corrective feedback, and reinforcement. She then began to withdraw her help so that Hsin could learn to perform the steps independently. First, Ms. Carlin gave a verbal reminder as Hsin completed each step. Gradually, she began only to point to a picture if he missed a step. Then, she placed herself farther and farther away from Hsin. Before long, Hsin was using the pictures on his own to prompt his behavior.

7. *Evaluate students' performance.* When training has been completed, teachers should periodically observe their students to determine whether their performance has maintained. Also, remember to continue to check whether their performance is similar to the performance of others in the environment. Finally, check the acceptability of your students' performance by asking others in the environment. Their opinion is as important as your students' actual behavior.

Example: Ms. Carlin occasionally watched Hsin (from a distance, of course) to determine how well he was doing at work and how his performance compared with that of his co-workers. She soon discovered that as Hsin became better at following the picture prompts, his speed and accuracy also improved. Conversations with the other prep cooks and the waitresses confirmed her observations— Hsin was making salads with the best of them! And, as it turned out, Hsin had put his own self-management program in place. If he finished all of his salads in time on his shift, he treated himself to his favorite dessert: a piece of "Sweet Indulgence Chocolate Cake." This job really was "a piece of cake" after all!

7.2.2 Teaching Students to Use Self-Instruction

Self-instruction involves teaching students to use their own verbal behavior, or "self-talk," to guide their performance. Put simply, *self-instruction* means that a student tells himself to do something and then does it. Self-instruction is an effective self-management strategy to teach if students are required to move around within an environment because students' verbal behavior is always available to them—whether they are interacting at work, riding the bus, getting dressed for school, or going to the movies with friends.

"I teach self-management by encouraging students to voice their activities for the day every morning. This helps them to learn their responsibilities and what they plan to do each day."

Teacher
Glencliff High School
Nashville, Tennessee

There are many different ways to self-instruct. Some students may use fairly sophisticated verbal or written self-instructions. For example, they may "talk" themselves through the steps of solving complex math problems or writing expository paragraphs. Other students may have limited speech and may use one word or sound to guide their behavior while completing a task, such as washing a window or brushing their teeth. Still others may not speak at all and may sign manually or tap a picture with their finger to self-instruct. In any case, students are using their own verbal behavior, or "self-talk," to guide their performance.

Evaluating Outcomes:

Teaching and Evaluating the Use of Self-Instruction

Teaching self-instruction is easy because the steps already have been developed for you. There is no need to start from scratch. Just identify a target behavior that a student is not performing independently, and follow the easy steps outlined in the Self-Instruction Training Sequence (Form 7.2 on page 202). You may adapt the steps to fit the behavior and your student's own strengths and needs. (Blank, reproducible forms for teaching self-instruction are included in the appendix.)

Self-Instruction Training Sequence[2]

1. Teacher models target behavior while self-instructing aloud. The first step in teaching self-instruction is to perform the target behavior yourself while the student is watching. For example, you may model for the student how to load a dishwasher or how to access the World Wide Web. As you perform the behavior, say aloud (self-instruct) each step of the task as you do it. *Example:* Mr. Wallace, the physical education teacher at Haverty High School, was trying to teach his class to dance a basic rumba step. He lined up all of the students on one side of the gym and stood with his back to them in front of them. Then he began to dance the basic rumba step over and over as the students watched. As he did so, Mr. Wallace loudly said, "Step-close-step," as he performed each of the foot movements of the pattern.

2. Student performs target behavior while teacher instructs aloud. Next, it's the student's turn to perform the target behavior. You continue to model how to self-instruct by saying the instructions aloud as the student performs each step. Provide prompts, corrective feedback, reinforcement, and, of course, plenty of opportunity to practice as the student learns to perform the behavior independently. *Example:* Next, Mr. Wallace turned around so that he could watch the students as they danced the basic rumba step. As they moved their feet in time to the music, he continued to instruct them aloud by saying, "Step-close-step." He also corrected the students if they missed any of their steps, had them practice their steps over and over, and praised them for learning the basic step so quickly.

[2]From *Student directed learning: Teaching self-determination skills,* by M. Agran. © 1997. Adapted with permission of Wadsworth Publishing, a division of Thomson Learning. Fax 800 730-2215.

3. Student performs target behavior while self-instructing aloud. Finally, it's time to turn all of the responsibility over to the student. This time the student performs the target behavior and self-instructs independently. You still may have to guide the student or provide corrective feedback, but you should discontinue your assistance as soon as possible. *Example:* Mr. Wallace now wanted the students to dance without his help. This time as they performed the basic rumba step, they self-instructed out loud, saying, "Step-close-step." Mr. Wallace was there to help a few who still had difficulty, but soon all of the students in the class were performing the step on their own to the beat of the music and their self-instructions.

4. If appropriate, teach the student to whisper or "think" the self-instructions. Talking aloud to themselves, although effective in guiding your students' behavior, may not be acceptable in some environments. You don't want your students to "stick out like a sore thumb"! If appropriate, instruct the student to whisper or to say the instructions in his or her head. *Example:* It might be all right for the students to say their dance steps out loud while they're learning them in class, but Mr. Wallace knew that would not be "cool" on the dance floor or at the prom. He decided to model dancing the rumba without self-instructions and reminded the students that talking out loud to themselves might be a big "turn-off" for their dates!

Self-Instruction Statements

The statements that students are taught to say as they self-instruct may be as simple as those used by Mr. Wallace to teach his students to do the rumba ("step-close-step"). Or, they may follow more of a problem-solving format, which prompts students to identify and respond to a problem. Students then evaluate their responses and reinforce themselves for doing a good job (or tell themselves to try another solution if theirs didn't work). The statements can be either complex or simple, as shown below.

1. *Identifying the problem:* "Here comes my boss. I always want to yell at her when I see her, but I don't want to get fired," or, "Not plugged in."

2. *Stating a possible response to the problem:* "Guess I'll try to smile and say 'Hi,'" or, "Got to plug in."

3. *Evaluating the response:* "Hey, that was pretty easy. She even smiled back," or, "That wasn't really a smile. I'll try better next time," or, "Fixed it."

4. *Self-reinforcing:* "It's a good idea to be nice. Then she's nicer to me," or, "Good."

7.2.3   Teaching Students to Use Permanent Prompts

Permanent prompts are visual, auditory, or tactile cues that are used to prompt a desired behavior. We often use some type of permanent prompt to remind us to do something, such as writing ourselves a note, setting an alarm on a wristwatch, or posting a daily schedule. In learning to use permanent prompts, students are taught to respond in a certain way when they see or hear the cue. That way, they don't need to have a teacher, parent, or someone else prompt them to do something.

The list of permanent prompts used by teachers is endless: picture recipes, taped auditory instructions, representative objects, color coding, posted signs, picture schedules, braille notes, tactile cues, and so forth.

Self-Instruction Training Sequence

Directions: *Describe the behaviors to be performed for each of these steps:*

1. Teacher models target behavior while self-instructing aloud:

Perform the basic rumba steps several times saying, "Step-close-step."

2. Student performs target behavior while teacher instructs aloud:

Ask students to perform the basic rumba step. While watching them, call out step instructions (step-close-step). Provide corrective feedback, give repeated opportunities for students to practice, and praise students who perform the steps correctly.

3. Student performs target behavior while self-instructing aloud:

Students will perform the basic rumba steps without instructions from the teacher. Students should self-instruct aloud (step-close-step). Continue to provide feedback to students who need assistance.

4. If appropriate, teach the student to whisper or "think" the self-instructions:

Teacher models how to dance the rumba without self-instructing "out loud." Next, students perform the dance steps on their own, without self-instruction.

Self-Instruction Statements

Directions: *Describe what the student will say (or do) for each of these statements:*

1. Identifying the problem: Someone is walking over here to ask me to dance, but I'm nervous that I'll forget the correct steps.

2. Stating the possible responses to the problem: As I dance, I'll "think" the steps to myself. "Step-close-step."

3. Evaluating the response: Wow! I only stepped on her feet twice.

4. Self-reinforcing: I danced much better than last time! I'll reward myself with something from the snack table.

Form 7.2.   Self-Instruction Training Sequence for Hsin Tu. (From *Student directed learning: Teaching self-determination skills,* by M. Agran. © 1997. Adapted with permission of Wadsworth Publishing, a division of Thomson Learning. Fax 800 730-2215.)

Starting Up:

- The use of permanent prompts is closely related to Modifying the Environment (4-5). Most environments already have many prompts for guiding behavior. Traffic lights indicate when to stop or go, clocks tell us what time to get off work, and telephones ring when we should answer them. Students, however, may need to be taught to respond appropriately to these naturally occurring prompts. Or, they may need additional permanent prompts to help them respond independently.

- Teach students to look for features of an environment that they can use to prompt their behavior. For example, a student who has difficulty remembering when medicine should be taken can be given a series of cues to remember, such as putting away her lunch after eating or when a certain television program comes on.

- Sometimes naturally occurring prompts in the environment must be adapted for them to cue a student's behavior. For example, a telephone may need to "ring" by flashing a light to signal a student with a hearing impairment of an incoming call, or exit signs in a building may need to be lowered for students in wheelchairs to be able to see them. Also, the way you adapt prompts must be socially acceptable—some students would not want to be "caught dead" carrying a picture schedule into their auto technology or art history class!

Cross-reference: Gaining Access to Existing Environmental Supports (4-4)

"Place empty cans of cleaning items in the areas needing to be cleaned; therefore, the student can remember the items needed in each area. This will help students learn on their own which items to use for cleaning and where to use them."
Teacher
Ripley High School
Henning, Tennessee

Evaluating Outcomes:

Teaching and Evaluating the Use of Picture Prompts

One way to use permanent prompts is to combine pictures with a task analysis of the steps needed to complete a job. For example, you could analyze each step for cleaning a bathroom in a motel or at home. Then take a photograph or draw a picture of each step of the job. Post the pictures on the wall, in a book, or on a board. Give the student a marker to check off each step as he completes it. If you laminate the pictures, they can be reused. The form on the next page is a series of picture prompts to use for cleaning a bathroom. Notice that the form also allows the student to evaluate how many steps toward his personal goal were completed (see Teaching Students to Use Self-Monitoring and Self-Reinforcement, 7.2.4). (A blank, re-producible form is included in the appendix.)

Cross-references: Conducting Environmental Assessments (4.1.1) and Observing Students' Performance (6.1.1)

Teacher-Proven Practices:

Teachers report that they have taught students to use picture prompts as self-management strategies in the following ways:

- Use a personal picture schedule at the beginning of the school year and at the worksite to increase students' autonomy and self-determination.

- Teach a young man to wash his hands by color coding each step of hand washing with a color-coded picture chart.

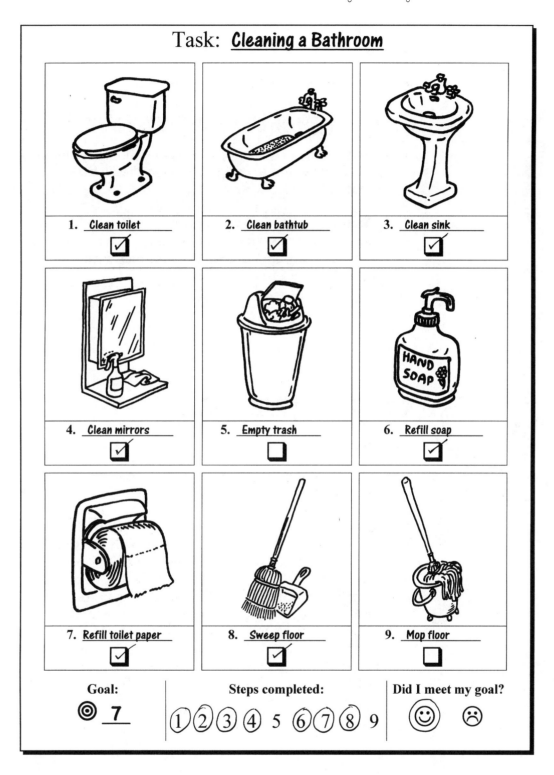

Task: **Cleaning a Bathroom**

1. **Clean toilet**
2. **Clean bathtub**
3. **Clean sink**
4. **Clean mirrors**
5. **Empty trash**
6. **Refill soap**
7. **Refill toilet paper**
8. **Sweep floor**
9. **Mop floor**

Goal: ◎ 7

Steps completed: ①②③④ 5 ⑥⑦⑧ 9

Did I meet my goal? ☺ ☹

Form 7.3.   Picture Prompt Form: Cleaning a Bathroom.

- Teach students to follow their morning routines by using checklists or picture schedules.

- Teach students to match their picture card schedules with a posted main schedule so that they can make the transition independently from one activity to the next.

- Use premarked envelopes with specified dollar amounts for students to use to budget their paychecks for monthly expenses.

- Require students to carry their personal schedules and wear wristwatches (adapted, if necessary) so that they can get to their daily appointments or take their medication on time.

Evaluating Outcomes:

Teaching and Evaluating the Use of Picture Schedules

Permanent prompts can be used to teach students to follow daily schedules. For students who don't tell time, use pictures of clocks with the hands set at, or showing digital faces of, the times of the day's activities. Students simply need to look at the picture clocks and match the times with those on a wall clock or their wristwatch. The picture schedule then tells them in words (like the following examples of Today's Schedule) or in pictures what to do at the specified time. They can mark off on their schedules when they initiate each activity to monitor their own behavior. Students can also use their picture schedules to communicate their activities to others, such as the driver of an accessible van or their roommates. (Blank, reproducible forms are included in the appendix.)

Today's Schedule

Student: ___Robert Scott___   **Day(s):** ___Thursdays___

Time	What should I do?	Time	What should I do?
	Meet bus on corner		Clock-out from work
	Arrive at work		Meet bus in front of store
	Take a break		Softball practice begins
	Return from break		End of softball practice
	Leave for lunch		Meet Randy for dinner
	Return from lunch		

Form 7.4.   Today's Schedule (with analog clock) for Robert Scott.

Today's Schedule

Student: Javier Alcarez   **Day(s):** Fridays

Time	What should I do?	Time	What should I do?
7:20	Meet Mike to walk to school	1:40	Computer Lab class
7:40	FCA club meeting (Room 212)	3:30	Pick up and deposit paycheck
8:10	American Literature class	5:30	Elias picks me up from home
9:47	Consumer Math class	6:00	Potluck dinner at church
11:24	Lunch with People First club	7:00	Choir practice
12:03	Industrial Arts class	8:30	Dessert with friends at EZ's

Form 7.5.   Today's Schedule (with digital clock) for Javier Alcarez.

7.2.4 Teaching Students to Use Self-Monitoring and Self-Reinforcement

A necessary part of self-determination is that students be aware of the consequences of their actions and the effect that their behavior has on their environment and people in that environment. For example, if a worker on quality control at an auto plant is negligent on the job, the effect may be that faulty parts are installed in newly produced cars and the worker is fired. Or if a student continues to talk about the same topic until it's "run into the ground," people may start avoiding the student in the lunchroom or breakroom. Unless we monitor our own behavior, we may be performing behaviors that have effects that we didn't intend and that undermine our own best interests. Luckily, students (and we!) can learn how to evaluate, change, and reinforce their (and our) behavior.

"Give a student a 'checkoff' system to complete a job or task. For example, when a student completes a task, she drops a chip into a jar. When all the chips are in the jar, that signals that the job is complete."

Teacher
LaVergne High School
Shelbyville, Tennessee

Evaluating Outcomes:

Using Checklists to Self-Monitor and Self-Reinforce Behavior

Learning how to evaluate your own behavior takes skill and practice. Many of us are so used to having other people evaluate us, such as our bosses, teachers, or supervisors, that we never have learned to look at and evaluate ourselves. When we first learn to evaluate our behavior, a checklist that lists steps in an activity, jobs to be completed, or reminders to use appropriate social skills with our co-workers may be helpful. The Daily Checklist form on page 211 shows a checklist used for completing a morning routine. The form can be adapted for nonreaders and others on the basis of their individual needs.

In teaching students to monitor their behavior with a checklist, there are three steps. First, teach the student to look at the first item on the checklist. The items can be listed as words, such as on the checklist for getting ready in the morning, or as pictures. Second, teach the student to look at (observe) herself as she performs the behavior indicated in the item. Third, show the student how to check off whether the behavior was performed. At the end of the day or the activity, the student can tally how many of the total behaviors were completed and reward herself if her behavior was acceptable to others and to herself.

You can also adapt the checklist for students to rate the quality of their performance, in addition to whether the behavior was performed. A videotape of their performance would be helpful, too. As always, when teaching a new behavior, use appropriate learning principles, such as prompting, corrective feedback, opportunities for practice, and reinforcement. Then withdraw your assistance as the student learns the new task. (A blank, reproducible form is included in the appendix.)

Cross-reference: Teaching Skills that Need Strengthening (6-4)

How to Do It:

- Teach students who are usually untidy to monitor on a chart their progress in keeping their work areas clean.

- Teach a student to use a self-monitoring chart to record his outbursts of anger when he goes to the gym to do his job as the basketball team manager.

- Teach students to use self-monitoring charts to complete routine jobs. Students learn to evaluate their own work and reward themselves for a job well done.

Daily Checklist

Student: __Stacey Dean__   **Week:** __January 20–25__

Activity: __Morning routines__

What do I need to do?	Monday	Tuesday	Wednesday	Thursday	Friday
Make my bed	X	X	X	✓	X
Brush my teeth	✓	X	X	X	X
Take a bath/shower	✓	✓	X	✓	✓
Put on clean clothes	✓	✓	X	✓	✓
Put on deodorant	X	X	✓	X	X
Comb hair	✓	✓	✓	✓	✓
Put on my makeup	✓	✓	✓	✓	✓
Eat breakfast	✓	X	X	✓	X
Make my lunch	✓	✓	✓	✓	✓
Feed the dog and cat	X	✓	X	X	X
Total completed:	**7**	**6**	**4**	**7**	**5**

✓ = I did this!!!   X = I did not do this!

Form 7.6. Daily Checklist for Stacey Dean.

Evaluating Outcomes:

Using Charts to Self-Monitor and Self-Reinforce Behavior

Self-recording charts, such as the one on page 213, can be used to teach students to monitor their own behavior. An advantage to charts like this is that students can observe and record more than one behavior at a time. In the example, a sales associate, Jefferson Lopez, is monitoring four of his behaviors: working hard, keeping the children's section clean, the number of customers greeted, and the number of items sold. These behaviors can be personal goals that a student has chosen to work on. Notice that Jefferson has stated a goal for each of the behaviors for his morning shift. For example, he has chosen as a goal to greet 20 customers from 9:00 to 10:30. After observing and recording the number of customers he greeted in 15-minute intervals, Jefferson counts the total number greeted. He records on his chart that he met his goal and chooses 28 customers as his next goal.

Meeting their goal on a self-recording chart can be rewarding in itself for your students. Just filling in the chart and knowing that they met their goals can be enough to keep them continuing to perform the desired behavior, even without praise, recognition, or assistance from others. If self-recording is not enough to maintain your students' behavior, however, they can try reinforcing themselves for meeting their goals with a desired reward, such as dining at their favorite restaurant at the end of the week.

Students can be taught to use self-recording charts to monitor and record their behaviors much in the same way that they learn to use checklists, through the application of proven learning principles such as modeling and corrective feedback. As students acquire their self-monitoring skills, of course, your assistance should be withdrawn. (See Teaching Skills that Need Strengthening, 6-4.)

In designing a self-recording chart, be sure to keep it attractive, easy to use, and easy to carry around. Use words, pictures, or symbols to match the strengths, needs, and preferences of your students. Involve your students as much as possible in constructing their charts; they are more likely to use them if they've had some choice in the behaviors and goals included. (A blank, reproducible form is included in the appendix.)

Self-Recording Chart

Name: Jefferson Lopez   **Date:** October 24

Activity: Working as sales associate on floor of G.L. Brownstein Clothing Store

Time	Behaviors			
	Am I working hard?	Am I keeping the children's section clean?	How many customers have I greeted?	How many items have I sold?
9:00	Y	Y	3	1
9:15	Y	Y	2	—
9:30	N	N	1	—
9:45	Y	N	6	4
10:00	Y	Y	3	1
10:15	Y	N	8	5
10:30	Y	Y	2	2
My total is:	6 yes	4 yes	25	13
My goal is:	7 yes	3 yes	20	15
Was goal met?	YES (NO)	(YES) NO	(YES) NO	YES (NO)

My goal for next time is . . .	7 yes	5 yes	28	15

_____Jefferson Lopez_____   _____Mr. Henderson_____
Student's Signature   **Teacher's Signature**

Form 7.7.   Self-Recording Chart for Jefferson Lopez.

7-3 INCORPORATING SELF-DETERMINATION INTO DAILY LIVING

The intent of the IDEA Amendments of 1997 is to increase students' participation in the mainstream of everyday life as active participants who are living independently and enjoying economic self-sufficiency. To do so, students must be self-determined. The amendments call for us to raise our expectations of students and empower them to lead productive, independent adult lives. By doing so, we raise these students' expectations of themselves in their everyday lives. By incorporating self-determination goals and objectives into students' daily living, we are being consistent with the legislative mandate.

7.3.1 Managing Everyday Living

All teachers hope that their students will use the skills they learn in high school in their everyday lives, both before and after graduation. The generalization of skills to new environments, activities, and people is an important outcome of any educational program. Self-determination and self-management can help students do just that. Teaching students to take greater responsibility for their own behavior will help them use their skills independently in places where teachers or other service providers are not there to provide support.

"How do I teach self-determination? By starting at the student's home. First, I ask where are the washer and dryer, and can she use them? Where does she keep her clean clothes, and does she know how to make her lunch? Where can she put everything in one place so she can get ready for work tomorrow? Can she use the alarm clock? Where can she put her eyeglasses so they are always in one place? These are the questions we need to ask."
Itinerant Transition Teacher
Nashville Public Schools
Nashville, Tennessee

Starting Up:

- Self-determination skills are important for every student to be successful on the job, in the classroom, and around the community. Everyone can benefit from learning to set goals for themselves, identify the steps needed to reach those goals, determine whether they are on-track, and adjust their behavior accordingly.

- Teaching students "generic" self-management strategies, such as making lists, can go a long way toward promoting self-determination in their daily lives. Students can easily adapt such strategies and use them at school or work or in other environments. For example, by learning how to make a list, students can plan meals at home, shop within their budgets at the mall, establish time lines for class assignments, or prioritize job tasks at work.

- If your (and your students') goal is to have students use self-determination and self-management skills at school and work, in their homes, and in the community, then you need to teach these skills in those environments. Remember, students are more likely to use a skill (even self-management) if they learn it where you (and they) expect them to use it.

- Becoming self-determined often means learning new skills to decrease dependence on others. By enrolling in home economics or family life classes, for example, students may learn housekeeping and cooking skills that will allow them to live more independently in the community.

Teacher-Proven Practices:

- Using a checklist, students can learn to write their own checks and balance their monthly bank statements.

- A young man with diabetes has learned which foods he should or should not eat. He is allowed to select his own foods in the lunchroom, in restaurants, and when he cooks meals.

"At the bowling alley, a student in a wheelchair independently requests an adaptive bowling ramp. With the ramp, she can successfully compete with her walking peers. She can get her own ball, place it on the ramp, throw the ball, and keep score."
Teacher
Central High School
Culleoka, Tennessee

- By using a written task analysis of her job requirements, a young woman is able to work independently on the job for the first time in the food-service department of a hospital.

- Providing photographs of clean motel rooms has helped housekeeping staff keep their jobs. They match the appearance of the rooms they are cleaning to the photos to determine whether they have completed each of their job tasks.

- Picture cards can help students find items by themselves in the store. If they can't count money, they can use the "next dollar up" method to pay for the items by themselves.

- Using a picture schedule, a young man matches the clock faces (analog or digital) on the schedule to his wristwatch. He has now learned to deliver papers on time to offices at his worksite.

- Have students plan their own community-based instruction activities. Have them choose an activity, call to make arrangements, plan the agenda, and determine the cost of the activity.

- For students who need help in putting on a uniform correctly for work, have them match their appearance in the mirror with a picture of themselves with their uniforms on correctly.

7.3.2   Providing Opportunities for Self-Determination

Being self-determined means being able to set your own goals in life and act toward achieving these goals. It means being able to make choices about "big things," such as whether to go to college or get married or which career to pursue. It also means making choices and decisions about the "little everyday things" that make up life, such as whether to take a sandwich to work or buy lunch, what to wear to a meeting, or how to spend Saturday night. Our self-determination is meaningless unless we have the chance to exercise our skills and rights every day—in our daily lives and in our plans for the future.

Communicating our needs and wants is a big part of self-determination. How else can we advocate for ourselves and let people know our decisions and choices? For some students, picture cards, manual signing, or communication devices help them communicate their ideas to others and to speak up for themselves.

"I provide opportunities for students to use self-determination by having them participate in personal management activities like shopping for clothes or hygiene. The students (with their families) select activities they think are needed for their independence."
Teacher
Volunteer High School
Jonesborough, Tennessee

How to Do It:

- Self-determination and self-management skills should not be taught in isolation. The point of teaching these skills is to allow students to have more control in all aspects of their daily lives. It's important to assist fellow teachers in incorporating units on self-determination into the general curriculum and extracurricular activities. For example, independent living skills could be embedded into a math or an English class.

- A home-living apartment affiliated with a high school transition program can be an ideal way for students to try out their self-determination skills in a safe environment. Students can spend several nights per week at the apartment with supervision as part of their high school curriculum before graduating and living more on their own. (See *The Wild Dream Team* video in the Careers and Employment Section of the Resources in the appendix.)

- With students and their parents, identify skills that each student needs to gain more independence. Then incorporate these into daily activities to provide opportunities for students to practice self-determination and self-management skills in their daily lives.

Cross-reference: Identifying Students' Opportunities for Choice and Decision Making (8-1)

REFERENCES

Hughes, C. (1997). Self-instruction. In M. Agran (Ed.), *Student directed learning: Teaching self-determination skills* (pp. 171–198). Pacific Grove, CA: Brooks/Cole.

Individuals with Disabilities Education Act Amendments of 1997, PL 105-17, 20 U.S.C. § 1400 *et seq.*

Lagomarcino, T.R., Hughes, C., & Rusch, F.R. (1989). Utilizing self-management to teach independence on the job. *Education and Training in Mental Retardation, 24,* 139–148.

Nirje, B. (1972). The right to self-determination. In W. Wolfensberger (Ed.), *Normalization: The principle of normalization* (pp. 176–200). Toronto, Ontario, Canada: National Institute on Mental Retardation.

Rehabilitation Act Amendments of 1992, PL 102-569, 29 U.S.C. §§ 701 *et seq.*

Chapter 8

Strategies for Increasing Students' Choice and Decision Making

OVERVIEW

The Individuals with Disabilities Education Act (IDEA) Amendments of 1997 require that students' preferences, choices, and interests as well as considerations for their cultural diversity be incorporated into their individualized education programs (IEPs). Research shows, however, that transition-age students often have little opportunity to make choices and decisions for themselves. For example, students may have little say in developing their own educational goals and may be placed in a career track that is not of their own choosing. Limited opportunity to choose, unfortunately, may continue into adulthood. Too often, choices about everyday living, such as what to wear or eat, how to spend free time, or where to live or work, are made by parents, teachers, or service providers, even after students leave school. No wonder students sometimes make poor choices! Making good choices and wise decisions is a skill that must be learned and that takes practice, sometimes by learning from one's mistakes.

Not only is including choice and decision making in a student's educational program a legal mandate, but it also can have many benefits for students. For example, by choosing to try new experiences, students have a chance to learn more about themselves, their interests, and their preferences. When students have the opportunity to choose, they may find that life has many possibilities! Teachers can learn to expand opportunities to choose and make decisions across many aspects of their students' lives. They can also teach students to improve their choice-making skills and to make wise decisions.

This chapter contains three main groups and seven subgroups of strategies for teachers to use to increase students' choice and decision making. These strategies include identifying and collaborating to increase students' opportunities for choice and decision making, teaching choice- and decision-making skills, and increasing students' choice and decision making.

We all value the right to make choices and decisions in our own lives. It's important, therefore, that we ensure that the spirit, not just the letter, of the law is enacted by providing students opportunities to choose and make decisions throughout their daily lives.

Case Study 8.1   No Choice

Angelo Rust used to get his hair styled at a salon called Choices. What a joke, he thought! Today, he had no choices. Whether to get up or just stay in bed all day was about the extent of his choices. When he used to have money, well, maybe then he had choices. But that was before he got busted for selling drugs. Before that, he could buy whatever he wanted. He wore jewelry around his neck and wrists, had new shirts and shoes, and had his hair styled every day. But still, he thought, looking up at the ceiling from where he lay on his mattress on the floor, even then he was a slave to his business. It's not like he could just take off work for the weekend and go to the lake or even go to the movies. He always had to be there to answer the pager, make a deal, or hide from the cops. Really, what kind of choices were those? What he really had wanted back then was just the chance to sit on a park bench in the sun, watching his nieces play in the sand and the men play chess at the tables under the trees. Well, now he had all the time in the world to do that since he dropped out of school 2 years ago at age 15, and now he hardly ever had work. Without even a general equivalency diploma (GED) or any kind of legitimate work experience, he never could find a job worth anything. So, what choice did he have now anyway but to sit on his mattress and wait for the next 24 hours to roll around?

All right, so maybe one time he did have choices. Maybe he did choose to start hanging out with the drug crowd, and maybe it was his idea to start selling drugs for some quick cash. And maybe he did decide to quit school. But let's face it: He hated school. He never had any choices there, that's for sure! For one thing, his counselor stuck him in auto tech classes all the time, and he hated working on cars. Dirty, greasy work, he thought! What he really had wanted to do, to tell you the truth, was to enroll in the child care classes they had at school and some-day become a preschool teacher. He loved little kids, just like his nieces, and he had wanted to teach them that they could have a better life than he had and to make better choices than he had. But nobody listened to him, and, finally, one day, he just quit going to school. And the only choice now was either to get up or to stay in bed. (See Case Study 8.3 for a different view of Angelo's life, had he been given career choices.)

"Our concern for choice is expressed in our mission statement: 'Making our dreams happen by having choices and control over our lives.'"

Southern Collaborative of Self-Advocates
People First of Tennessee, Georgia, and Alabama
Murfreesboro, Tennessee

"Choice-making opportunities exist all day long. People who work with individuals with disabilities are too accustomed to making choices for these individuals. They simply need to stop talking, stop using their hands, and stand back."
Itinerant Transition Teacher
Metropolitan Nashville Public Schools
Nashville, Tennessee

8-1 IDENTIFYING STUDENTS' OPPORTUNITIES FOR CHOICE AND DECISION MAKING

How do we find out what our own preferences and interests are? Well, we try lots of different things, such as jobs, hobbies, hairstyles, CDs, movies, or people to hang out with. We don't know if we like them until we try them!

8.1.1 Observing Students' Choices

It's important to find out what kind of choices students have in their everyday lives in and out of school. Research shows that they may have surprisingly little opportunity to make choices or decisions, especially regarding their own lifestyles. Observing students over a period of time and in different environments is one way to gain information about students' opportunities to choose.

Starting Up:

- When trying to identify a student's opportunities for choice, focus on the student's actions, what is going on around the student, and how others react to the student. You may observe that many opportunities for choice making occur throughout the day, such as choosing to walk or to ride the bus to work. Does the student, however, have access to these opportunities to choose?

- You can't be everywhere in a student's life at all times. Learn to rely on the reports of others sometimes. Encourage all teachers and service providers with whom the student comes in contact to observe the choices a student makes during the day, such as choices of social partners or free-time activities. Peers and family members can help, too.

- Choice making can be included as an objective in a student's IEP. Some examples include the following: "Given a snack machine at school, a student goes independently at the appropriate times and makes his or her own selection," or "given an outline of job descriptions, a student indicates several jobs that he or she would like to try." Observing the student's behavior will tell you at least two things: whether the student independently makes a choice and what the student's preferences are (choices that a student continues to make over time).

The IDEA Amendments of 1997 state that, beginning at age 14 and updated annually, all students receiving special education services must have included in their IEPs a statement of their transition service needs as determined by their courses of study. These services must be based on each individual student's needs, taking into account the student's preferences and interests. Teachers must learn to observe and identify their students' individual preferences, interests, and choices to meet the IDEA mandate.

Everyone has choices and preferences. With students who communicate in nontraditional ways, such as pointing, making facial expressions, or gesturing, it's important to observe them carefully to determine what choices they are trying to communicate.

"To observe students' choices, I watch how much involvement they have during extracurricular activities like homecoming events. I encourage them to work on different jobs with their classmates, and I see which jobs they choose and with whom they choose to work."

Teacher
McEwen High School
McEwen, Tennessee

"Observe students during their social interactions. Listen as students discuss opportunities for choice in their daily lives. Provide examples for making choices, and discuss why certain choices should or should not be made."

Teacher
South Side High School
Memphis, Tennessee

Teacher-Proven Practices:

- Observe a student making everyday choices, such as whether to attend an optional school assembly or an afternoon play. Or, observe a student selecting menu items that are within her budget when ordering lunch at a restaurant.

- Observe students' participation in school clubs, service organizations, and social activities. Keep your eye on which activities they appear to enjoy and how students choose to be involved with their peers. For example, do they like to hold offices in their clubs, or do they prefer to take more of a position on the sidelines?

- Observe students' participation in recreational options available in the school gym, the local YMCA, the Boys' and Girls' Club, or around the neighborhood. Do they usually skateboard, swim, or play basketball? Recreational activities frequently chosen by them are likely to be preferred ones.

- Observe a student and his peers as they make choices about their activities, such as which movie to go to or which assignment to begin first. Who makes the decisions and what role does the student play in the decision-making process?

- Observe opportunities for choice that are available for students during lunch, pep rallies, parties, and clubs or while shopping, traveling, or working. Note whether students independently make choices during these times.

Cross-references: Observing Students' Performance (4.1.2 and 6.1.1), Observing Students' Interactions (5.1.2)

"To learn about students' recreational and leisure choices, I expose students to several recreational activities over a period of months and observe their performance. I do this across employment-training sites too. For students who can't tell me their preferences, I note differences in their behavior as signs of preference."

Teacher
McGavock High School
Nashville, Tennessee

8.1.2 Collecting Data on Students' Choices

Most of us have the opportunity to make many choices in our own lives. For example, we usually choose when to get up in the morning, what to wear, what to eat for breakfast, and whether to read the paper or listen to the radio as we eat. We usually have choices throughout the day at work, and, after work, we may decide whether we want to stay home and watch television, work out at the gym, or spend time with friends. In fact, we have so many choices that we may tend to take them for granted. We may not realize how few choices some people have or how limited their choice-making skills are. Taking data on students' opportunities for choice making gives us information on their current situation and whether their opportunities change over time.

"Quietly observing a student and carefully collecting data can provide a good picture of the number of choices a worker has or does not have over a period of time."

Itinerant Transition Teacher
Nashville Public Schools
Nashville, Tennessee

How to Do It

- There are many ways to collect data on students' choices. One way is to observe the choices that students make in role-play situations, such as ordering a meal or choosing a date for the prom. Students' choices can be recorded on checklists. You can also "set up" choice-making opportunities, such as alternative ways to complete a job task or whom to sit next to at a restaurant. Observe students' choices unobtrusively, and record their choices on the Choice-Making Opportunities form shown on pages 229–230.

- Opportunities for choice in students' curricula can be identified by checking their class schedules and looking for diversity across curricular areas. Record the variety of courses in which they have been enrolled over time, such as drama or calculus, and ask students how well these represent their own choices.

- Journal writing is a good way to learn about students' choices. Have students keep journals in which they write about choices they have or have not made and their reactions to these experiences. Discuss these experiences with students on a regular basis (e.g., when a student wanted to ask a friend to go to the mall, but didn't).

- Survey students and teachers about choices available in students' daily activities, such as alternative assignments available in their classes and choices of partners with whom to work.

Cross-reference: Observing Performance and Collecting Data (6-1)

"When I first get to know a student, I record, as much as possible, how the student reacts to choice making—how long it takes to come to a decision, how many prompts must be given, what influences the decisions, and so forth."

Teacher
Hunters Lane High School
Nashville, Tennessee

Evaluating Outcomes:

Observing Choice

How do you observe students' opportunities for choosing and the choices they make in their daily lives? It's easy if you use the Choice-Making Opportunities form on pages 229–230. (A blank, reproducible form is included in the appendix.) By using this form, you can gain important information about the opportunities for choice that exist in an environment and whether a student makes a choice when given the opportunity. You can also observe whether the student made a choice independently or the student needed support.

Notice that the form allows you to observe opportunities and choices across all important environments in which a student spends time, such as at home, at work, in school, or around the community. If you are not in an environment to observe the student, have someone else (or the student) record information on the form. Notice that you can also observe the student in these environments for an entire week using the form. Take a look in the next case study at two opportunities for choice that Rafael had on Tuesday during the week of December 6, which were recorded in the sample Choice-Making Opportunities form.

Case Study 8.2   Makin' Choices

Opportunity 1: Rafael got on the city bus with his sister Buelah. There were two seats available—one by itself and one next to someone whom Rafael knew from school. Rafael, who boarded the bus first, sat down next to his schoolmate. Buelah, who was recording observations on a form for Rafael's teacher, wrote down that Rafael had an opportunity to choose a bus seat and that he had chosen to sit next to someone he knew. The form also allowed Buelah to indicate whether Rafael had made his choice independently (which he did) or whether he needed assistance. This was important information because one of Rafael's IEP goals was to increase his independent choice-making skills, and another goal was to increase his social interaction with his peers. Of course, Buelah was careful to record the information discreetly; she didn't want Rafael to appear different from anyone else on the bus.

Opportunity 2: When they got off the bus downtown, Rafael and Buelah stopped first at an ice cream parlor to get an ice cream cone. Rafael got in line first. When he reached the counter, the counterperson asked, "May I take your order?" Rafael said nothing. After a while, the counterperson asked Buelah, "What does he want?" Buelah asked Rafael to point to his choice of ice cream displayed in containers in the freezer under the counter. After looking around for a while, Rafael pointed to the container of chocolate chip ice cream. The counter person filled a cone with ice cream and handed it to Rafael, who eagerly began licking it.

After she had placed her own order, Buelah quickly jotted down on her observation form that Rafael had had an opportunity to choose but had needed a verbal prompt from her to make a choice.

It is important to identify not only how many choices a student has but also how important those choices are to a student. For example, if a student can make choices only about types of snacks to eat but not about her free time or future plans, then you would probably consider her opportunities to choose to be quite restricted.

"Monitor choice of friends a student sits with at lunch, in class, in homeroom, on the bus, and so forth. Discuss choices with students, and have them self-monitor their choices. Monitor students' participation in extracurricular activities through observation and discussion. Have peer tutors attend class and record students' choices of friends, tasks, and so forth."

Teacher
Karns High School
Knoxville, Tennessee

8.1.3 Assessing Students' Choices and Preferences

People who have had little opportunity to choose are not likely to know what their choices and preferences are. They also may not know how realistic their choices are unless they can act on and experience the consequences of these choices. We can assess the choices and preferences of some students by simply asking them. With other students—those who communicate in nontraditional ways, such as gesturing—we must find alternative ways to assess their choices and preferences.

"I evaluate students' choice making by observing how they actually make choices. What I have found interesting is looking at what influences a student's final choice."

Teacher
Hunters Lane High School
Nashville, Tennessee

 # Starting Up:

- To find out about students' employment choices, allow them to experience different job situations. Observe their behavior at different worksites using the Student Job His-

Choice-Making Opportunities

Student: Rafael Laguzamo   **Date:** December 6

	Check one ✓				What opportunities for choice were there?	What choice was made (including no choice)?	Was assistance provided? How?
	School	Work	Community	Home			
Monday — Bedroom				✓	Rafael had to decide what to wear to school	Rafael chose his favorite summer outfit	Father helped him choose from his winter clothes
Science class	✓				Teacher asked students to choose partners for chemistry lab	None	Teacher made choice for Rafael—paired him up with Jon
Cafeteria	✓				Had to decide what he wanted to eat	Rafael went into the pizza line	None—Rafael always goes into the pizza line
Tuesday — Drama class	✓				Students were asked to get in groups for an exercise	Rafael quickly chose to be with Seth and Ali	None—chose independently
Auditorium	✓				Sign-ups for extracurricular clubs and activities	Rafael signed up for every single club (all 32)	Students at booths showed him where to sign
City bus			✓		Only two seats were empty on the bus	Rafael chose to sit next to a friend from school	None—chose independently
Ice cream parlor			✓		Employee asked, "May I take your order?"	Rafael was quiet at first but chose chocolate chip	Sister had to provide him with a verbal prompt
Wednesday — Coffeeshop		✓			Given a choice of when to take his break	Rafael chose to take it with a co-worker	None—chose independently
Guidance office	✓				Selecting courses for next semester	None	Counselor chose classes for him
Science class	✓				Teacher asked students to pick a topic for an upcoming project	None	Teacher assigned him to work with partner on "plants"

(continued)

Form 8.1.   Choice-Making Opportunities for Rafael Laguzamo.

Form 8.1. (continued)

	Location	Check one ✓				What opportunities for choice were there?	What choice was made (including no choice)?	Was assistance provided? How?
		School	Work	Community	Home			
Thursday	Homeroom	✓				Students given a chance to vote for "Most likely to…"	Rafael made his selections	Peer had to read choices and show Rafael pictures
	Special education classroom	✓				Teacher asked Rafael which job he would like to try next	Rafael chose the Taco Cocina	Teacher showed Rafael pictures of potential worksites
	School lobby	✓				Rafael missed the bus and had to decide how to get home	Rafael asked a friend for a ride	Teacher helped him think through his options
Friday	Taco Cocina		✓			Manager asked Rafael what shifts he would like to work	Rafael chose Monday, Friday, and Saturday	Teacher helped him look through a calendar
	Taco Cocina		✓			Manager offered Rafael a free lunch	Rafael chose the chalupa combination	Teacher showed Rafael a picture menu
	Video store			✓		Father said Rafael could pick out one movie for himself	Rafael picked "Star Wars"	None—chose independently
Weekend	Living room				✓	Rafael could decide how he wanted to spend the day	Chose to watch television for a while	None—chose independently
	Mall			✓		Rafael could decide which stores he wanted to go in	Chose a record store, hobby shop, and gadget store	None—chose independently
	Mall			✓		Clerk asked if Rafael would like to listen to a CD	Rafael chose a country CD	Rafael was quiet at first, friend pointed to some choices
	Bedroom				✓	Mom asked if Rafael wanted to join them for church	Rafael was extremely tired and decided not to go this time	None—chose independently
	Living room				✓	Rafael could decide how he wanted to spend the afternoon	Rafael decided to call a friend	Mom prompted him to find something to do

"Evaluate a student's opportunities for choice making across different environments and daily activities. This is very important because many of our students have had limited opportunities to make choices."
Teacher
Cumberland High School
Crossville, Tennessee

tory (Form 8.2) on page 234. Differences in performance at different jobs may indicate their job preferences. Discuss students' performance and interests with them.

- Track students' careers throughout high school by monitoring their progress using the Student Job History form. Ensure that their job preferences are addressed in their worksites and that their job histories reflect professional growth throughout their high school years.

- Give students frequent options throughout the day, such as choosing the topic of a class project or which employer to interview with at a job fair. Allow them to choose which options are most acceptable to them. Interview students to identify their preferences for jobs or general education classes.

- Provide job sampling on and off the high school campus. Complete work experience résumés with notes regarding students' preferences for different worksites.

"Give students time for leisure activities in the community so they have opportunities for choices. Observe the choices they make when given freedom to choose during leisure time."

Teacher
Lebanon High School
Lebanon, Tennessee

"To assess students' job preferences, I go on the job with them. I am there with the students all day during a typical day at each of their jobsites. I observe their behavior and talk to those who are in each environment to determine their job preferences."

Teacher
Cleveland High School
Cleveland, Tennessee

Evaluating Outcomes:

Job Sampling

Job sampling is a process that provides students with a variety of employment experiences during their middle and high school years. Job sampling means having the opportunity to work at a variety of worksites over a period of time, either as a trainee or as a paid employee. Each worksite opportunity may last a few months or longer, giving the student the chance to find out what the job is like.

By sampling different jobs that have a variety of task, social, and environmental characteristics, students can begin to identify their preferred employment options. From middle school to the time they leave high school, students may sample as many as 5–10 different job opportunities. Teachers need to keep records of students' job experiences, their performance on the job, and their preferred job types. Three forms help teachers keep records of students' job experiences and preferences. These are the Job Analysis Survey, the Work Performance Evaluation form, and the Student Job History form.

The Job Analysis Survey (Form 4.1 in Conducting Environmental Assessments, 4.1.1) is used to identify important task, social, environmental, and support characteristics at a worksite. A Job Analysis Survey should be completed for every worksite in which a student participates during job sampling. By doing so, you can identify important factors that may relate to a student's success on a particular job and why a student may prefer one job to another. A student's performance on the job is evaluated using the Work Performance Evaluation form (Form 4.2 in Observing Students' Performance, 4.1.2). This form allows you to evaluate the student's performance in relation to relevant factors at the worksite and to evaluate the support that is available to the student or that may be needed.

The final form to complete is a Student Job History. The Student Job History form is based on the information on the Job Analysis Survey and Work Performance Evaluation, which are filled out for each job experience that a student has. Be sure to complete the Student Job History form while a student is working at each new worksite. If you wait until a student leaves, you may forget what his performance was like. By comparing a student's performance on different jobs, you can identify the best "job match"—that job where the characteristics of the job best match the student's skills, interests, and preferences.

One way to identify a student's job preferences is to compare her performance on different jobs. This is because people usually perform better on jobs they like better. After completing a Student Job History form, you should have a pretty good idea of which job a student prefers. Next, you need to discuss your findings with the student and her parents, employers, and important others to determine whether they agree. When a good "job match" is identified, the student's job-training experiences can focus on the identified career area, such as word processing, journalism, forestry, or medical arts. Continue to keep a record of the student's job experiences on the Student Job History form—as it can also be used to develop a résumé for a student to use when applying for new jobs.

Cross-reference: Conducting Site Visits and Observations (4-1)

Student Job History

Student: __Amanda Jocz__

		Dates: 8/99 to 12/99	Dates: 1/00 to 5/00	Dates: 8/00 to 12/00
Basic information	Worksite	Community Blood Bank	Heimer, Lief, & Ali Law Offices	Varner's Family Restaurant
	General job types or positions experienced	receptionist, front desk, courier	janitor, copy person	wait staff, bus staff, cashier
	Job tasks experienced	answering phones, filing, customer service, deliveries	mopping, painting, photocopying, filing	washing dishes, food prep, cashier, customer service
	Location and transportation	1 (2) 3 N/A	1 (2) 3 N/A	(1) 2 3 N/A
Task characteristics	Job task requirements	1 (2) 3 N/A	1 2 (3) N/A	(1) 2 3 N/A
	General mobility	(1) 2 3 N/A	1 (2) 3 N/A	1 (2) 3 N/A
	Gross motor demands	(1) 2 3 N/A	1 (2) 3 N/A	(1) 2 3 N/A
	Fine motor demands	1 (2) 3 N/A	1 2 (3) N/A	(1) 2 3 N/A
	Length of work tasks	1 (2) 3 N/A	1 2 (3) N/A	(1) 2 3 N/A
	Variability of daily job tasks	(1) 2 3 N/A	1 2 (3) N/A	1 (2) 3 N/A
	Problem-solving requirements	(1) 2 3 N/A	1 (2) 3 N/A	1 (2) 3 N/A
	Production rate	(1) 2 3 N/A	1 2 (3) N/A	(1) 2 3 N/A
	Work product quality	1 (2) 3 N/A	1 2 (3) N/A	(1) 2 3 N/A
	Continuous working requirements	(1) 2 3 N/A	1 2 (3) N/A	(1) 2 3 N/A
Task-related characteristics	Co-worker presence	(1) 2 3 N/A	1 2 3 (N/A)	(1) 2 3 N/A
	Nontask social contacts	1 2 (3) N/A	1 2 (3) N/A	(1) 2 3 N/A
	Social atmosphere of worksite	1 (2) 3 N/A	1 2 (3) N/A	(1) 2 3 N/A
	Interaction with customers	1 2 (3) N/A	1 2 (3) N/A	(1) 2 3 N/A
	Supervisory contact	1 2 (3) N/A	1 2 (3) N/A	(1) 2 3 N/A
Environmental characteristics	Distraction level	1 (2) 3 N/A	1 (2) 3 N/A	1 (2) 3 N/A
	Comfort factors	(1) 2 3 N/A	1 (2) 3 N/A	1 (2) 3 N/A
	Equipment/tool use	(1) 2 3 N/A	1 (2) 3 N/A	(1) 2 3 N/A
Natural supports	Environmental support	(1) 2 3 N/A	1 (2) 3 N/A	(1) 2 3 N/A
	Supervisor/co-worker support	1 (2) 3 N/A	1 2 (3) N/A	(1) 2 3 N/A

1 = Excellent job match   2 = Fair job match   3 = Poor job match   N/A = Not applicable

Form 8.2.   Student Job History for Amanda Jocz. (From Renzaglia, A., & Hutchins, M. [1995]. Materials developed for *A model for longitudinal vocational programming for students with moderate and severe disabilities.* Grant funded by the U.S. Department of Education, Office of Special Education and Rehabilitation Services; adapted by permission.) (Key: 1 = excellent job match; 2 = fair job match; 3 = poor job match; N/A = not applicable.)

Case Study 8.3   If Angelo Had Tried Job Sampling

Angelo Rust entered Walt Whitman High School as a freshman at age 15. He had no work experience when he walked into the office of Ms. Gustafson, the high school vocational counselor, early in September. Ms. Gustafson explained to Angelo that besides taking his regular academic courses, he could enroll in Whitman's Job Experience Program if he wanted to. The Job Experience Program would give Angelo the chance during his high school years to try out, or sample, different kinds of jobs. Counselors in the program would help Angelo find jobs, and they would make sure that he had the opportunity to try out a variety of work experiences so that he could begin to figure out which career areas most interested him. By targeting a particular area, Angelo could determine the skills that he needed and whether he could get them through his high school classes or if he needed postsecondary training or education. The counselors would also keep a record of his job experiences to help him identify his career preferences and to begin to develop a résumé for potential employers.

The Job Experience Program sounded like a good idea to Angelo. He could use some part-time work while he went to school, and he really did need some help to find a job. Also, he wasn't sure what kind of jobs were available and what he really wanted to do when he finished school. He did know that he liked being with little kids like his nieces. He didn't know, however, whether there even was a job where he could work with little kids all day. Maybe he could find out in the job program.

During the next few years, Angelo discovered that Ms. Gustafson was right! He did get to try out new jobs when he wasn't in school. Some he liked, such as the child care program, and some he didn't like at all, such as the auto body shop. Each time he sampled a new job, his vocational counselor would complete his Student Job History. By the time he entered his senior year, his job history was getting really long! Besides the child care center and the auto body shop, he already had had jobs in an office, a landscaping business, and an advertising company. When Angelo and his counselor, his parents, and his employers discussed Angelo's job history, they all agreed: The job he liked best and in which he performed best was working as an aide at the child care center. Because of this interest, Angelo enrolled in the child care classes at school. His instructor, Ms. Chickie, was thrilled with his exceptional performance in class and was overjoyed that a male was interested in going into preschool teaching! Male teachers were desperately needed in preschool, but Angelo was the first young man to enroll in her child care classes during the 8 years she had taught at Walt Whitman High School.

Angelo was grateful for the job sampling he had had in Whitman's Job Experience Program. He had learned which career he wanted in life by having the chance to try different jobs. By comparing his jobs and how he performed on them, Angelo learned that child care was the best job match for him. Now he had some real career plans. When he finished high school, Angelo planned to go to college, where he could complete his certification program as a preschool teacher. And wait until those little kids find out what a great teacher he is!

Teacher-Proven Practices:

- The Home Inventory Form (Form 6.5 in Using Informal Assessment Methods, 6.2.1) is a good source of information about a student's preferences, choices, and interests. In completing the form, students, their parents, and important others provide information about the student's likes and dislikes at home and work and in the community. By listing activities in which they frequently engage, such as dancing or playing racquetball, students tell us much about their own preferences.

- Assess students' preferences through role plays. Give them choices in role-play situations that sample a variety of options, such as leisure activities or career options. Compare these findings with preferences they indicate when filling out an interest inventory or questionnaire. Discuss with each student your findings as well as the skills needed in their chosen options.

- It's important to maintain frequent communication with students regarding their choices and preferences. You may not always agree with them, such as their choice of CDs, clothes, or hairstyles, but you need to allow them to express their preferences.

- Pictures are helpful in assessing some students' choices and preferences. After a student has been to several worksites, help him make a connection between each site and a picture. Then use the pictures when asking the student where he would like to work.

- Have students sample a variety of jobs while in high school, such as clerical, industrial, and service jobs. The student's performance on these tasks should speak for itself as far as showing the student's preferences.

- Give students a choice of community-based training sites and options for different job choices at the sites. Allow them to experience each job for at least 2 weeks so that they can begin to learn what their preferences are. Then help them make a choice of their preferred job and arrange for them to work there for at least 12–18 weeks.

"Assess job preferences by providing as many types of job training as possible. Keep records of previous jobs, and take pictures and videos so the student can remember the site. Stay at one site long enough so the student can get to know it. Keep a logbook of students' feelings and comments, and discuss these with the student."

Itinerant Transition Teacher
Metropolitan Nashville Public Schools
Nashville, Tennessee

Evaluating Outcomes:

Assessing Preferences Using Alternative Communication

Some students can simply tell us what their preferences are, provided they have had the opportunity to experience different options. For example, students who have had the chance to participate on different sports teams during high school probably can tell us that they prefer, for example, soccer to basketball or volleyball. Other students, however, may not communicate their preferences and choices in traditional ways. These students may speak in one- to two-word phrases or use manual signs, picture boards, or computer aids. Some may communicate by gesturing, grabbing, or hitting others. Others may communicate by eye gazing, pointing, vocalizing, or moving away. Also, some may not hear or see or may walk or grasp objects only with assistance. How do we identify the preferences of those who do not speak to us in conventional ways? How can they tell us, for example, what they want to eat or wear, what they want to do during leisure time, what kind of job they want, or where they want to live?

Several strategies have been developed to assess the preferences and choices of people who communicate in alternative ways. Look at the following descriptions of these strategies and case study examples and pick which ones would be best suited to your students and the preferences you are assessing.

Activating an Electrical Switch

One way to assess preferences of students who have little or no speech and who cannot pick up or manipulate objects unaided is to teach them to use an electrical switch to indicate a preference. An electrical switch is connected individually to each of two or more objects, such as a radio and a videotape player. By moving, or "activating," one of the switches, the object connected to that switch is turned on for a short period of time (e.g., 15 seconds). For example, if the switch connected to the radio were activated, the radio would play for 15 seconds.

To assess preferences using electrical switches, the student must first be taught how to activate a switch by moving it. Be sure to use recommended instructional methods when you do so, such as prompting, opportunities for practice, and corrective feedback (see Teaching Skills that Need Strengthening, 6-4). For students with limited mobility, there are many different kinds of switches that can be activated in different ways, such as pressing with an elbow or blowing through a straw. (See the Technology and Augmentative Communication section of the Resources in the appendix.) Next, the student is taught that activating one switch, such as the yellow one, will cause the radio to play and that activating the red one will cause the videotape player to turn on.

Now, you're ready to assess the student's preferences. Allow the student to have access to both switches, then observe what happens. Does the student activate the radio or the videotape player? Be sure that you give the student many opportunities to choose switches. Preferences are choices that people continue to make over time, so you must see which switch the student chooses most of the time, such as 80% of opportunities to choose. Choices may change over time, too, so even if you have determined today that the student prefers the radio to the videotape player, this may change after a few weeks or months.

Case Study 8.4   Jared Pushes a Switch

Jared's IEP called for increasing his social interactions with his general education peers. When he was with his peers, however, Jared usually just sat around looking disinterested. Mr. Blount, his teacher, thought that if he could find an activity that

Cross-reference: Teaching Skills that Need Strengthening (6-4)

Jared liked and would engage in with his peers, this might increase their social interactions. Because Jared didn't talk, Mr. Blount decided to use switches to check Jared's preferences for activities. He hooked one switch to a computer game and another to a CD player. Then he taught Jared to use the switches to operate each of the electronic devices for a short, preset amount of time. Over the next few days, Mr. Blount watched which switch Jared pressed when he was given a chance. The computer game was definitely his favorite—he picked it practically every time! Mr. Blount then had Jared's peers join him in playing the game. Mr. Blount smiled as he watched them play. Jared was like a new person—lively, with his head up, laughing and smiling with his peers. Assessing Jared's preferences was certainly worth the effort. It helped meet one of his IEP goals and was a load of fun!

Approaching or Selecting an Object

If students can walk or move about, one way to assess their preferences is to observe which objects they approach consistently. Or, if students can't move easily, you can see which objects they prefer by noting the ones they touch or pick up when the objects are placed nearby. For example, you could assess a student's preferences for clothes by having two items of clothing, such as two shirts, lying on a bed. Then see which shirt the student approaches. Or you could place the shirts on a student's wheelchair tray or a nearby table and see which one he touches or picks up. In either case, you need to give the student the choice of the same two shirts several times until you can clearly see that the student picks one shirt over another. By varying the two choices over time, such as several other choices of shirts, you could identify a group of shirts that a student likes and another group that she dislikes. You can use the "approach" or "selecting" method to assess students' preferences for people, recreational activities, seating arrangements, foods, and vocational and academic tasks. You may want to use pictures or items that represent some choices that are not convenient to show to students, such as community housing, relatives who are out of town, sports events, or career choices.

Case Study 8.5   Ms. Aubrey Keeps Her Shirt Clean

Hannah sometimes was a "bear" in the cafeteria. Ms. Aubrey, her teacher, just couldn't figure it out! When they sat down at the table to eat, sometimes Hannah was "as good as gold," as her peer buddy assisted her with eating with her adapted spoon and cup. Other times, however, you just didn't want to be anywhere around Hannah, especially if you were wearing a white shirt on the days they ate anything with tomato sauce, as Ms. Aubrey had found out! Finally, Ms. Randall, a veteran English teacher who ate near Hannah, suggested that Hannah maybe just didn't like anything with tomato sauce in it. Ms. Aubrey was certain that couldn't be the problem—more likely it was one of her "moods" or the cycle of the moon—but she thought she would try it anyway. Over the next 2 weeks, she set a choice of two entrées in front of Hannah as she approached the lunch table: One always had tomato sauce, such as lasagna or spaghetti, and one did not, such as hamburgers or pasta salad. Hannah *never* picked the entrée with tomato sauce! She had a definite preference, which was for *not* eating anything with tomato sauce in it. Ms. Randall was right, after all. As long as Hannah ate anything else, Ms. Aubrey's shirts stayed "as white as snow!"

Gesturing, Signing, Vocalizing, or Affect

Although some students don't talk in complex sentences, they may make gestures, sounds, or facial expressions that can communicate a choice. For example, a student may point at the horse he wants to ride at a riding stable, or another may say, "Eeeeh!" and smile or laugh to show which channel he wants to watch on television. Or a student may hold up a card or use a communication device to show that he wants to go bowling after dinner. Remember, just as when assessing preferences with any strategy, observe a student's choices many times until you see that he chooses the same thing consistently, which indicates his preference. Otherwise, you may jump to the wrong conclusion, as illustrated next.

Case Study 8.6   Coach Jarvis Jumps Too Fast!

When Coach Jarvis got out the volleyballs in physical education (PE) one day, Ji-won started to shriek. She also played the best volleyball game that day that Coach had seen her play. Naturally, he assumed that volleyball was Ji-won's favorite PE activity. So when Coach Jarvis was going to an in-service session and knew he would have a substitute during third period, he wrote in his lesson plans that Ji-won should be assigned to volleyball that day—just to avoid any possible hassles. When third period rolled around, Mr. Ray, the substitute teacher, announced to the class the options that were available during the period: aerobics, weightlifting, volleyball, and walking around the track. He then handed Ji-won a volleyball and pointed to the volleyball court. Right then and there, Ji-won threw a fit unlike anything Mr. Ray had seen before. After a while, one of Ji-won's friends said, "She wants to do aerobics. See how she's pointing over there?" Mr. Ray had to agree that she definitely was pointing and agreed to let Ji-won accompany her friend to the aerobics room, where she promptly began quietly and enthusiastically to participate in an aerobic routine. Mr. Ray scratched his head and reminded himself to ask Coach why he wanted Ji-won to play volleyball that day.

Observing Students' Performance

Just like most of us, students are likely to perform better or show more enthusiasm when engaged in tasks or activities that they prefer. You may have noticed that you have much more gusto when you are waterskiing, watching a movie, or vacationing in a new city than you are when you are grading papers, cleaning house, or working in the yard. Students are just the same! They often show us by their behavior, if not their words, what they prefer to do. For example, when assigned an academic task that a student finds boring, he may make many careless errors or refuse to complete the assignment. The same student, however, may enthusiastically begin a more challenging assignment and make fewer mistakes simply because he prefers it and finds it more interesting. Observing a student's performance can be used to assess preferences for many types of activities, including vocational, recreational, academic, and social. As always, when assessing preferences, be sure to observe the student enough times to determine which activities are consistently associated with improved performance; these activities are likely to be the ones that are preferred by the student.

Cross-references: Observing Students' Performance (4.1.2 and 6.1.1), Observing Students' Interactions (5.1.2)

Case Study 8.7   Wayne Joins the Band

Although Wayne didn't speak, he seemed to have a yen for music. He was always tapping his toe to the beat of the music, had almost perfect pitch when he hummed, and could even pick out tunes on the piano. His mother, Sandra, thought he might like to play a musical instrument in the school band. For one thing, it might be a fun free-time activity he could do at home. For another, he might make some new friends in band class. However, which instrument would he like to play? Sandra didn't want to purchase one that Wayne might later quit playing—they were too expensive! She approached Mr. Cotton, the band teacher, who had some "loaner" instruments that Wayne could try. Over the next few weeks, Mr. Cotton showed Wayne how to play a few simple notes on each instrument, such as the trumpet and French horn. Then he let Sandra borrow each one for a few days. Sandra gave Wayne a chance to try each of the instruments several times. Soon it was obvious to the whole family which instrument Wayne preferred: the alto saxophone. Every time he picked it up, his eyes glowed! He had already taught himself to play a scale, whereas he hardly was interested in touching the flute. Maybe it was all those John Coltrane CDs his father listened to. At any rate, you could tell that Wayne was going to shine on the saxophone!

8-2   COLLABORATING TO INCREASE STUDENTS' CHOICE AND DECISION MAKING

Increasing students' choice- and decision-making skills and opportunities requires the efforts of many people. Choice does not exist in a vacuum. The opportunity to choose has value only when a student's choices can be acted on and supported by others, whether in school, at home, at work, or around the community.

8.2.1 Communicating with Parents, Teachers, and Others

Students' choices must be communicated to important others in their environments who can work together to enable students to act on their choices and decisions. Employers and other community leaders, in turn, can communicate to students the variety of choices they do have—for careers, community living arrangements, recreational options, clubs, and social opportunities.

"Have various speakers from the community come to class or take the students to them. Have them speak about their jobs, the education and training they had to have, and the chances for advancement on their jobs."
Teacher
McEwen High School
McEwen, Tennessee

"I set up situations for students to practice choice making in school. Then I interview parents about students' opportunities for choice at home, and I interview the student. I also expand students' areas of choice through field trips and through guest speakers who discuss different careers in class."

Teacher
Central High School
Ashland City, Tennessee

How to Do It:

- Work with a student's parents to provide a schedule of leisure and recreational activities in which the student can choose to participate at school and in the community, such as at the YMCA, Boys' and Girls' Club, or a community center. If parents are more involved in their children's recreational activities, the chances that a student can act on her leisure-time choices are increased.

- Brainstorm with guidance counselors and general education teachers about possible choices of classes for each student. Have the counselor and teachers describe the content and range of courses available, such as theater arts, journalism, or horticulture, so that the student is knowledgeable about choices.

- Have students visit different worksites and "shadow" employees to find out what their jobs are like. Invite guest speakers into the classroom to explain different jobs and the skills required. Have open discussions with students, parents, and representatives of community businesses about realistic expectations and requirements of potential careers, such as landscaping, carpentry, or radio announcing.

Cross-references: Communicating Environmental Support Needs (4-2), Communicating Social Support Needs (5-2), and Communicating Students' Strengths and Needs (6-3)

"It's difficult to observe a student's opportunities for choice throughout the day. I can do this only if I talk to all the student's teachers, parents, and employers."

Teacher
Jefferson County High School
White Pine, Tennessee

 # Starting Up:

- Communicate to students and their parents that students can try out for different school sports teams of their choice, such as the track team. Remind them, however, that they must accept the responsibilities that accompany their choices. For example, members of the track team must provide their own transportation to practice and meets.

- Have speakers from the community, including staff from a mental health center and drug and alcohol program, speak in class to discuss choices that students have in their lives. Have them discuss with students that they have options—to control their anger, not to use drugs or alcohol, and other healthy choices.

- Use the Home Interview form (see Form 6.5 in Using Informal Assessment Methods, 6.2.1) to survey parents' as well as students' choices. How do parents' goals for their children compare with the students'? Discuss areas of disagreement with them, and help them negotiate a compromise. Also, help employers provide students with options that are consistent with their choices and goals for advancement so that students don't feel they are "stuck in a rut."

"Expose students to career opportunities that would stimulate their interests and are within their skill levels. For example, we take trips to area vocational schools to see the programs offered, skills needed for different careers, financial obligations, salary possibilities, and job placement success in different fields."

Teacher
Whitehaven High School
Memphis, Tennessee

8.2.2 Involving Students in the Individualized Education Program Process

The IDEA Amendments of 1997 state explicitly that educational personnel should ensure that students develop the "skills and knowledge necessary to enable them to meet…challenging expectations…and to be prepared to lead productive, independent, adult lives, to the maximum extent possible" (Section 601). Students' educational programs, which are designed to develop their skills and knowledge, must be based on the students' needs, preferences, and interests. The amendments also state that students, whenever appropriate, should be members of their IEP teams. The IEP team is responsible for developing students' educational programs, which are designed to achieve the outcomes stated in the amendments. Teachers, therefore, need to know how to help students become actively involved in the IEP process.

"Involving students in their IEP teams and meetings is critical. They have the right to have input into their programs. The total outcome of their education will be improved because they will have made their own choices—with help from their family and teachers."

Teacher
Volunteer High School
Jonesborough, Tennessee

"All students should be responsible for striving to do the best they can no matter what their abilities or disabilities are. This is a philosophy that should be included in an educational curriculum. Student input and student self-evaluation should be incorporated into each student's high school program."

Teacher
Treadwell High School
Memphis, Tennessee

"Any worker will be more productive if given the opportunity to be a part of the decision-making process. I realize that for many of my students this would require more support than for others. This is an area where a good working knowledge of the individual is needed."

Teacher
Cleveland High School
Cleveland, Tennessee

Evaluating Outcomes:

The Student-Directed Individualized Education Program

How do you support students so that they may become more involved in the IEP process? There are already several programs that have been developed for teaching students the skills they need to become active participants in developing and implementing their IEPs. Some of these include *ChoiceMaker, Whose Future Is it Anyway?, Next S.T.E.P., TAKE CHARGE,* and *Making Actions Plans* (MAPs; originally *McGill Action Planning System*). (See Self-Determination in the Resources section of the appendix for complete references and additional programs.)

The *ChoiceMaker* program (Martin & Marshall, 1995) includes a curriculum, the *Self-Directed IEP* (Martin, Huber Marshall, Maxson, & Jerman, 1996), for teaching students to develop their own educational goals and lead their IEP meetings. Through role playing, modeling, and corrective feedback, students learn the skills needed to take an active leadership role in their IEP process. The curriculum contains videotapes, a teacher's manual, student workbooks, and a curriculum-based assessment. The *Self-Directed IEP* lessons can be adapted as a checklist for students to assess the extent of their involvement in their IEP process, using the Self-Directed IEP Self-Assessment form (Form 8.3). (A blank, reproducible form is included in the appendix.)

Teacher-Proven Practices:

- Include students in IEP meetings and decision making about their educational programs. Provide any assistance needed to support students in selecting their courses and setting their own transition goals, including vocational and social aspirations.

- Help students incorporate their plans for personal development into their IEPs. Discuss their personal goals with them, such as learning to control their anger, being more assertive, or becoming a better tennis player. Help them list their goals on a self-survey to use to monitor their progress toward their goals.

- If students are going to be involved in developing their own IEPs, they must be aware of what their interests, preferences, and options are. One way to do this is by having a variety of job and community experiences. This helps students develop their preferences and learn more about their own skills in relation to a job or community activity. (See Job Sampling in Assessing Students' Choices and Preferences, 8.1.3.)

"Assist students in planning and choosing appropriate courses to enroll in in high school according to their interests. If job sampling has been done, students should have a good idea where their interests and abilities lie. Enlist help from the school guidance counselor and the vocational rehabilitation counselor. Give students options and allow them to make their own choices."
Teacher
Whites Creek High School
Nashville, Tennessee

The Self-Directed IEP
Self-Assessment

Name: _Lori Dunlop_   **Date:** _February 14_

	Step	How did I do?			Did I have the chance?		
1	Begin the meeting by stating its purpose.	1	2	③	1	2	③
2	Introduce everyone I invited.	1	2	③	1	2	③
3	Review my past goals and performance.	1	②	3	1	②	3
4	Ask for others' feedback.	①	2	3	1	2	③
5	State my school and transitional goals.	1	②	3	1	②	3
6	Ask questions if I did not understand.	①	2	3	①	2	3
7	Address differences in opinion.	1	②	3	1	2	③
8	State what supports I'll need.	1	2	③	1	2	③
9	Summarize my goals.	1	②	3	1	2	③
10	Close the meeting by thanking everyone.	1	2	③	1	2	③
11	Work on my IEP goals all year.	1	2	③	1	2	③
		1 Didn't do it **2** So-so **3** Great!!!			**1** Not at all **2** So-so **3** Yes!!!		

Form 8.3.   The Self-Directed IEP for Lori Dunlop. (From Martin, J.E., Huber Marshall, L., Maxson, L.L., & Jerman, P.A. [1996]. *Self-directed IEP*. Longmont, CO: Sopris West; adapted by permission.)

How to Do It:

- Help students choose their schedules for the school year, and allow them to make changes at the semester if they are dissatisfied or if a change is needed. It may be that the class was not a "good fit." For example, a young man may decide that he prefers computer applications to keyboarding. Be sure to continue to consult with students throughout the year to find out their level of satisfaction with their educational programs. Are they happy? Did they make the best decision in choosing a class, an extracurricular activity, or a job placement? Should they make a change?

- Sometimes setting their own goals and making their own academic choices means that students will have to act against their parents' expectations. For example, a student may decide to enroll in a general math class instead of pre-algebra even though her parents want her to go on to take algebra. The student may realize, however, that her career choice does not require algebra.

- Teachers can provide guidance in course selection, and parents can provide advice. Ultimately, however, the choice must be the student's.

- Talking with students is the first step toward finding out their plans and hopes for the future. Use an alternative mode of communication, such as pictures or communication devices, for students who don't talk. Choose whatever method of communication is necessary for students to give input into their IEPs and transition plans.

Cross-references: Promoting Students' Self-Determination (7-1) and Incorporating Self-Determination into Daily Living (7-3)

"I try to help students have realistic career and personal goals. For example, it may be difficult for some students with physical limitations to play football. I try to let them know that they have other options, such as being manager of the football team or participating in other ways. By getting out and trying different options, students learn more about what they can do."

Teacher
Henry County High School
Paris, Tennessee

8-3 TEACHING AND INCREASING STUDENTS' CHOICE AND DECISION MAKING

"I think student independence is very important. Students are not always going to have the close supervision of a teacher or job coach. It is important for students to be able to make their own decisions and to know how to go about making appropriate choices."

Teacher
Pearl-Cohn High School
Nashville, Tennessee

8.3.1 Teaching Choice and Decision Making

The IDEA Amendments of 1997 state that more than 20 years of research and experience have demonstrated that the education of students with diverse abilities can be more effective when we have high expectations for them that lead to successful adult outcomes, such as independent living and economic self-sufficiency. We can achieve these outcomes by applying proven methods of teaching and learning so that students can acquire the skills needed for independence and full participation in adult life. Teaching students to make good choices and wise decisions about their lives is essential to achieving the outcomes addressed in the amendments.

"We teach decision making by providing options for assignments (with equal content and on the same level). We use computer software that provides a variety of experiences all with the same educational objective. We incorporate decision making, goal setting, logical consequences, time management, and esteem-building skills into the academic curriculum."

Teacher
Treadwell High School
Memphis, Tennessee

Case Study 8.8   Winnie Makes a Choice

As far as Winnie was concerned, her life was a mess! She was so far behind in her classes, she didn't think she could ever get caught up. She had a D in French already for the semester because she'd failed the last two exams, she hadn't even started the semester biology project that was due on Friday, and her last two book reports in English had been handed back to her because they were incomplete. In algebra, she had gotten a mid-semester deficiency because she was in danger of failing the course. She knew she was completely lost in that class and didn't know what was going on, but she was afraid to ask Ms. Hersey anything because she would look too stupid. Instead, she simply started cutting class.

Winnie really did want to get good grades; after all, it was just her freshman year at the new magnet school in town. In middle school, her grades were always Bs or better. Back then, she never did let anything slide—her assignments were always in on time. What happened this year, she just didn't know. But the worst thing was that her guidance counselor, Mr. Perry, had asked for a meeting during second period tomorrow. She just knew what he was going to say to her!

Evaluating Outcomes:

Teaching Choice and Decision Making
Using the Adaptability Model

Some students have limited experience with making choices, or the choices or decisions they make may be unwise. Learning to make healthy choices and decisions requires several steps. These steps are having the opportunity to choose, practicing making choices, acting on these choices, evaluating the consequences of these choices, and making adjustments, if needed, if the outcome of a choice is not acceptable. Making good choices is a skill; even adults need practice at it!

One program for teaching students to improve their choice- and decision-making skills is the Adaptability Model (Mithaug, Martin, & Agran, 1987). The Adaptability Model has four components made up of nine steps. The four components are decision making, independent performance, self-evaluation, and adjustment. Decision making requires students first to identify a personal goal, such as learning a new job skill. Next, students list different options for attaining their goal, such as attending the area vocational school or learning while on the job. Then, they list possible consequences of each option, such as the cost of school or difficulty of getting a job without training. Finally, they choose one of the options, weighing the consequences of each.

During *independent performance*, students act on the option they chose during decision making; for example, a student might enroll in school to learn secretarial skills.

The goal is for students to act as independently as possible. For many students, however, this will require support, at least initially. Self-management strategies can also be helpful in increasing students' independence. (See Teaching Self-Management and Self-Determination Skills, 7-2.) Next, students evaluate their own performance during *self-evaluation*. They compare their performance with the goal they set and decide whether their goal was met. For example, did the student learn the job skills identified as a goal?

The last step of the model is *adjustment*. Here students choose one of two actions. If their goal was not met, they go back to the decision-making steps of the model. It may be that their initial goal should be adjusted or a different option should be chosen to meet their goal. For example, maybe learning a new job skill was not a realistic goal because a student was just recovering from a serious illness. Or perhaps a student planned to learn the job skill on the job but the opportunity never happened. Rather than simply concluding that, "Nothing ever works!" the student just starts the process again, revising the goal or the option chosen. If students met their goal the first time going through the steps, however, they should remember to reward themselves for a job well done! (See Teaching Students to Use Self-Monitoring and Self-Reinforcement, 7.2.4.)

The Adaptability Model can be adapted as a checklist for students to use to monitor themselves as they complete each step of the model. Two variations of the Choice-Making Self-Check form are shown (Figure 8.4 and 8.5). (Modify the forms as needed on the basis of students' skills and preferences.) Using the forms, students fill in or check off each step when completed, as shown in Case Study 8.8. (Blank, reproducible forms are included in the appendix.) The following case study shows how students may use this form.

Cross-reference: Teaching Self-Management and Self-Determination Skills (7-2)

What was surprising was that, when Winnie walked into Mr. Perry's office the next day, he didn't look angry at all. Winnie was expecting him to start yelling the moment he saw her. Instead, he asked her to sit down and tell him how her classes were going. Of course, he already knew because of her deficiency slip, but she told him anyway. Somehow, it seemed to help just saying what the problem was. Then, Mr. Perry surprised her for the second time. Instead of just asking why she was so behind in her classes, he simply said, "Winnie, you have some important decisions to make, and I'm going to help you do it." Mr. Perry then explained that getting good grades was really Winnie's choice. She had the skills she needed—she just had to start using those skills in class.

Next, Mr. Perry pulled a piece of paper out of his drawer and handed it to Winnie. He told her that it was a "Choice-Making Self-Check" and that she could use it to get caught up in her classes. He suggested they start with algebra first because that was the class in which she had received the deficiency notice. Mr. Perry said he would go through the checklist on the form with her, step by step. Then she could use the form herself for her other classes. Winnie sighed. It looked hard, but, because nothing else was working, she agreed to give it a try.

First, they looked at Step 1: Identify my goal. Winnie wrote down quickly that her goal was to get a B in algebra class and checked off Step 1 on the form. Then, Mr. Perry asked her to list her options and their consequences. That was a little harder. If she talked to Ms. Hersey, Winnie might be able to find out which assignments she was missing and what she could do to get caught up. However, that would mean having to risk feeling stupid. Another option could be just to start going to class again, hoping that she could figure out what she had missed. But, there was the chance that she never could get caught up without help. She could always drop the class, but it would show up on her record as her current class average, which was an F. Even though Winnie knew it would be hard, she decided that talking to Ms. Hersey would be the best idea. She decided to do that during fourth period, which was Ms. Hersey's free period.

Mr. Perry then asked Winnie to begin Step 5, to act on the option she chose, immediately. Next, she should complete Steps 6–9, making adjustments in her goals or the options chosen, if necessary, and remembering to reward herself when she met her goal. She could complete a Choice-Making Self-Check for each of her other classes when she felt ready. Mr. Perry didn't want to overwhelm her, so he said it was better to start with one class first. Winnie felt a sense of relief just knowing she had a plan. She thanked Mr. Perry and left his office after making an appointment with him to check back in a week.

Talking with Ms. Hersey was hard, but, when it was over, Winnie was glad she had done it. Ms. Hersey thanked Winnie for talking with her, and together they came up with a plan. Ms. Hersey gave Winnie a list of her missing assignments to complete. Of course, they would be late, so her grade would be marked down. However, she would have the option of doing some extra-credit assignments. She also would have the help of one of the peer tutors—students in class who received extra credit by helping classmates. Because she had missed so much work, Winnie's grade for the semester would never exceed a C−. Winnie winced because her goal was a B, but a C− was better than an F, so she decided to adjust her goal.

Choice-Making Self-Check

1. Identify my goal . . .

Get a "B" in algebra
_____
_____

2. What are my options?

1. Find out missing work from Ms. Hersey
_____

2. Go to class—hope to catch up!
_____

3. Just drop the class
_____

3. What might happen?

1. Might feel stupid or embarrassed
_____

2. Won't get caught up without help
_____

3. I'll get an F on my class record
_____

4. The Best Choice

Talk to Ms. Hersey
_____

5. TAKE ACTION!!!

6. How did I do?

Ms. Hersey helped me develop a plan; I completed
_____
finished assignments; highest grade possible is C-
_____

7. Did I meet my goal?

Yes!

No!

8. My NEW goal is . . .

Pass Algebra with at least a C-
_____

9. Reward Yourself!

When I meet my goal, I'M GOING ON THE
_____
CLASS SKI TRIP!
_____

Form 8.4.   Choice-Making Self-Check for Winnie Reynolds. (From Adaptability instruction: The goal of transitional programming, by Mithaug, D.E., Martin, J.E., & Agran, M., *Exceptional Children, 53,* 500–505. Copyright 1987 by The Council for Exceptional Children. Adapted with permission.)

Choice-Making Self-Check

Student: Winnie Reynolds   **Date:** October 17

	Steps	Did I do it?
Decision making	1. **Identify my goal:** *My goal is:* Get a B in algebra	(Yes) No
	2. **List my options:** a. Find out missing work from Ms. Hersey b. Go to class—hope to catch up! c. Just drop the class	(Yes) No
	3. **List possible consequences of the options:** a. Might feel stupid or embarrassed b. Won't get caught up without help c. I'll get an F on my class record	(Yes) No
	4. **The best choice:** Talk to Ms. Hershey	(Yes) No
Independent performance	5. **Act on the option I chose.**	(Yes) No
Self-evaluation	6. **Evaluate my performance:** *How did I do?* Ms. Hersey helped with a plan: I finished my work	(Yes) No
	7. **Decide if I met my goal:** *Was goal met?* Highest grade I can get is a C-; goal not met	(Yes) No
Adjustment	8. **If I didn't meet my goal, go back to Step 1 and try again!**	(Yes) No
	9. **If I did meet my goal, remember to reward myself.**	Yes No

Form 8.5.   Another Choice-Making Self-Check for Winnie Reynolds. (From Adaptability instruction: The goal of transitional programming, by Mithaug, D.E., Martin, J.E., & Agran, M., *Exceptional Children, 53,* 500–505. Copyright 1987 by The Council for Exceptional Children. Adapted with permission.)

By the end of the semester, Winnie was pleased with her performance. She had completed all of her assignments and even some for extra credit. The peer tutor was really good at explaining the assignments, and by going to class, Winnie was beginning to feel like she knew what was going on. It was great not to feel stupid in there anymore. When she got her report card and saw that she had gotten a C–, she was as happy as if it were an A! And her other grades had improved, too.

Winnie couldn't wait to do Step 9 of the Self-Check, which was to reward herself if she met her goals. She had promised herself to go on the school ski trip if she had met her goals, and she knew this was a reward she deserved after all of her hard work. But the greatest reward, she realized, was just what Mr. Perry had said—she had learned to make the right choices all by herself!

"Help students realize the consequences of their choice. For example, given the choice to continue work or stop due to work slowing down, the student says, 'If I stop now, that means my paycheck will be less. So I guess I'll stay the other 30 minutes.'"

Teacher
Central High School
Culleoka, Tennessee

"Observe a student who is going to work and how she is dressed. Help her decide whether her choice of dress is suitable for her particular job position."
Teacher
Beech High School
Hendersonville, Tennessee

Starting Up:

- Teach students to use a self-monitoring system to evaluate their choices and decisions. On a regular basis, discuss with students the choices they have made and whether the choices were good ones. Discuss their plans for the future, such as living independently or participating in college athletics, and help them prioritize their goals.

- First, provide students with opportunities for choice, and then encourage students to exercise their right to choose. Question students about how they made a choice, such as getting angry with a friend or changing jobs, and whether they think they made a good decision.

- Students can learn much about making good choices through community and job-training experiences. They can learn to compare their expectations about a career area with their actual experiences at the worksite. For example, they may think they are interested in child care as a career; however, after some time on the job, they realize this is not a good choice for them because they cannot tolerate noise.

- Keep an ongoing log of activities in which students are involved. If you see that they are not choosing to participate in many activities, provide suggestions for making choices and interacting with others. Give them positive feedback when they do make choices and increase their active participation. (See Observing Students' Social Participation in At Work and in the Community, 3.4.2.)

Teacher-Proven Practices:

- Teach choice making to students who have had little opportunity to make choices by starting with everyday decisions. For example, give them the lunch menu ahead of time so that they can choose their entrée before going to the cafeteria. Then, work up to having them plan a weekly menu with the school cafeteria manager.

- Discuss choice making by using daily living examples and their consequences. For example, what are the consequences of getting angry or not bringing the necessary materials to class? Using this strategy, students can learn to avoid situations that have undesirable consequences. For example, a young man may learn to avoid situations in the cafeteria that have caused problems for him in the past.

"Be aware of naturally occurring opportunities to make choices, such as whether to save money for new clothes or a trip, and help students to recognize and take advantage of those opportunities. Throughout the day, we encourage choice making in every area as a way of developing independence and maturity."
Teacher
Rutledge High School
Rutledge, Tennessee

- Students learn to make good choices by having frequent opportunities to choose and to experience the consequences of their choices. Assess school, work, and home environments to identify specific areas in which students might have choices. Then, support students in making choices within those areas, such as leisure-time activities.

- Role-play choice-making scenarios in class. Present a choice-making situation, and see how students would respond. For example, have students role-play stating their job preferences and goals to employers and agency representatives at a transition fair.

"Whenever reasonable, I'll give students an alternative choice. This has helped a student with autism in communication. I started with soft drinks—having him circle a desired choice, then have him write a choice, then progressed from there."

Teacher
Henry County High School
Paris, Tennessee

8.3.2 Increasing Students' Choice and Decision Making

We all have the right to choose. There are many ways to increase students' choices and the opportunity to practice choice-making skills. At school, let students fill up their own plates so that they can choose their own food. Also, let them choose their classes each year. During community-based training, let students choose their worksite. At the community center, let students pick whether they want to walk laps, play basketball, or use the weight room.

"Making career choices takes time! If you start at age 14, your vocational training will allow your students enough time to sample a variety of jobs, including summer jobs. This is important to helping them choose a career area."

Teacher
Halls High School
Halls, Tennessee

We always allow choice of food in the school cafeteria and when students eat in the community. During their IEP meetings, all students choose at least one general education class to enroll in. We allow students to choose the order of activities they do in their classrooms. We try to encourage them to choose friends. We observe a student's day and brainstorm ways and times to increase opportunities for choices."
Teacher
Rutledge High School
Rutledge, Tennessee

How to Do It:

- Remember that most activities in the community require choices, such as which movie to see, where to eat, or what to wear. Provide opportunities for students to make choices with regard to recreation and leisure activities, community or adult education classes, places to shop, and friends to interact with.

- The use of augmentative communication can give the opportunity to make choices to some students who have never had it before. All students can make choices, even if they seem simple to someone else! For example, picture schedules can give students choices throughout the day regarding their activities and the order in which they do them (see Assessing Preferences Using Augmentative Communication in Observing Students' Choices, 8.1.3).

- Let students visit different classrooms and meet the teachers and students to decide in which classes they would like to enroll. Provide them with a choice of electives that are associated with various careers. For example, a sophomore may choose to take a health occupation class because he wants to be an emergency medical technician, or a senior who wants to own her own child care center may take courses at the vocational center.

- Provide opportunities for students to "job shadow" by accompanying employees to work to see what their jobs are really like. Have students review catalogs of vocational-training programs to see what they offer. For example, a young man may choose to go to a vocational school to get training as an electrician before trying to look for a job and live on his own.

- Allow students to choose their own rewards for a job well done. What we may think is a reward to a student, for example, a pat on the back, may not be. Remember, different strokes for different folks!

"Students choose courses they are interested in. Even if they cannot do all that is required in that class, partial participation with assistance is always an option."

Teacher
Maryville High School
Maryville, Tennessee

Cross-references: "Strategies for Increasing Environmental Support" (Chapter 4) and "Strategies for Increasing Social Support" (Chapter 5)

REFERENCES

Hutchins, M., & Renzaglia, A. (1993). *Model for longitudinal vocal programming.* Unpublished manuscript.

Individuals with Disabilities Education Act Amendments of 1997, PL 105-17, 20 U.S.C. § 1400 *et seq.*

Martin, J.E., Huber Marshall, L., Maxson, L.L., & Jerman, P.A. (1996). *Self-directed IEP.* Longmont, CO: Sopris West.

Martin, J.E., & Marshall, L.H. (1995). ChoiceMaker: A comprehensive self-determination transition program. *Intervention in School and Clinic, 30,* 147–156.

Mithaug, D.E., Martin, J.E., & Agran, M. (1987). Adaptability instruction: The goal of transitional programming. *Exceptional Children, 53,* 500–505.

C h a p t e r   9

Strategies that Promote
Social Interaction

OVERVIEW

Let's face it: We live in a social world! There are very few activities that don't involve other people. When we shop at the store, stand in line for a movie, or deposit money at the bank, we deal with clerks, tellers, or other customers. Applying for a job, working out at the gym, dining out, and ordering with a credit card over the telephone involve interacting with others. At work, there's our boss, our co-workers, the secretary down the hall, or the guy at the other end of the assembly line. And, of course, there are our families, friends, and loved ones—those "special" people we usually interact with often. When our social interactions with others are going well, it seems that we usually feel great. When they're not, we often feel pretty lousy.

Part of having satisfying social interactions with others is the social skills we bring into a situation. If students are perceived as lacking social skills, they may be less accepted by their peers at school or in the community. They also may find it harder to get and keep a job, become involved in clubs or organizations, make friends with their neighbors, or experience the other benefits of youth and adulthood. Because so much importance is placed on social skills, not meeting social expectations within an environment may lead to isolation and feelings of loneliness for a person. For example, if a clerk in a hardware store continually talks about her personal problems at break, her co-workers may try to avoid sitting near her. When students perform expected social skills, however, such as greeting others or starting a conversation about a topic of common interest, they are more likely to be accepted by their peers and others in an environment.

Sometimes, students with diverse abilities have had little opportunity to interact with their peers either in or out of school. Teachers can collaborate with fellow teachers, worksite supervisors, and others to increase opportunities for social interaction, such as suggesting that a student ride home with a co-worker. Or, teachers may modify an environment or curriculum to promote social interactions, such as having students work in small cooperative learning groups. As students begin to increase their involvement with their peers, they may need support to fit in socially, such as when they participate in general education classes and activities or are on the job or in the community. "Peer buddies" or co-workers can be a great source of support in helping students know what behavior is "cool," such as sharing a snack at break, and what is not, such as criticizing a peer's choice of clothes in front of others. Teachers can also teach social interaction skills directly through activities such as role playing, problem solving, and peer involvement.

This chapter contains four main groups and ten subgroups of strategies that teachers may use for promoting social interaction among students. It includes such strategies as increasing students' social interactions, promoting peer involvement, increasing opportunities for social interaction, and teaching social interaction skills.

Case Study 9.1   The Student Nobody Knows

Olmos High School is like many schools: full of activity and life. On any given school day, visitors will notice students eating lunch together in the courtyard,

"I provide as many social interaction opportunities as possible in daily activities. I achieve this through inclusion in general education classes, mingling in the hallways, learning to walk appropriately in the hall with other students, and by including general education students into the classroom. I also encourage families to provide opportunities for interaction as well."
Teacher
Pearl-Cohn High School
Nashville, Tennessee

congregating in the parking lot, and lining up around the snack machines. On the practice fields, football players talk on the sidelines, band members take breaks from the heat together, and JROTC officers talk about their plans after graduation. Inside the building, students are gathered in groups around lockers, laughing together and hoping the late bell will never ring. The students at Olmos are friends and enjoy the time they spend together—if only there weren't classes, homework, and tests to get in the way!

Hank had been a student at Olmos for almost 2 years. Still, most of the other members of his sophomore class had never met him. Of the few students who did know Hank, most agreed that he could be a pretty uncomfortable person to hang around. Maybe it was because Hank hardly ever started conversations with anyone. When he did, it was usually about the same thing or something embarrassing or really weird. Or, maybe it was Hank's habit of walking up and hugging you, smelling your hair, and saying something such as, "Tomorrow's a half-day," over and over. Hanging out with Hank was just not that much fun.

Except for physical education (PE) and lunch, Hank spent his school day in his self-contained classroom. Although he had some friends in his class, he never saw his classmates outside of school. Because Hank always took the special education bus home with classmates, he never had the chance to join any extracurricular activities after school. That was too bad because as the bus left the school grounds, Hank always looked longingly at the other students out on the field doing warmups, running track, or playing baseball. He would have loved to be out there too—hanging out with "the guys" and making friends. But, the truth was, he really didn't know *how* to hang out with the guys—he never had had the chance!

Hank's family was getting concerned that unless Hank had a chance to interact with some of his peers and join in their activities, he probably never would learn how to socialize with others and make friends. They believed that if Hank could just spend more time with general education students in classes and extracurricular activities, he could learn from them what was appropriate and not appropriate when he was interacting with others. But how could they make this happen? Hank didn't even know a single general education student's name!

9-1   INCREASING STUDENTS' SOCIAL INTERACTIONS

"Involve students in social situations as often as
possible to allow them to interact with many
students and practice their social skills."
Teacher
Northside High School
Memphis, Tennessee

9.1.1   In General Education Classes

Many benefits result from including all students in general education
courses. Students receiving special education services benefit from participating in an academic or career preparation environment as well as from
having peers with whom they can learn and practice social skills. General
education students benefit by having the opportunity to interact with students with diverse abilities. Research shows that general education students often report feeling better about themselves and having more understanding of others when they have the chance to interact often with
their peers in special education.

Starting Up:

- Curriculum content is just one aspect of what is taught in
  general education classrooms. Students are also expected
  to learn to interact cooperatively with their peers. Even in
  academic classes such as history, there are opportunities
  for social interaction through cooperative learning groups,
  class debates, and group projects.

- In any school, you can see students walking to class together, helping each other with homework, and working
  on class projects together. Social relationships and social
  interactions are what high school is all about. Make use of
  the natural support of peers when involving students in
  classes. Assign general education "buddies" to assist stu-

"Inclusion in general education classes such as PE, health, home economics, or academics provides opportunities for social interaction skills and friendships to develop. We have many general education students who have become good friends of our students through inclusive programs."
Teacher
Maryville High School
Maryville, Tennessee

dents whenever possible in completing assignments or participating in class discussions. Let students have free time to interact with each other at the end of class when their work is done or before the bell rings at the beginning of class.

- Going to a class for the first time can be frightening for anyone. Pair students with peers in their classes to ease the transition. Having a buddy can go a long way toward making a student feel welcome in a classroom of strangers.

- Career preparation courses, such as commercial art, automotive technology, culinary arts, and child care, often provide frequent opportunities for social interaction, such as when students work together on a car in the auto body shop or when they're preparing a meal for a group of visiting principals. Find peers within these classes to encourage interactions among classmates and help new students become full members of the class.

"My students interact daily during PE, lunch, and classes with their general education peers. We work on socialization skills continuously during the school day. This area generally is a problem with my students, so we constantly work on it."

Teacher
Hillsboro High School
Nashville, Tennessee

Inclusion in general education curricula and activities is a major thrust of the Individuals with Disabilities Education Act (IDEA) Amendments of 1997 (PL 105-17). The amendments state that "over 20 years of research and experience has demonstrated that the education of children with disabilities can be made more effective by having high expectations for such children and ensuring their access in the general curriculum to the maximum extent possible" (Section 601).

Cross-references: Developing Social Support Plans (5-3) and Gaining Access to Existing Social Supports (5-4)

"Within the school environment, provide as many social opportunities as possible. Do 'PR' work with general education teachers and principals on behalf of your students. Get students involved in regular activities. Don't isolate them from the rest of the student body. Make your students visible—acceptance will eventually follow."

Teacher
Whites Creek High School
Whites Creek, Tennessee

9.1.2 In Extracurricular Activities

Being a true member of a school community involves more than simply attending classes each day. It means playing on an athletic team, joining a club, attending a school play or concert, voting in school elections, or decorating for a homecoming dance. It also means greeting friends in the hall, sitting together at lunch, or hanging out together by the lockers before the first bell rings. By participating in extracurricular and nonacademic activities, not only do students find increased opportunities for interacting with their peers, but they also experience the benefits of being part of a community.

"A student who is nonverbal spends a lot of time with a peer helper. For example, they eat lunch together, attend school club meetings together, and interact over the weekend, like going to ball games or movies."

Teacher
LaVergne High School
Shelbyville, Tennessee

How to Do It:

- Lunchrooms are often the social center of a high school. Encourage students to eat lunch with their general education peers. Establish a Lunch Bunch program in which students from different classes eat lunch together and get to know each other's friends.

• Between classes, students congregate in hallways, around lockers, and in courtyards to greet friends, share a quick conversation, or discuss weekend plans. Encourage your students to be outside the classroom before school and between classes to join and interact with their peers.

• Some students may not have transportation to or from after-school events, such as a tennis tournament, or may need help finding a Future Teachers of America meeting room. Recruit peers who are already participating in an event to help students get to and from the activity.

• Going to the school library or attending a basketball game for the first time can be confusing for any student. Have a general education peer help a student check out a book, pay for a ticket to a game, or read the scoreboard in the gym. It will make these activities more fun for both partners.

"Help students start clubs and volunteer organizations that encourage the involvement of *all* students, such as Unified Sports or a Red Cross volunteer club. Have PE class members help students participate in team sports or small group activities, such as leading a warm-up session."
Teacher
Southside High School
Memphis, Tennessee

Teacher-Proven Practices:

• Invite general education students to a meeting of the school's chapter of People First. They can become involved as volunteers, interact with People First members, and learn about the self-advocacy process.

- Have a general education peer meet a student in her homeroom and go together to a pep rally, school assembly, school club, or the lunchroom. It's always more fun when you go with someone else!

- Brainstorm the variety of ways students can participate in extracurricular activities. Students can sort through photos as a school yearbook staff person, be in charge of equipment as a soccer team member, signal the crowd to start a cheer as a cheerleader, or help choose songs to sing as a choir member.

- Provide opportunities for different groups to interact socially. Have a picnic, dance, or party during which different school clubs, such as photography or fencing, can get together and meet each other's members.

Cross-references: Increasing Students' Social Participation (3-4) and In the Community and at School (5.4.1)

"One of my students has difficulty remembering things. He was given one position to play on the football team, so the number of plays he has to learn is shortened. He was able to learn these plays and has become a key player on the team. At school, he receives many compliments on his performance in the games."

Teacher
McEwen High School
McEwen, Tennessee

9.1.3   At Work and in the Community

Although it may not always seem like it, students do spend the majority of their day outside their school classrooms—working or playing in their communities with friends or at home with their families. It makes sense, then, that students need opportunities to develop their social interaction skills across *all* of these environments. When students practice their skills outside the school environment, they increase the likelihood that they will maintain these skills and that they will develop satisfying and supportive relationships.

"I arrange for each student to view a movie with a general education peer. This gives them a chance to purchase concession items, interact with a friend, and practice acceptable behavior in a social setting."

Teacher
Maplewood High School
Nashville, Tennessee

Evaluating Outcomes:

Evaluating Social Interaction

Just how much *are* your students interacting with their general education peers and participating in general education activities? Sometimes it's hard to know, especially when you're busy doing so many other things. The Social Interaction Observation Form can be used to keep track of a student's social interactions over a week's time. (See page 271 for an example. A blank, reproducible form is included in the appendix.) To complete the form, simply jot down every time you notice the student interacting with a general education peer during a class or an activity. Try to estimate how long the interaction occurred, and use the code on the form to indicate the length of the interaction. Also, note the name of the peer with whom the student was interacting. If you're not around the student throughout the day, ask others who are in contact with the student, such as a general education teacher, a peer, or a job coach, to help you.

By the end of the week, you will have a good idea of the amount of time the student spends interacting, with whom, and during which activities. You may find that a student has many social interactions with a variety of peers throughout the day during different classes and extracurricular activities. Some ways teachers report that students interact include the following:

- A student in a wheelchair joins in a game of basketball with co-workers after work.

- A person in a parking lot helps a student get out of the way of an oncoming car.

- A student signs and interacts with her co-workers. To communicate with the student, the co-workers have learned to sign, too.

- A student with a visual impairment participates in PE activities with the help of general education peers in her class.

- A student with a physical disability who uses a wheelchair is the football manager for the school team.

- A student with a visual impairment participates in racing and swimming events with his co-worker at a company picnic.

- During a discussion in a world history class, a student shares ideas and participates in decision making.

- A student with a cognitive disability tries out for the track team and is chosen to join.

- At the school prom, a student using a wheelchair dances with general education friends.

- A young man with a speech impairment sings a solo at church, backed up by the choir.

- A student's peers make sure that he is on the school bus, help him change buses if the bus is late or broken down, and sit and talk with him as they ride the bus to and from school.

- A student is a member of a school academic club and attends the club's out-of-town functions with a peer helper.

Or, you may find that a student has few social interactions even though he attends general education classes and activities. In that case, you may want to use some of the strategies in Chapter 3 for increasing students' social participation. Just because students are in proximity doesn't ensure that they are interacting with each other!

Cross-references: Increasing Students' Social Participation (3-4) and Observing and Collecting Data (6-1)

Social Interaction Observation Form

Student: __Sharon Kay__   Week of: __October 15–19__

	In the courtyard before school	1st period class	2nd period class	Lunch	3rd period class (math)	Opryland Hotel worksite	Volunteering at the Community Center
Monday	Marco—A Stephanie—B	*Industrial Arts* Jessica—C	*Student Council* Mica—C Shirley—C Amanda—B	Erik—C	Briana—C Liz—B Janice—C	Caleb—A	Scott—C Robert—C Marjie—B
Tuesday	Travis—A	*PE*	*Library Aide*	Erik—C	Liz—B Emily—A	Michael—A	Scott—C Gerald—B
Wednesday	Leslie—B	*Industrial Arts* Toni—C	*Student Council* Mica—C Terry—B Pat—C	Erik—C	Gretchen—C Janice—A	Casey—B	Scott—C Robert—B Phyllis—C
Thursday		*PE*	*Library Aide*	Erik—C	Briana—C	Jennifer—A	Scott—C Volunteer?—B Gerald—C
Friday	Klassing—B	*Industrial Arts* Jessica—B Toni—C	*Student Council* Mica—C Terry—C Amanda—C	Erik—C	Briana—B Janice—C	Leah—B	Scott—B Marjie—C Robert—C

Activity/class

Form 9.1.   Social Interaction Observation Form for Sharon Kay. Record each interaction with a general education peer by listing the name of the peer and the estimated length of the interaction. (Key: A = less than 1 minute; B = 1–5 minutes; C = more than 5 minutes.)

Starting Up:

- The skills needed for asking for help at a store differ from those needed for striking up a conversation after church. Because social expectations vary from environment to environment, students should have opportunities to interact with others in as many different community locations as possible.

- To improve students' job interview skills, arrange for them to interview with several different store managers. Evaluate their interviewing skills by creating a short checklist that the employer can complete.

- Eating lunch at restaurants around the community can provide students with opportunities to practice many social interaction skills, such as ordering, thanking and tipping the waitperson, and conversing socially with peers.

- Create opportunities for out-of-school interactions. Help students work together to plan a party or picnic for school clubs in which they are members. Fundraising activities also can get them actively involved in the community.

- Encourage students to go on field trips with their general education classes, such as when an English class goes to a Shakespeare play or a music history class attends a concert. In addition to being educational, these community outings provide an opportunity for students to interact with each other in a variety of situations.

- A job is not just a place to work! Observe how employees at a worksite interact with each other, such as participating in a walking club at noon, chatting as they deliver mail to different offices, or celebrating a co-worker's birthday at break. Support students in getting involved in these activities and becoming a part of the social life of a workplace.

- Helping others is a great way to interact. Serving a meal at a homeless shelter, fixing up a halfway house, and building a wheelchair ramp are opportunities for students to interact with others and to contribute to the community.

- Relax! Some of the best opportunities for interaction occur when we throw away our planning schedules and just take time to enjoy the moment! Give your students a chance just to relax and spend time in a leisurely way with their peers.

Cross-reference: Teaching Skills that Support Acceptance (3-3)

"I plan activities that are educational in nature but that also incorporate social skills like eating out at a restaurant, shopping at the mall, or working out at a health club."
Teacher
Whitehaven High School
Memphis, Tennessee

9-2 PROMOTING PEER INVOLVEMENT

Who do teenagers want to spend time with? That's right! For the most part, it's their peers—at school, work, or in the community. There are many ways to increase students' involvement with peers, whether they are fellow students, co-workers, or club members or friends in the neighborhood.

Case Study 9.2   Why Does He Do It?

For many of the teachers sitting in staff orientation meetings at Lee High School, the beginning of the school year meant having to listen to one long speech after another. Some quietly doodled on their notepads while others covertly read through the newspaper. Mr. Kort, however, had other ideas in mind. As a special education teacher, he was a jack-of-all-trades—community-based instruction teacher, job-training coordinator, and classroom teacher. Recognizing the importance of having general education students involved in his programs, he was already searching the auditorium for faculty who might assist him in promoting student involvement. In the back was Ms. Greiner, the Student Council sponsor. By the door was Coach Nichols, head of the athletic program. Two rows ahead was Mr. Luna, the school secretary, who knew all of the students!

Evaluating Outcomes:

Evaluating Social Opportunities

It's impossible to interact with others if we never have the opportunity! If you filled out the Social Interaction Observation Form (in 9.1.2), you may have found that a student has very little social interaction with her peers. It may be that she has had little opportunity to do so. By examining a student's daily schedule, you can determine what opportunities for social interaction are actually available throughout the day. You can also identify what supports are available to and needed by the student to increase her opportunities for interaction. These supports could include the following:

- *Personal supports* such as "peer buddies," interpreters, or notetakers

- *Scheduling adaptations* such as changing or rearranging classes

- *Instructional methods* such as cooperative groupings, class projects, or lab partners

- *Environmental supports* such as moving the location of a desk, creating a study area, or providing a communication device

Cross-references: "Strategies for Increasing Environmental Support" (Chapter 4) and "Strategies for Increasing Social Support" (Chapter 5)

The Social Opportunities Chart on page 276 can help you identify the frequency and quality of opportunities for social interaction that occur throughout the day for a student. You can also record the supports that exist and additional supports that are needed to increase a student's opportunities for social interaction. (A blank, reproducible form is included in the appendix.)

The following additional methods are used by teachers to evaluate opportunities for social interaction:

- Make a list of school activities in which general education students are typically involved, such as pep rallies, club days, homecoming events, and field trips. Next, compare your students' involvement in school activities with those on your list. You may discover that your students are more (or less) involved than you think.

- When observing students' social interactions in the community, interview parents, teachers, and the students themselves to determine which community locations they currently visit and in which locations they plan to be involved in the future.

- Interview important others, such as peers, employers, co-workers, general education teachers, family members, and the student him- or herself, to obtain their perception of a student's social interactions. Their views may be very different from yours.

Of course, Mr. Kort knew that the best way to increase general education students' involvement with his students was to increase his own involvement in school activities. The more that students knew him, the more willing they would be to spend time with his students. That's one of the reasons he had volunteered to be a faculty sponsor for the Beta Club and the Spanish Club. He also helped as a student advisor during fall registration. That was a good time to get students signed up as "peer buddies" in his class. He even tutored some students he didn't have in a class. Sure, it took some extra time, but Mr. Kort realized that the long-term benefits would make it worth it.

Why would a teacher work so hard to increase general education peer involvement? Mr. Kort would tell you that the answer lies in the Lee High School's mission statement to "develop citizens who participate in productive partnerships with staff, peers, parents, and community members to serve the long-term best interests of students and the community." Mr. Kort knew that *all* students benefit from involvement in relationships with their peers and that *all* students have something to learn from the differences and similarities found in others!

Social Opportunities Chart

Student: __Maricella Longmont__   Date: __January 19__

Activity/class	Time	Opportunities for social interaction	Quality of social interaction	Supports needed	Supports available
Before school	7:50 to 8:10	1 2 3 4 (5) — none / few / many	(1) 2 3 4 5 — not good / so-so / great	Assistance getting to the courtyard; help getting over curb	Peers could walk with her from the bus; officer in courtyard could help lift
Drama/theater	8:10 to 9:10	1 2 3 4 (5) — none / few / many	1 2 (3) 4 5 — not good / so-so / great	Help getting onto the stage where most of the class rehearses	Woodworking class could build a portable ramp; peers/teacher could set up ramp daily
Civics/government	9:10 to 10:05	1 2 3 (4) 5 — none / few / many	1 2 (3) 4 5 — not good / so-so / great	Someone to change overlay on communication device; help learning to use device	Teacher could train peers to work with Maricella; teach her to ask/sign for assistance
Morning break	10:05 to 10:20	1 2 3 4 (5) — none / few / many	1 2 3 (4) 5 — not good / so-so / great	Assistance getting from class to hallway/break room	Peer buddy and educational assistant are willing to help
Consumer math	10:20 to 11:15	1 (2) 3 4 5 — none / few / many	1 2 (3) 4 5 — not good / so-so / great	Closer proximity to her peers; activities that allow for interaction	Teacher willing to plan small–group projects; room could be rearranged
Lunch	11:15 to 12:00	1 2 3 4 (5) — none / few / many	1 2 3 4 (5) — not good / so-so / great	None	Maricella eats lunch with a close group of friends
Community-based vocational instruction	12:00 to 3:20	(1) 2 3 4 5 — none / few / many	(1) 2 3 4 5 — not good / so-so / great	Help completing job tasks; reminders to use device to greet customers	Adjust work routine to match a co-worker's routine; picture prompts set up as reminders
Extracurricular club (Mon, Tue, & Thur)	3:20 to 4:00	1 2 3 (4) 5 — none / few / many	1 2 3 (4) 5 — not good / so-so / great	Accessible ride to and from service projects	One club member's parents have an accessible van

Form 9.2.   Social Opportunities Chart for Maricella Longmont.

9.2.1 In-School Activities

When it comes to social interaction in high school, students are definitely the experts! After all, they are the ones who determine what fashions are "in," what sayings are "cool," and what hairdos are definitely "out"! They are also the best models of how teenagers act. By involving general education peers in school activities with your students, you can help ensure that your students are interacting socially in ways that are acceptable to and expected and practiced by others.

"General education students are involved with my students in many ways. They work with my students to complete assignments in class, train for Unified Sports, rehearse for dance presentations for a school assembly, and help in styling their hair in cosmetology class."

Teacher
Austin-East High School
Knoxville, Tennessee

How to Do It:

- Students may have fears about getting involved in new classes and unfamiliar activities such as intramural tennis or French Club. Encourage general education peers to support them and ease their transition.

- Inform general education peers about the many ways they can get involved with your students, such as walking with a student to class, hanging out in the halls, sitting next to each other at a pep rally, or working together in a study hall.

- During lunch, general education peers can invite students to eat lunch with them and include them in conversation with their friends. That way, everyone benefits by making new friends.

- Pair a verbal student with one who uses signing; together they can complete a class project and make a presentation to the class.

9.2.2   By Peer Buddies and Co-workers

Teenagers get along best with other teens. Peer Buddy programs are one effective way of getting high school students together. Whether through a volunteer program or a credit course, peer buddies provide their partners with social support, assistance, and, ultimately, friendship. On the job, co-workers can provide this support, too.

"Clubs like the debate club provide excellent opportunities for the development of social interaction skills. In classes, student leadership can be rotated so that students have the chance to lead part of the class. Peer tutoring uses the concept of 'every person knows less in some areas than you do and more in other areas than you do.' You can develop short questionnaires that allow pairing of students with unlike areas of knowledge in content areas, such as cosmetology or auto mechanics."

Teacher
Fairley High School
Memphis, Tennessee

Teacher-Proven Practices:

- Setting up a peer buddy program doesn't have to be difficult. Seven steps for starting up a program in your school, which have been tried and tested by other schools, are in Form 3.3 in Teaching Skills to Others, 3.3.2.

- Involve peer buddies in as many activities throughout the school day as possible, including trips to community sites, pep rallies, lunch, after-school events, and school assemblies.

- Ask peers in a general education class to keep track of the social interactions of a student who is nonverbal. They may have a different perspective than you do.

- Peer buddy and co-worker relationships can extend beyond the school day or workday, such as when a peer buddy invites a partner to attend a soccer game or when co-workers stop at a local restaurant on their way home from work.

- Roles can change in a peer-tutoring relationship. Depending on the participants' strengths and needs, some of the

"One of my students was afraid to join the basketball team and stay after school for practice. A general education peer encouraged her by going with her to practice. She now suits up for each game."
Teacher
Greenville High School
Greenville, Tennessee

time each is a teacher and, at other times, a learner. The same can be true on the job when peers mentor each other on work- or social-related issues.

- Peer buddies do not have to be the top academic students in your school. Sometimes students who are struggling find their niche as a peer buddy and begin to develop their own talents while they interact with their special education peers.

- On the job, notice which co-workers tend to "buddy up" with or work near a student. Try to promote these relationships without "getting in the way"—sometimes the presence of a teacher or job coach can inhibit these interactions even if you don't mean to!

Cross-references: Teaching Skills to Students (3.3.1) and Teaching Skills to Others (3.3.2)

The IDEA Amendments of 1997 reaffirm the importance of educating all students together. The amendments state that students with diverse abilities should, to the maximum extent appropriate, be educated with their general education peers. Having peer buddies may provide one avenue for supporting students in general education environments. In addition to assisting students with class routines and assignments, peer buddies can encourage interaction between their partners and other members of a class.

Q: *What are some things you do with your peer buddies?*

A: Katie comes to my house, and I go bowling with Jenni.
They came to my birthday party at my house. We had a barbecue.
We listen to the radio and just talk.
We go to the mall, restaurants, and other places. We go play video games.
We tell jokes and eat lunch together. We talk "boy talk" with David.
We lift weights, go to work, and play games.
My peer buddy's friend and I went to the prom. We went there in a limousine, and I got her a corsage. It was cool!

Q: *Why do you like to spend time with your peer buddies?*

A: Because they are my best friends.
He is a good friend—a good pal.
Because she introduces me to her friends, and now I have a lot of friends.
Because it's fun!
We go hear country music downtown. We talk with them.
I like him. He's fun and makes me laugh.
They're great! We have friendships."

Students
Metropolitan Nashville High Schools
Nashville, Tennessee

9-3 INCREASING OPPORTUNITIES FOR SOCIAL INTERACTION

"Every educational experience can be presented in such a way that appropriate social interactions are encouraged. Students can talk and physically participate together in groups. Adopting a philosophy that values and encourages positive social interaction is important for all teachers."
Teacher
Treadwell High School
Memphis, Tennessee

9.3.1 Modifying Environments and Curricula

Simply attending a general education class or activity does not ensure that a student is fitting in socially with his peers and having quality interactions

"I encourage as much socialization as possible with general education peers. I include peers in the classroom as tutors and as someone to help my students in initiating interactions. Sometimes these interactions develop into friendships but not in all cases. It's tough to get sincere friendships that really last."
Teacher
Hunters Lane High School
Nashville, Tennessee

"This year I have a student in my class who has severe autism. When Kim first came into my room, she appeared to have no interest in others and only initiated interactions when she wanted to eat or go to the restroom. Then Kim developed a friendship with her peer buddy, Corie. Now she watches the door for Corie every day. When they are together, Kim makes eye contact with her buddy frequently, laughs often, and even initiates conversation. We never saw her do these behaviors before. Kim also has increased her vocal repertoire from 4 words to 11 words. We have been truly amazed with the difference peer buddies have made in the lives of our students."
Teacher
McGavock High School
Nashville, Tennessee

with other students. Sometimes an environment must be altered or changes must be made in a curriculum to accommodate a student. For example, in keyboarding class, students often work alone on their assignments using individual computers. To maintain a business-like atmosphere, teachers generally don't wish to promote social interaction. It may be that a naturally occurring break time, such as at the beginning or end of class, could be used as acceptable time for students to socialize with each other, such as co-workers do on their breaks at work. During class time, there may be projects that students could work on in groups or students could rotate as "managers" who supervise the work of others. These simple modifications can promote appropriate social interactions and are consistent with the requirement of the IDEA Amendments of 1997 to accommodate students' individual needs.

"Provide class time even in academic classes for students to engage in activities that promote the development of conversation and social skills. For example, work in cooperative groups, have peers tutor each other, and assign a buddy to assist a student when necessary."
Teacher
Hillcrest High School
Memphis, Tennessee

Starting Up:

- Some classes support only infrequent social interaction among students. If increasing social interaction is an important educational goal for a student, help the student schedule classes that are of interest to her *and* allow opportunities to interact socially.

- Survey a student's typical school, work, or community environments to identify changes that will increase opportunities for social interaction. Often, these changes are simple, such as pulling desks together during a class assignment, coordinating co-workers' breaks so that they occur at the same time, or encouraging a student to join a community fitness center instead of exercising at home alone.

- In classes, rotate student leadership throughout the school year. By providing students with opportunities to direct a portion of the class, such as moderating a discussion, students gain confidence in their social abilities and learn valuable leadership skills.

The IDEA Amendments of 1997 clearly mandate making accommodations for students to promote their inclusion in general education classes and activities. According to the amendments, students' individualized education programs (IEPs) must include a statement of the program modifications or supports that will be provided to ensure that they will be involved and progress in the general education curriculum, participate in extracurricular and other nonacademic activities, and be educated and participate with general education students. In addition, an explanation must be provided of the extent, if any, to which a student will not participate with students without disabilities in the general education curriculum and activities.

Cross-references: Developing Environmental Support Plans (4-3) and Modifying the Environment (4-5)

9.3.2 Collaborating with Others to Promote Social Interaction

Throughout high school, most students have an increasing number of opportunities to be involved in different school, work, and community environments. For example, many service clubs at school sponsor food drives, neighborhood cleanups, or other community projects. Many students hold part-time jobs while they go to school; some play in bands or sing in a choir; and others pursue hobbies, such as working on cars, climbing the wall at a local recreation center, or taking dance lessons. As students increase their involvement in these environments, it becomes particularly important for teachers to collaborate with parents, peers, fellow teachers, co-workers at students' worksites, and community members when seeking to increase students' levels of social interaction. By working together, those involved in students' lives can ensure support for and access to social interaction.

"We have students call and set up appointments with local employers or personnel managers who interview the students in mock job interviews. They evaluate the students' performance and provide opportunities to practice for an actual job interview. Often, the employers end up hiring the students who have participated in the mock interviews!"

Teacher
Huntington High School
Huntington, Tennessee

"You can't force students to interact with each other. First, you need to build acceptance of yourself and your program. Then, inclusion of your students will follow in time. Host parties and meetings in your classroom, or serve as a coach for sports teams. Having the teacher be a part of the overall school helps general education students accept and realize that it is "cool" to sit and talk with students with disabilities."

Itinerant Transition Teacher
Metropolitan Nashville Public Schools
Nashville, Tennessee

How to Do It:

- Other teachers may not even be aware of the need for creating opportunities for social interaction for your students. Conversations in the faculty lounge, a guest speaker at a district in-service session, or a brief video at a faculty meeting may be effective in getting the word out.

- Talk with family members about the types of relationships and opportunities in which they would like to have a student involved. By working together, you can encourage a student's involvement in social relationships both in and out of school.

- Help students plan an after-school party for their peer buddies and other students with whom they have interacted during the school year. Include an honors recognition for achievements that students have made, such as "Volunteer of the Year" in the Red Cross Club, an accuracy award in keyboarding class, or "Most Valuable Player" on the girls' volleyball team.

- Brainstorm with co-workers or work supervisors ways they can encourage a student who is hesitant to talk to interact with them during break and other opportunities to socialize throughout the day.

- Contact your local college or university to see if there is a Best Buddies chapter. Best Buddies matches college students (College Buddies) with people with cognitive disabilities (Buddies) on a one-to-one basis to become friends and spend time together. The mission of Best Buddies is to enhance the lives of people with mental retardation by providing opportunities for socialization and employment. There are 230 college chapters nationwide. You may find some willing volunteers eager to befriend your students and interact with them on an ongoing basis.

Cross-references: Communicating an Attitude of Acceptance (3-1) and Communicating Social Support Needs (5-2)

"I like being a Best Buddy because I see the joy that I can bring into someone's life and that makes me feel good and wanted. Being a Best Buddy is a reciprocal relationship—it's a 50/50 deal. As much as my Buddy gets from me, I get back from him. He means as much to me as I do to him. It's a special relationship—it's a real friendship. We both like spending time together. It's not work; it's rewarding!"

Best Buddy
Vanderbilt University Chapter
Nashville, Tennessee

9-4 TEACHING SOCIAL INTERACTION SKILLS

Social interaction is a natural occurrence in classrooms, at worksites, and around the community. In fact, the desire for social interaction may be the main reason that many students like to go to school, choose a workplace, or get involved in their neighborhood. Some students, however, must be taught skills that will allow them to interact socially with their peers in ways that are acceptable and enjoyable.

9.4.1 Using Direct Instruction

Whether we like it or not, our social behavior influences the degree to which we are liked and accepted by others. Most of us learn expected social skills through our interactions and relationships with others. Some students, however, may need direct instruction in these skills. Luckily, there are many ways to teach social interaction skills.

"I can't stress how important social skills are and how this area is one of the weakest for my students. I reward them for shaking hands, greeting people appropriately, giving others "space," and so forth. They lose privileges for hugging, touching, talking loudly, and so forth. They need constant practice in this area."

Teacher
Hillsboro High School
Nashville, Tennessee

Teacher-Proven Practices:

- When eating out, model socially appropriate behaviors for students, such as using the correct piece of silverware and taking small bites of food.

- Sometimes students just don't know what behavior is expected in public. Have discussions with students on appropriate behaviors for different situations, such as when inviting a friend to the movies, accepting criticism from a boss, or asking for clarification of an assignment in class.

- Use direct instruction techniques to teach social skills, just as you would with any other skill. Model appropriate behavior, use prompting and corrective feedback, reinforce correct performance, and decrease your assistance as students become more proficient.

- Embed opportunities to practice social skills throughout the day—during academic classes, career preparation, and working or recreating in the community. Social skills are best taught in the context in which they will be used.

- Teach students to replace inappropriate behaviors with more appropriate alternatives. For example, students should learn to shake hands rather than hug a stranger and say, "I love you."

- Provide opportunities for students to interact with people of different backgrounds and cultures. They will learn different methods of greeting and interacting.

- Make sure that a student who uses a hearing or visual aid knows how to use it properly when interacting socially with others. Otherwise, the aid may hinder rather than help the student interact.

- Teach students to be aware of others' behavior and to watch those around them for cues on what's expected.

- Eat out often! Eating out at restaurants, shopping at the mall, ordering pizza over the telephone, and attending social functions all provide opportunities for practicing social skills by interacting with others.

- Working in the school office with a peer buddy or participating in student council with a peer can help students learn new social skills, such as providing information or speaking in front of groups.

- Encourage students to enroll in career preparation classes. Many of these classes, such as keyboarding, health sciences, and automotive trades, instruct students on how to interact appropriately on the job.

Cross-reference: Teaching Skills that Need Strengthening (6-4)

"For challenging, antisocial behaviors, I develop a plan, take data, and have a consistent set of reinforcements and consequences."

Teacher
Henry County High School
Paris, Tennessee

"I evaluate students' social skills by using a work habits checklist. I also have a social skills behavior sheet for each student that I check every day."

Teacher
Gallatin High School
Gallatin, Tennessee

Evaluating Outcomes:

Evaluating Students' Social Skills

There are several published social skills programs for adolescents, such as the *Walker Social Skills Curriculum* (Walker, Todis, Holmes, & Horton, 1988), that you can use to evaluate your students' social skills. (See the Social Supports section of the Resources in the appendix for others.) Often, these programs contain checklists that you can use to observe and assess a student's social behavior in different situations, such as in school or in the community. You can also create your own checklist of social skills that focuses on only the skills that are critical within a particular environment. For example, see the Employee Social Skills Checklist (Form 6.4) in 6.2.1. Information can be gathered either by your directly observing the student or by interviewing others who have observed the student. Check Section 6.1.1 for other informal, teacher-devised forms to use to evaluate students' social skills, such as when tallying the occurrence of appropriate behaviors (e.g., greeting customers [Event Recording Form]) or when observing how long a behavior occurs (e.g., engaging in conversation [Interval Recording Form]).

You can also use the Home Inventory Form in Section 6.2.1 to gather information from parents and other family members to determine which of a student's social skills are viewed as a problem at home and outside school. Similar information can be obtained from employers or peers. You can then focus on these skills in your daily instructional programming and evaluation.

When evaluating a student's social skills, it's important to know what the "norm" is for performing social skills. Observing Students' Performance, Section 6.1.1, provides directions for conducting comparative observations to establish a norm for a particular behavior. This is done by comparing a student's performance with that of peers or co-workers who are considered proficient within a particular environment. You then have a standard by which to evaluate a student's social skills as well as an instructional goal for educational programming. For example, by conducting comparative observations, you may determine that high school students usually talk more about their peers than about the weather; people usually initiate conversation at a rate of three times per minute; and co-workers at a particular worksite usually tease and joke with each other when on break. You can then compare a student's behavior with these standards.

Social behaviors that have been the focus of teachers' evaluations include the following:

• How a student greets and introduces a guest speaker in class

- Whether an employee says, "Thank you," and, "Yes, sir," or "Yes, ma'am," to her boss

- Whether a student's choice of clothing is similar to high school peers' choices

- In gaining a co-worker's attention, whether a student says, "Excuse me," before asking a question

- Whether a student shakes hands when greeting a new-comer rather than hugging the person

- On breaks at work, whether a student gets to know other co-workers

- If a student addresses the school principal by name rather than by yelling, "Hey, principal!"

- The extent to which others accept the student as a re-flection of a student's social skills

- At the recreation center, in student council, or at a dance, whether a student's social behavior is similar to his peers' behavior

- How often an employee offers to help a customer lo-cate an item at the grocery store

- The extent to which a student is attentive during a school assembly or an after-school play

- How often a student greets peers and co-workers ap-propriately

- Whether a student shakes hands, has eye contact, and introduces herself without hesitation in a new situation

- Whether a student provides help to a co-worker when asked, rather than giggling and running away

- Whether a student tells a supervisor about a mistake he has made rather than crying

- Whether a student who has had anger-management counseling handles herself appropriately in a potentially explosive situation

- The number of peers with whom a student interacts and gets along in his general education classes

Cross-references: Observing Performance and Collecting Data (6-1) and Assessing Students' Strengths and Needs (6-2)

9.4.2   Using Role-Playing and Problem-Solving

One very effective means of teaching students social interaction skills is providing them with frequent opportunities to practice those skills. Through role-playing common social scenarios or problem-solving solutions to typical social encounters, teachers can help students be prepared and feel confident when interacting with others.

"My students need to be taught appropriate social skills from day one. A teacher needs to provide opportunities for practice—in general education, everyday school activities, and community outings. I have found role playing and having frank discussions about different situations helpful."

Teacher
Whites Creek High School
Whites Creek, Tennessee

Teacher-Proven Practices:

- Using acceptable social skills during an interview can mean the difference between getting a job and being passed over for another applicant. If scheduling problems make it difficult to interview with business managers off campus, try having students rehearse their skills in mock interviews with a school administrator on campus. Principals and school counselors are experienced in interviewing and can provide valuable feedback about a student's social skills.

• Although teaching social skills in the actual environments in which they will be used is usually the best context for learning, role-playing social behaviors at school can provide students with additional practice and preparation for future interactions. For example, a student could role-play and get feedback from her peers on how to ask her mother to let her choose her own clothes.

• Students can be very creative when brainstorming which behaviors are appropriate in a particular situation. Hold small-group discussions with peers in which students problem-solve which social behaviors would be acceptable during a certain interaction, such as when telling a clerk that you have not received the correct change.

• The IDEA Amendments of 1997 emphasize the need for teachers to be good role models for their students. During the school day, remember that you are one of the most visible models of appropriate social skills that your students will see. For example, if you treat others kindly and with respect, your students are more likely to do so, too.

• Role playing can be helpful in encouraging students who are hesitant or shy to participate in groups. Peers can provide a nonthreatening atmosphere in which students can practice new social skills, such as speaking up in class or asking a friend for her telephone number.

• Have students role-play interviewing each other. Then follow up these sessions by having students interview guest speakers in class.

"Role-play communication techniques and problem-solving strategies in groups. Have groups of peers problem-solve together. That way, everybody learns together!"

Teacher
Central High School
Ashland City, Tennessee

9.4.3 Peer-Delivered Social Skills Programs

"The best way to have students learn social skills is through peer-tutoring programs and integration into general education settings. Teach peer tutors to interact and teach social interaction to students. I encourage peers to tell students when they are acting or talking inappropriately. I tell peers, 'If you would allow another friend to act or say that, then allow the students. If you wouldn't, then don't allow them to get away with it.'"
Teacher
Karns High School
Knoxville, Tennessee

"Social skills are easier taught in the natural environment with peers than in the classroom because there the interactions are natural. For example, one day in class a student said he had chased some girls at school, although previously I had lectured the student not to. The next day, a peer approached me and said the student had chased her at the bus stop. I asked her to tell the student to stop chasing her. He has not chased another girl since. The peer was able to teach what I was not!"

Teacher
Warren County High School
McMinnville, Tennessee

 # Starting Up:

- Peer buddies provide many opportunities for students to practice social skills. Take time to have students just socialize with their peer buddies—talking casually, playing cards, or looking at magazines. Students' social skills will improve.

- Peers are not "shy" about providing feedback to students. If students are acting inappropriately—such as mumbling, talking too loudly, or repeating themselves continuously, or if they forget to shut the bathroom door when using the toilet—their peers will let them know. Teachers report that peers have often been much more effective in changing students' social behavior than the teachers have.

- Special education students can serve as peer buddies, too. In some schools, students tutor younger children in general education classes. Cross-age tutoring helps both parties improve their communication, social, and academic skills. Students with learning disabilities or emotional disabilities also may have much to offer to students with cognitive disabilities—and benefit greatly from the experience themselves.

Cross-reference: Teaching Skills that Support Acceptance (3-3) (in particular, Beginning a Peer Buddy Program, 3.3.2)

"Start with the bus line and lunchroom first. Then, you will have many peers together at one time. Work with several of the students, and share your goals for your students. Often, they will step in and correct the student naturally."

Teacher
Warren County High School
McMinnville, Tennessee

"Integration into the general high school program automatically provides many opportunities to learn and practice social skills. The peer tutor program is an important part of this, because the tutors are trained to work with my students to bridge the gap."

Teacher
Rutledge High School
Rutledge, Tennessee

Evaluating Outcomes:

Peers as Teachers of Social Skills

With a little training and coaching, peers can be effective teachers of social skills to students with even very limited verbal skills. In the Metropolitan Nashville Peer Buddy Program, peers have learned to teach students to use "communication books" to increase their conversational initiations. Peer buddies teach students to turn pages in the book, which serves to prompt their initiations with a variety of peers. Because the students have varying abilities to speak, some can verbalize their conversational initiations aloud, whereas others show written questions to peers to initiate conversational topics. The peer buddies have been successful in teaching all their partners to increase their conversational interactions—with peers who are both familiar and unfamiliar to them. In teaching social skills, the peer buddies use the following script:

Peer Buddy Social Skills Teaching Script

1. Rationale
   a. "I'd like to help you learn to talk to your friends and other people at school. Would you like to try?"
   b. "I'm going to teach you a way to talk so that it will be easy for you to talk with other people."

2. Training Sequence
   a. "Watch me and listen to what I say. I'll show you how to talk to friends by using this book." (You model using the book). Go through all the pictures in the book. Look at each picture, and ask the question.
   b. "Now you talk to me and I'll tell you what to do." (You instruct student while student uses book to ask questions.)
   c. "Now it's your turn to use your book while you're talking to me." (Student uses book to ask questions.) Be sure to give lots of verbal praise for using the book. Also, correct the student if he or she misses a step. Be sure to prompt the student to use the book (if he or she doesn't on his or her own) by asking, "Look at the picture," or, "What do we say?"

3. Reminder
   a. "Now you remember to use your book when you want to talk to somebody."
   b. "You be the one to start talking and do all the talking when you talk to your next friend."

How do you know if the peer buddy is following the script correctly? That's easy! Just use the Peer Buddy Social Skills Teaching Checklist on page 295. (A blank, reproducible form is included in the appendix.) As the peer buddy and partner perform each step on the script, simply mark it off on the checklist. Then, follow up by observing the students with peers who did not provide social

Peer Buddy Social Skills Teaching Checklist

Student: Pamela Vidal

Date: November 21

Observer: Mica Downs

Peer buddy: Delores Walls

Time start: 9:30

Time stop: 9:50

Number of minutes: 20 minutes

Location: Cafeteria

Rationale

☑ **1.** Peer buddy explains that he or she wants to help student learn to talk to his or her friends at school.

☑ **2.** Peer buddy explains that he or she is going to teach student a way to talk.

Training Sequence

☑ **3.** Peer buddy models using the book.

☑ **4.** Peer buddy goes through all of the pictures in the book.

☑ **5.** Peer buddy looks at each picture and asks the question.

☑ **6.** Peer buddy instructs student while student uses book to ask questions.

☐ **7.** Student uses book to ask questions.

☑ **8.** Peer buddy provides lots of verbal praise for using book.

☑ **9.** Peer buddy corrects student if student misses a step.

☑ **10.** Peer buddy prompts student to use book.

Reminder

☐ **11.** Peer buddy reminds student to use book when student wants to talk to somebody.

☑ **12.** Peer buddy reminds student to start talking and do all of the talking when student talks to his or her next friend.

Comments: Delores did a fantastic job of explaining how to use the communication book. She modeled use of the book well but should give more verbal praise to her partner. Delores also missed several great opportunities to remind her partner to use the book at the lunch table.

Form 9.3. Peer Buddy Social Skills Teaching Checklist for Delores Walls. (From Hughes, C., Harmer, M.L., Killian, D.J., & Niarhos, F. [1995]. The effects of multiple exemplar self-instructional training on high school students' generalized conversational interactions. *Journal of Applied Behavior Analysis, 28,* 206–207. Copyright *Journal of Applied Behavior Analysis;* adapted by permission.)

skills training. Do they continue to prompt themselves to talk by using their communication books? Are they having more conversations and interacting with their peers more often? If so, there's a good chance that the peer-delivered social skills training is working! You can also ask peers with whom the students interact to see how they enjoy the conversations by asking them to fill out the following Peer Perception Questionnaire. (A blank, reproducible form is included in the appendix.)

Metropolitan Nashville Peer Buddy Program
Nashville, Tennessee

Peer Perception Questionnaire

Student: Janelle Ibute   **Date:** November 21

Partner: Mica Ackridge   **Location:** Cafeteria

INSTRUCTIONS: Please circle the number that best represents the way you feel about the interaction you just experienced with your partner.

	Never	Rarely	Sometimes	Usually	Always
Did you feel that your partner interacted with you appropriately?	1	2	3	(4)	5
Did you enjoy this interaction?	1	2	3	(4)	5
Would you like to have this kind of interaction again?	1	2	3	4	(5)
Do you think that your partner enjoyed this interaction?	1	2	3	4	(5)
When you are with your friends, do you have similar interactions?	1	2	3	(4)	5

Comments: It took a little time to get used to, but I enjoyed talking with Janelle! I'd like to hang out with her again.

Form 9.4.   Peer Perception Questionnaire for Janelle Ibute (completed by Mica Ackridge).

"My second semester as a Peer Buddy I spent mostly with Kim in Ms. Dye's room. And that girl–whew! She was a handful. When I first got into the classroom, she would just sit there and either sleep all day or cry about something or kind of just wander around with her eyes and look and not do anything. After my first semester, I noticed how she wouldn't deal with anybody. She was just always by herself. So I would go over there and tickle her and, all of a sudden, she just livened up! It was like someone had to just talk to her one time and she burst out with life. When I first started talking to her, she really didn't have many words that she could say. Mostly she just said "milk" if she wanted milk, or if she had to go to the bathroom, she would tell us. That was about it. Then I got to talking to her and toward the end of the year, she developed more language and everything. We played games like hand-slap games and tickled each other. The bean bag chair was the best because she just loved that thing. Kim would just lay on it and wallow all over the floor and just laugh. It was so cool! Well, that's Kim! She's cool now."

Peer Buddy
McGavock High School
Nashville, Tennessee

REFERENCES

Hughes, C., Harmer, M.L., Killian, D.J., & Niarhos, F. (1995). The effects of multiple exemplar self-instructional training on high school students' generalized conversational interactions. *Journal of Applied Behavior Analysis, 28,* 201–218.

Individuals with Disabilities Education Act Amendments of 1997, PL 105-17, 20 U.S.C. §§ 1400 *et seq.*

Walker, H.M., Todis, B., Holmes, D., & Horton, G. (1988). *The Walker social skills curriculum.* Austin, TX: PRO-ED.

SECTION IV

Epilogue

Chapter 10

Epilogue

I Must Be Invisible

I'm at the door knocking
Trying to get in
No look no stare
They just don't care

I must be invisible
They can't see me
Why not rare up my wheelchair
And ride straight up a tree

I go to the movies
I laugh out loud
No one can hear me
I must be in a cloud

I must be invisible
They can't see me
Why not throw down my cane
And hop around on one knee

A child smiles and waves
It was just a small babe
But before I said hi
She was rushed quickly by

I must be invisible
They can't see me
Or is that just the way
They want me to be.

Pam Townsend
Board Member
The Arc of Davidson County
Nashville, Tennessee

"LIFE"—WHAT'S IT ALL ABOUT?

One thing everyone has in common, even if we each may feel very different, is that we all are living "life" right now—that's one thing we know for sure! But what's it all about? What is this thing called "life," and what do we want out of "life," anyway?

Social Acceptance

We can pretty much count on one thing: We don't live in this world alone, and many of us probably would not want to. Instead, most of us seek social acceptance and want to fit in with others and be a part of the social makeup of our immediate environments. No one wants to feel "invisible" as described in Pam Townsend's poem—to walk into a room where no one greets us, to be in a family where we don't feel loved or included, to sit in a class or a meeting and have no one ask our opinion, to work alongside someone who never jokes with or smiles at us, or to exercise at the gym or eat in our favorite restaurant and always feel like an outsider, as if no one sees or knows us, even though we're there almost every day of our lives! As people, we want to be participants in an environment, actively engaging in interactions with others, rather than feeling like we are visitors in our own hometowns, neighborhoods, or workplaces.

Social and Environmental Supports

Most of us want to engage in some sort of social relationships that offer mutual and reciprocal supports as friends, family members, co-workers, or associates. We may not want to be interacting with others *all* the time; sometimes we may want to be alone or just quietly observe others around us or "do our own thing" and not pay any attention to anyone. But when we've had our fill of being alone, we're ready to jump back in and be a part of the action and the people around us. And then, we want our relationships and our environments to be accepting, supportive, and accommodating. Social acceptance and social and environmental supports—these are some things that life is all about!

Personal Competence

What else is life all about? Well, let's face it: We also want to feel competent with respect to the expectations of the environments in which we spend time. No one wants to feel like a "klutz" or a "dork," feeling as if we mess up everything we try to do! Instead, we want to feel good about ourselves, like we do when we feel we're doing a good job at something we think is important, such as our jobs, our schoolwork, our hobbies, or our relationships with others. None of us likes to be handed a job we think we can't do, to be asked to sing in front of a crowd if we think we can't sing, to play a game of cards if we don't know the rules, or to take a new class if we feel we don't have the prerequisites. When we feel competent, however—when we feel we have the skills needed for a situation—we're ready to accept new challenges and expand our competence. That's another thing that life is all about: personal competence.

Competence, Acceptance, and Support

Our feelings of competence and the support and social acceptance in an environment relate to each other. The more accepting an environment is and the more support it offers, the more competent we feel in that environment. In turn, when we feel competent at what we're doing, we're more likely to feel a part of and accepted by an environment and the people in it. Acceptance, support, and personal competence go hand-in-hand, and that's why we've included them all in *The Transition Handbook* as integral parts of our Transition Support Model.

THE TRANSITION HANDBOOK: A TRANSITION SUPPORT MODEL

What Do High School Students Want out of Life?

Sometimes, it seems that high school students are very different from everyone else! We (the authors) know colleagues who have walked into high schools and felt "shocked." Not being high school students themselves, they feel that high schools (and high school students) are very different from other schools, such as elementary or middle schools or almost everywhere else "on earth" they've been lately. Some people think teenagers are "scary," and some say they wish teenagers would just "disappear" until they reach age 21 or older and are finished with those "horrible growth years." But are high school students so different, and is what they want so different from what everyone else wants in life? Don't they also want social acceptance and support and the opportunity to feel competent at what they do? One premise of *The Transition Handbook* is that these "wants" are universal among all of us—high school students included!

Transition to Adult Life: A Unique Situation

Although high school students' ultimate "wants" in life may be basically the same as everyone else's, remember that high school students are in the unique position of being engaged in making a transition from school to adult life. What does making a transition to adult life mean? It means that *all* high school students are going through the following changes at some time:

- Growing up
- Becoming increasingly independent from but still involved with their parents and families
- Choosing to go on to further education, training, or employment with the eventual goal of becoming financially independent
- Finding a satisfying and fulfilling career
- Maintaining current social relationships and developing new ones at college or other postsecondary training or on the job
- Becoming involved in important, long-term relationships, such as being married and becoming a parent

- Expanding their leisure and recreational repertoires and activities

- Becoming members of a community and building social support networks

- Trying to live up to their ideals, such as "making a difference" in the world or contributing to society

- Experiencing a personal sense of "quality of life" in their everyday lives

Of course, there are many variations in how students make the transition from high school to adult life. We believe, however, that the overall lifetime goals of high school students are similar to what we all want: to feel accepted, supported, and competent within our environments. High school students, like all of us, don't want to feel "invisible" as they enter their adult lives.

Supporting Students in the Transition to Adult Life: *The Transition Handbook*

Some students who are making the transition from high school to adult life may need more support than others in achieving the lifetime goals of feeling accepted, supported, and competent. Without more support than is provided in a typical secondary educational program, some students will experience the same adult outcomes that Lester Anthony did in Case Study 1.1 in Chapter 1: high school dropout, lack of job skills, unemployment, lack of family involvement, and dissatisfying social relationships. With support, however, we see in Case Study 4.4 in Chapter 4 how a life such as Lester's can be turned around. Lester and his educational support team designed a plan that included environmental and social supports that helped Lester build his competence. Rather than drop out of high school, Lester graduated at age 18, chose a job in an auto body shop, and now has a life full of social and recreational activities with his friends and family.

What Can You Do?

What can you do to help students achieve the outcomes of social acceptance, support, and personal competence? How do you, as parents, teachers, friends, employers, job coaches, or others, work with students to provide support that reflects a student's choice, preferences, interests, and self-determination; that is culturally sensitive; and that is socially accepted within a student's immediate environments? To you—those who are providing support directly to students—and to students themselves, we offer the Transition Support Model in Table 1.1 of Chapter 1 as an overall guide for a model of support. To you and the students, we offer *The Transition Handbook* as a user-friendly resource with a menu of teacher-tested and research-based support strategies derived from both researchers and practitioners.

PUTTING *THE TRANSITION HANDBOOK* TO WORK

Collaboration Is the Key

No one can provide transition support to a student alone. Collaboration is mandated by the Individuals with Disabilities Education Act (IDEA) Amendments of 1997 (PL 105-17) and is the key to providing a comprehensive support plan for any student. Build a support team for yourself *and* for your students, and stress collaboration throughout the entire support process.

As an aid to collaboration, all of the strategies included in *The Transition Handbook* address the individual or small-group level of interaction, such as peer support, rather than the large organization or community level, such as urban renewal (Bronfenbrenner, 1977). That is why we defined support strategies as "any assistance or help provided *directly* to a student to promote a successful transition from school to adult life" (see Chapter 1). This is a critical concern because you may be more likely to have opportunities and resources to implement strategies within the immediate environment than across an entire agency, city, or state. Although you may also want to seek supports on a larger level, perhaps regional or statewide, your collaborative efforts at providing transition supports to individual students will always ultimately be provided directly on the individual or small-group level of interaction, over which you may have more direct input.

Be Consistent with IDEA

Finally, one concern of teachers and other providers is that they are in compliance with laws that mandate services to students. Rest assured! All of the strategies in *The Transition Handbook* are consistent with and tie in to current transition legislative requirements and exemplary secondary transition practices, such as community-based instruction, inclusion in general education, interagency collaboration, and employment training. In using *The Transition Handbook* with your students, not only are you providing exemplary support strategies to assist their transition from school to adult life, but you are also staying true to the letter and the spirit of the law! Now, let's get together and get busy. We *can* make a difference in students' lives by providing support, increasing acceptance, and building competence. And isn't that what life is all about?

REFERENCES

Bronfenbrenner, U. (1977). Toward an experimental ecology of human development. *American Psychologist, 32,* 513–531.

Individuals with Disabilities Education Act Amendments of 1997, PL 105-17, 20 U.S.C. §§ 1400 *et seq.*

APPENDIX

Blank Forms

Behavior Checklist

Person completing checklist: _____ **Date:** _____

Student: _____

	Strongly disagree	Mildly disagree	Don't feel strongly either way	Mildly agree	Strongly agree
	1	2	3	4	5
	1	2	3	4	5
	1	2	3	4	5
	1	2	3	4	5
	1	2	3	4	5
	1	2	3	4	5
	1	2	3	4	5

Comments: _____

_____

_____

Form 3.1.   Behavior Checklist. (From Hughes, C., Lorden, S.W., Scott, S.V., Hwang, B., Derer, K.R., Rodi, M.S., Pitkin, S.E., & Godshall, J.C. [1998]. Identification and validation of critical conversational social skills. *Journal of Applied Behavior Analysis, 31,* 438. Copyright © 1998 *Journal of Applied Behavior Analysis;* adapted by permission.)

Data Collection System

Student: _____   **Date:** _____   **Observer:** _____

Behavior: _____

Date	Yes or no	Comments

Y = _____   **N =** _____

Form 3.2.   Data Collection System.

Seven Steps to Starting a Peer Buddy Program

Step 1: Develop a one-credit course

☐ Incorporate into your school's curriculum a peer tutoring course that allows peer buddies to spend at least one period each day with their partners in special education.

☐ Begin building a base of support with the administration, guidance personnel, and teachers in your school for the inclusion of students receiving special education services in general education activities.

☐ Follow the established procedures of the local and state educational agencies when you apply for the new course offering.

☐ Include the course description in your school's schedule of classes.

Step 2: Recruit peer buddies

☐ Actively recruit peer buddies during the first year. After that, peer buddies will recruit for you.

☐ Include announcements, posters, articles in the school newspaper and PTA newsletter, videotapes on the school's closed-circuit television, and peer buddies speaking in school clubs and classes.

☐ Present information about the new program at a faculty meeting.

☐ Start slowly while you establish the course expectations.

Step 3: Screen and match students

☐ Have guidance counselors refer students who have interest, good attendance, and adequate grades.

☐ Arrange for students to interview with the special education teachers.

☐ Have students provide information regarding their past experience with students with diverse abilities and about clubs or activities that they are involved in and that their partners could join.

☐ Allow students to observe in the classroom to learn about the role of a peer buddy and whether they would be an appropriate match for the class.

Form 3.3.   Seven Steps to Starting a Peer Buddy Program. (From "They are my best friends": Peer buddies promote inclusion in high school, by Hughes, C., Guth, C., Hall, S., Presley, J., Dye, M., & Byers, C., *TEACHING Exceptional Children, 31*(5), 32–37. Copyright 1999 by The Council for Exceptional Children. Adapted with permission.)

The Transition Handbook: Strategies High School Teachers Use that Work!
by Carolyn Hughes, Ph.D., and Erik W. Carter, M.Ed.
© 2000 by Paul H. Brookes Publishing Co., Baltimore

(continued)

Form 3.3. *(continued)*

Step 4: *Teach peer buddies to use instructional strategies*

☐ Model the use of prompting and reinforcement techniques.

☐ Conduct a peer buddy orientation that includes the concept of "people first," disability awareness, communication strategies, and suggested activities.

☐ Communicate teachers' expectations for the peer buddy course including attendance and grading policies.

☐ Provide suggestions for dealing with inappropriate behavior, setting limits, and modifying general education curricula.

Step 5: *Evaluate the program*

☐ Schedule observations and feedback sessions with peer buddies to address their questions or concerns.

☐ Provide feedback on their interaction skills, time management, use of positive reinforcement, and activities engaged in with their partners.

☐ Have peer buddies keep a daily journal of their activities and reflections, which should be reviewed weekly by the classroom teacher.

☐ Establish a Peer Buddy Club, which allows students to share experiences and ideas as well as gives the teacher an opportunity to offer ongoing training and feedback.

Step 6: *Hold a Lunch Bunch*

☐ Invite peer buddies to join students in special education for lunch in the cafeteria.

☐ Encourage the peer buddies to invite their general education friends to join the group, increasing social contacts for their partners.

☐ Remind general education students who, because of class conflicts, are unable to enroll in the course to join the Lunch Bunch.

Step 7: *Establish an advisory board*

☐ Develop an advisory board that includes students (peer buddies and partners), students' parents, participating general and special education teachers, administrators, and guidance counselors.

☐ Include community representatives to expand the Peer Buddy Program to community-based activities, such as work experiences.

☐ Meet at least once each semester to obtain insight and suggestions for evaluating and improving the program. Thank all members for their participation.

Community Activity Participation Form

Student: _____   **Month:** _____

Activity	Monday	Tuesday	Wednesday	Thursday	Friday	Weekends	Total

Form 3.4.   Community Activities Form.

The Transition Handbook: Strategies High School Teachers Use that Work!
by Carolyn Hughes, Ph.D., and Erik W. Carter, M.Ed.
© 2000 by Paul H. Brookes Publishing Co., Baltimore

Job Analysis Survey

Worksite: _____   **Date:** _____

Basic Information

1. General job type or position: _____

2. Job tasks involved in the position: _____

_____

_____

_____

Three most time-consuming job tasks: _____

3. Worksite location and access to public transportation: _____

_____

_____

_____

Task Characteristics

Job task requirements: _____

_____

_____

_____

General mobility requirements: _____

_____

_____

Physical demands—gross motor: _____

_____

_____

Physical demands—fine motor: _____

_____

_____

Length of work tasks: _____

_____

Form 4.1.   Job Analysis Survey. (From Renzaglia, A., & Hutchins, M. [1995]. Materials developed for *A model for longitudinal vocational programming for students with moderate and severe disabilities.* Grant funded by the U.S. Department of Education, Office of Special Education and Rehabilitation Services; adapted by permission.)

The Transition Handbook: Strategies High School Teachers Use that Work!
by Carolyn Hughes, Ph.D., and Erik W. Carter, M.Ed.
© 2000 by Paul H. Brookes Publishing Co., Baltimore

Variability of daily job tasks: _____

Problem-solving requirements: _____

Production rate requirements: _____

Work product quality requirements: _____

Continuous working requirements: _____

Task-Related Characteristics

Co-worker presence/task-related contact: _____

Nontask-related social contacts while working: _____

Social atmosphere of worksite: _____

(continued)

Form 4.1.   *(continued)*

Interactions with customers: _____

_____

_____

_____

Supervisory contact: _____

_____

_____

_____

Environmental Characteristics
Distraction level (noise/visual): _____

_____

_____

_____

Comfort factors (temperature, space available, lighting, odor, sensory):

_____

_____

_____

_____

Equipment/tool use requirements: _____

_____

_____

_____

Natural Supports
Environmental support: _____

_____

_____

_____

_____

Supervisor and co-worker support: _____

_____

_____

_____

_____

_____

Job Task Analysis

Approximate times   **Tasks performed**

1 _____   _____

2 _____   _____

3 _____   _____

4 _____   _____

5 _____   _____

6 _____   _____

7 _____   _____

8 _____   _____

9 _____   _____

10 _____   _____

11 _____   _____

12 _____   _____

13 _____   _____

14 _____   _____

15 _____   _____

16 _____   _____

17 _____   _____

18 _____   _____

19 _____   _____

20 _____   _____

21 _____   _____

22 _____   _____

23 _____   _____

24 _____   _____

25 _____   _____

26 _____   _____

27 _____   _____

_____   _____
Person completing the form   **Signature of employer or supervisor**

Work Performance Evaluation

Student: _____ Date: _____ Worksite: _____ Evaluator: _____

Job task requirements	Performance	Implications

General mobility requirements	Performance	Implications

Form 4.2. Work Performance Evaluation. (From Renzaglia, A.,, & Hutchins, M. [1995]. Materials developed for *A model for longitudinal vocational programming for students with moderate and severe disabilities.* Grant funded by the U.S. Department of Education, Office of Special Education and Rehabilitation Services.; adapted by permission.)

The Transition Handbook: Strategies High School Teachers Use that Work!
by Carolyn Hughes, Ph.D., and Erik W. Carter, M.Ed.
© 2000 by Paul H. Brookes Publishing Co., Baltimore

Physical demands—Gross motor	Performance	Implications

Physical demands—Fine motor	Performance	Implications

Length of work tasks	Performance	Implications

(continued)

Form 4.2. *(continued)*

Variability of daily job tasks	Performance	Implications
Problem-solving requirements	**Performance**	**Implications**
Production rate requirements	**Performance**	**Implications**

320

Work product quality requirements	Performance	Implications
Continuous working requirements	Performance	Implications
Co-worker presence/task-related	Performance	Implications

(continued)

321

Form 4.2. *(continued)*

Nontask-related social contacts	Performance	Implications
Social atmosphere of worksite	Performance	Implications
Interactions with customers	Performance	Implications

322

Supervisory contact	Performance	Implications
Distraction level	Performance	Implications
Comfort factors	Performance	Implications

(continued)

323

Form 4.2. *(continued)*

Equipment/tool use requirements	Performance	Implications
Environmental support	Performance	Implications
Supervisor and co-worker support	Performance	Implications

324

Individual Support Plan

Student: _____   Date: _____

Component	Action steps

Form 4.3.   Individual Support Plan. (From *Beyond high school: Transition from school to work,* by F.R. Rusch & J.G. Chadsey. © 1998. Adapted with permission of Wadsworth Publishing, a division of Thomson Learning. Fax 800 730-2215.)

The Transition Handbook: Strategies High School Teachers Use that Work!
by Carolyn Hughes, Ph.D., and Erik W. Carter, M.Ed.
© 2000 by Paul H. Brookes Publishing Co., Baltimore

Individual Social Support Plan

Student: _____   Age: _____   Date: _____

Support needs	Support strategy	Person or agency responsible	Outcome	Target date	Evaluation method
Vocational needs					
Community needs					
Residential needs					
School needs					

Form 5.1.   Individual Social Support Plan.

The Transition Handbook: Strategies High School Teachers Use that Work!
by Carolyn Hughes, Ph.D., and Erik W. Carter, M.Ed.
© 2000 by Paul H. Brookes Publishing Co., Baltimore

Event Recording Datasheet

Student: _____   **Date:** _____

Location: _____   **Observer:** _____

Activity: _____

Total					

Comments: _____

_____

_____

Form 6.1.   Event Recording Datasheet.

The Transition Handbook: Strategies High School Teachers Use that Work!
by Carolyn Hughes, Ph.D., and Erik W. Carter, M.Ed.
© 2000 by Paul H. Brookes Publishing Co., Baltimore

Interval Recording Datasheet

Students: _____   **Date:** _____

Location: _____   **Observer:** _____

Activity: _____

Interval: _____						
Total						
% of intervals						

✓ = Occurrence   — = Nonoccurrence

Comments: _____

_____

_____

Form 6.2   Interval Recording Datasheet.

The Transition Handbook: Strategies High School Teachers Use that Work!
by Carolyn Hughes, Ph.D., and Erik W. Carter, M.Ed.
© 2000 by Paul H. Brookes Publishing Co., Baltimore

Task Analysis

Student: _____

Setting: _____

Goal: _____

_____

Coding:
4 = Independent response
3 = Verbal prompt
2 = Gestural prompt
1 = Physical prompt

Steps	Trial									
	1	2	3	4	5	6	7	8	9	10
20										
19										
18										
17										
16										
15										
14										
13										
12										
11										
10										
9										
8										
7										
6										
5										
4										
3										
2										
1										
Total										
Date										

Form 6.3.   Task Analysis.

The Transition Handbook: Strategies High School Teachers Use that Work!
by Carolyn Hughes, Ph.D., and Erik W. Carter, M.Ed.
© 2000 by Paul H. Brookes Publishing Co., Baltimore

Employee Social Skills Checklist

Student: _____   **Interview/observation date:** _____

Work environment: _____

Skill	Always	Sometimes	Never	N/A	Comments
➢ Does the student greet co-workers when arriving to or leaving work?	☐	☐	☐	☐	
➢ Is the student punctual and on time?	☐	☐	☐	☐	
➢ Does the student look approachable (e.g., smiling, well-groomed)?	☐	☐	☐	☐	
➢ Is the student polite (e.g., jokes, uses social amenities)?	☐	☐	☐	☐	
➢ Does the student greet/interact with customers in an acceptable way?	☐	☐	☐	☐	
➢ Does the student greet/interact with co-workers in an acceptable way?	☐	☐	☐	☐	
➢ Is the student meeting expected work performance goals?	☐	☐	☐	☐	
➢ Does the student turn to co-workers for assistance when needed?	☐	☐	☐	☐	
➢ Does the student give and receive directions/instructions well?	☐	☐	☐	☐	
➢ Does the student give and receive praise/criticism well?	☐	☐	☐	☐	
➢ Does the student get along well with his or her peers?	☐	☐	☐	☐	
➢ Does the student seem to fit in with a social group at work?	☐	☐	☐	☐	
➢ Does the student spend break or lunch with co-workers?	☐	☐	☐	☐	
➢ Does the student interact with co-workers outside work?	☐	☐	☐	☐	

Form 6.4.   Employee Social Skills Checklist.

The Transition Handbook: Strategies High School Teachers Use that Work!
by Carolyn Hughes, Ph.D., and Erik W. Carter, M.Ed.
© 2000 by Paul H. Brookes Publishing Co., Baltimore

Home Inventory Form

Personal Information

Student: _____ Age: _____ Interview date: _____

Where do you live? ____ House _____ Apartment **How long have you lived there?** _____

Who lives with you? _____

Do you have relatives who live near you? _____ Who? _____

Likes and Dislikes

	What do you like?	What do you dislike?
Foods (snacks, treats, special diet)		
Activities (hobbies, sports, places, events)		
Work (jobs, chores, volunteer events)		

Concerns

Are there issues that keep you from enjoying community events?
(e.g., toileting accidents, hitting others, loud screaming)

What issues?	Where do they occur?	What is the result?

Form 6.5.   Home Inventory Form. (From Allen, W.T. [1988]. *Read my lips: It's choice*....St. Paul, MN: Governor's Council on Developmental Disabilities, Department of Administration; adapted by permission of Allen, Shea & Associates.)

The Transition Handbook: Strategies High School Teachers Use that Work!
by Carolyn Hughes, Ph.D., and Erik W. Carter, M.Ed.
© 2000 by Paul H. Brookes Publishing Co., Baltimore

(continued)

Form 6.5.   *(continued)*

Your Community

A "map" of your community will help develop a picture of where neighbors live, work, and play. Make sure to fill this out completely.

Streets	**Which streets in your neighborhood do you use frequently?**	**How do you use them?**			**Are there . . .**	
		Walk	Car	Bus	Signals	Crosswalks

Family & Friends	**Whom do you visit?**	**How far away?**		**How do you get there?**			**How often do you visit?**			
		1–5 blocks	5 + blocks	Walk	Car	Bus	Daily	Each week	Each month	Other

Community Activities	**Where do you go?**	**How do you get there?**			**When?**		**How often do you go?**			
		Walk	Car	Bus	Week-day	Week-end	Daily	Each week	Each month	Other

Strengths and Training Needs

Here is an opportunity to talk about what you like to do, the talents that you have, and which supports might help you become more independent in the community!

Circle area: Community   Recreation/Leisure   Home   Work   Other

Strengths

What activities do you do?	What is involved in that activity?

Training Needs

What things would you like to learn to do?	What things get in the way?

Potential supports: _____

_____

_____

_____

(continued)

Form 6.5. *(continued)*

What do we know . . .

. . . about your community?

. . . about your likes and dislikes?

. . . about your strengths?

What things have you decided you would like to work on with us?

Community	•
	•
	•
	•
Recreation/leisure	•
	•
	•
	•
Home	•
	•
	•
	•
Work	•
	•
	•
	•
Other	•
	•
	•
	•

Modified Grading System for Students in General Education Classrooms

Grading period (circle one): 1   2   3   4   5   6

Student: _____

General education teacher: _____

Course title: _____

Suggested modifications: _____

Objectives	Date											Average
	8/11	8/14	8/19	8/21	8/25	8/27	9/1	9/4	9/8	9/10	9/16	

Scoring: You may assign either a letter grade or a numerical grade.

Suggested Codes:

I = 100   Meets objective independently
P = 90   Needs a prompt to meet objective
S = 80   Requires several prompts to meet objective
U = 70   Unable to meet objective

Directions: Each time you grade the class members on assigned work or tests, you may choose to grade this student on the above modified criteria, if appropriate. Please return this sheet to me at the end of the grading period. Thank you!

Signed: _____
Special Education Teacher

Form 6.6.   Modified Grading System for Students in General Education Classrooms.

The Transition Handbook: Strategies High School Teachers Use that Work!
by Carolyn Hughes, Ph.D., and Erik W. Carter, M.Ed.
© 2000 by Paul H. Brookes Publishing Co., Baltimore

335

Teaching and Evaluating Self-Management

Student: _____   **Environment:** _____

1. **Identify the problem:**

   _____

   _____

   _____

2. **Verify the problem:**

   _____

   _____

   _____

3. **Determine acceptability:**

   _____

   _____

   _____

4. **Identify natural supports in the environment:**

   _____

   _____

   _____

5. **Select a self-management strategy:**

   _____

   _____

   _____

6. **Teach self-management skills:**

   _____

   _____

   _____

7. **Evaluate student's performance:**

   _____

   _____

Form 7.1.   Teaching and Evaluating Self-Management. (From "Utilizing self-management to teach independence on the job," by Lagomarcino, T.R., Hughes, C., & Rusch, F.R., *Education and Training in Mental Retardation, 24*, 1989, 142. Copyright 1989 by The Council for Exceptional Children. Adapted with permission.)

Self-Instruction Training Sequence

Directions: Describe the behaviors to be performed for each of these steps:

1. Teacher models target behavior while self-instructing aloud:

_____

_____

2. Student performs target behavior while teacher instructs aloud:

_____

_____

_____

3. Student performs target behavior while self-instructing aloud:

_____

_____

_____

4. If appropriate, teach the student to whisper or "think" the self-instructions:

_____

_____

Self-Instruction Statements

Directions: Describe what the student will say (or do) for each of these statements:

1. Identifying the problem: _____

_____

2. Stating the possible responses to the problem: _____

_____

3. Evaluating the response: _____

_____

4. Self-reinforcing: _____

Form 7.2.   Self-Instruction Training Sequence. (From *Student directed learning: Teaching self-determination skills,* by M. Agran. © 1997. Adapted with permission of Wadsworth Publishing, a division of Thomson Learning. Fax 800 730-2215.)

Task: _____

1. _____ ☐	2. _____ ☐	3. _____ ☐
4. _____ ☐	5. _____ ☐	6. _____ ☐
7. _____ ☐	8. _____ ☐	9. _____ ☐

Goal:
◎ _____

Steps completed:
1 2 3 4 5 6 7 8 9

Did I meet my goal?
☺   ☹

Form 7.3.   Picture Prompt Form

The Transition Handbook: Strategies High School Teachers Use that Work!
by Carolyn Hughes, Ph.D., and Erik W. Carter, M.Ed.
© 2000 by Paul H. Brookes Publishing Co., Baltimore

Today's Schedule

Student: _____   **Day(s):** _____

Time	What should I do?	Time	What should I do?
(clock)	_____	(clock)	_____
(clock)	_____	(clock)	_____
(clock)	_____	(clock)	_____
(clock)	_____	(clock)	_____
(clock)	_____	(clock)	_____
(clock)	_____	(clock)	_____

Form 7.4.   Today's Schedule (with analog clock).

The Transition Handbook: Strategies High School Teachers Use that Work!
by Carolyn Hughes, Ph.D., and Erik W. Carter, M.Ed.
© 2000 by Paul H. Brookes Publishing Co., Baltimore

Today's Schedule

Student: _____   **Day(s):** _____

Time	What should I do?	Time	What should I do?
[:]	_____	[:]	_____
[:]	_____	[:]	_____
[:]	_____	[:]	_____
[:]	_____	[:]	_____
[:]	_____	[:]	_____
[:]	_____	[:]	_____

Form 7.5.   Today's Schedule (with digital clock).

Daily Checklist

Student: _____   **Week:** _____

Activity: _____

What do I need to do?	Monday	Tuesday	Wednesday	Thursday	Friday
Total completed:					

✓ = I did this!!!   X = I did not do this!

Form 7.6.   Daily Checklist.

The Transition Handbook: Strategies High School Teachers Use that Work!
by Carolyn Hughes, Ph.D., and Erik W. Carter, M.Ed.
© 2000 by Paul H. Brookes Publishing Co., Baltimore

Self-Recording Chart

Name: _____   **Date:** _____

Activity: _____

Time	Behaviors			
My total is:				
My goal is:				
Was goal met?	YES NO	YES NO	YES NO	YES NO

My goal for next time is . . .				

_____   _____
Student's Signature   **Teacher's Signature**

Form 7.7.   Self-Recording Chart.

The Transition Handbook: Strategies High School Teachers Use that Work!
by Carolyn Hughes, Ph.D., and Erik W. Carter, M.Ed.
© 2000 by Paul H. Brookes Publishing Co., Baltimore

Choice-Making Opportunities

Student: _____   Date: _____

Location	Check one ✓				What opportunities for choice were there?	What choice was made (including no choice)?	Was assistance provided? How?
	School	Work	Community	Home			
Monday							
Tuesday							
Wednesday							

Form 8.1.   Choice-Making Opportunities.

The Transition Handbook: Strategies High School Teachers Use that Work!
by Carolyn Hughes, Ph.D., and Erik W. Carter, M.Ed.
© 2000 by Paul H. Brookes Publishing Co., Baltimore

(continued)

Form 8.1.   *(continued)*

Location	Check one ✓	What opportunities for choice were there?	What choice was made (including no choice)?	Was assistance provided? How?
Thursday	Home / Community / Work / School			
Friday	Home / Community / Work / School			
Weekend	Home / Community / Work / School			

Student Job History

Student: _____

		Dates:		to		Dates:		to		Dates:		to	
Basic information	Worksite												
	General job types or positions experienced												
	Job tasks experienced												
	Location and transportation	1	2	3	N/A	1	2	3	N/A	1	2	3	N/A
Task characteristics	Job task requirements	1	2	3	N/A	1	2	3	N/A	1	2	3	N/A
	General mobility	1	2	3	N/A	1	2	3	N/A	1	2	3	N/A
	Gross motor demands	1	2	3	N/A	1	2	3	N/A	1	2	3	N/A
	Fine motor demands	1	2	3	N/A	1	2	3	N/A	1	2	3	N/A
	Length of work tasks	1	2	3	N/A	1	2	3	N/A	1	2	3	N/A
	Variability of daily job tasks	1	2	3	N/A	1	2	3	N/A	1	2	3	N/A
	Problem-solving requirements	1	2	3	N/A	1	2	3	N/A	1	2	3	N/A
	Production rate	1	2	3	N/A	1	2	3	N/A	1	2	3	N/A
	Work product quality	1	2	3	N/A	1	2	3	N/A	1	2	3	N/A
	Continuous working requirements	1	2	3	N/A	1	2	3	N/A	1	2	3	N/A
Task-related characteristics	Co-worker presence	1	2	3	N/A	1	2	3	N/A	1	2	3	N/A
	Nontask social contacts	1	2	3	N/A	1	2	3	N/A	1	2	3	N/A
	Social atmosphere of worksite	1	2	3	N/A	1	2	3	N/A	1	2	3	N/A
	Interaction with customers	1	2	3	N/A	1	2	3	N/A	1	2	3	N/A
	Supervisory contact	1	2	3	N/A	1	2	3	N/A	1	2	3	N/A
Environmental characteristics	Distraction level	1	2	3	N/A	1	2	3	N/A	1	2	3	N/A
	Comfort factors	1	2	3	N/A	1	2	3	N/A	1	2	3	N/A
	Equipment/tool use	1	2	3	N/A	1	2	3	N/A	1	2	3	N/A
Natural supports	Environmental support	1	2	3	N/A	1	2	3	N/A	1	2	3	N/A
	Supervisor/co-worker support	1	2	3	N/A	1	2	3	N/A	1	2	3	N/A

Form 8.2.   Student Job History. (From Renzaglia, A., Hutchins, M. [1995]. *A model for longitudinal vocational programming for students with moderate and severe disabilities.* Grant funded by the U.S. Department of Education, Office of Special Education and Rehabilitation Services; adapted by permission.) (Key: 1 = excellent job match; 2 = fair job match; 3 = poor job match; N/A = not applicable.)

The Transition Handbook: Strategies High School Teachers Use that Work!
by Carolyn Hughes, Ph.D., and Erik W. Carter, M.Ed.
© 2000 by Paul H. Brookes Publishing Co., Baltimore

The Self-Directed IEP
Self-Assessment

Name: _____   Date: _____

	Step	How did I do?			Did I have the chance?		
1	Begin the meeting by stating its purpose.	1	2	3	1	2	3
2	Introduce everyone I invited.	1	2	3	1	2	3
3	Review my past goals and performance.	1	2	3	1	2	3
4	Ask for others' feedback.	1	2	3	1	2	3
5	State my school and transitional goals.	1	2	3	1	2	3
6	Ask questions if I did not understand.	1	2	3	1	2	3
7	Address differences in opinion.	1	2	3	1	2	3
8	State what supports I'll need.	1	2	3	1	2	3
9	Summarize my goals.	1	2	3	1	2	3
10	Close the meeting by thanking everyone.	1	2	3	1	2	3
11	Work on my IEP goals all year.	1	2	3	1	2	3
		1 Didn't do it **2** So-so **3** Great!!!			**1** Not at all **2** So-so **3** Yes!!!		

Form 8.3.   The Self-Directed IEP. (From Martin, J.E., Huber Marshall, L., Maxson, L.L., & Jerman, P.A. [1996]. *Self-directed IEP.* Longmont, CO: Sopris West; adapted by permission.)

The Transition Handbook: Strategies High School Teachers Use that Work!
by Carolyn Hughes, Ph.D., and Erik W. Carter, M.Ed.
© 2000 by Paul H. Brookes Publishing Co., Baltimore

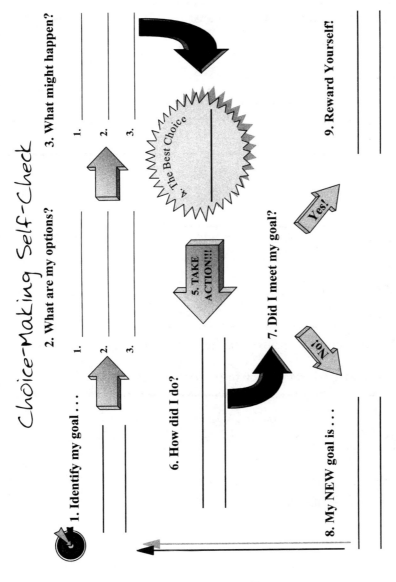

Choice-Making Self-Check

1. Identify my goal . . .
_____
_____

2. What are my options?
1. _____
2. _____
3. _____

3. What might happen?
1. _____
2. _____
3. _____

The Best Choice
_____

5. TAKE ACTION!!!

6. How did I do?
_____
_____

7. Did I meet my goal?

Yes!

No!

8. My NEW goal is . . .
_____
_____

9. Reward Yourself!
_____
_____

Form 8.4. Choice-Making Self-Check. (From Adaptability instruction: The goal of transitional programming, by Mithaug, D.E., Martin, J.E., & Agran, M., *Exceptional Children, 53,* 1987, 500–505. Copyright 1987 by The Council for Exceptional Children. Adapted with permission.)

The Transition Handbook: Strategies High School Teachers Use that Work!
by Carolyn Hughes, Ph.D., and Erik W. Carter, M.Ed.
© 2000 by Paul H. Brookes Publishing Co., Baltimore

Choice-Making Self-Check

Student: _____   **Date:** _____

	Steps	Did I do it?	
Decision making	**1. Identify my goal:** *My goal is:* _____	Yes	No
	2. List my options: a. _____ b. _____ c. _____	Yes	No
	3. List possible consequences of the options: a. _____ b. _____ c. _____	Yes	No
	4. The best choice:	Yes	No
Independent performance	**5. Act on the option I chose.**	Yes	No
Self-evaluation	**6. Evaluate my performance:** *How did I do?* _____	Yes	No
	7. Decide if I met my goal: *Was goal met?*	Yes	No
Adjustment	**8. If I didn't meet my goal, go back to Step 1 and try again!**	Yes	No
	9. If I did meet my goal, remember to reward myself.	Yes	No

Form 8.5.   Another Choice-Making Self-Check. (From Adaptability instruction: The goal of transitional programming, by Mithaug, D.E., Martin, J.E., & Agran, M., *Exceptional Children, 53,* 1987, 500–505. Copyright 1987 by The Council for Exceptional Children. Adapted with permission.)

Social Interaction Observation Form

Student: _____   **Week of:** _____

Activity/class							
Monday							
Tuesday							
Wednesday							
Thursday							
Friday							

Form 9.1.   Social Interaction Observation Form. Record each interaction with a general education peer by listing the name of the peer and the estimated length of the interaction. (Key: A = less than 1 minute; B = 1–5 minutes; C = more than 5 minutes.)

The Transition Handbook: Strategies High School Teachers Use that Work!
by Carolyn Hughes, Ph.D., and Erik W. Carter, M.Ed.
© 2000 by Paul H. Brookes Publishing Co., Baltimore

Social Opportunities Chart

Student: _____

Date: _____

Activity/class	Time	Opportunities for social interaction	Quality of social interaction	Supports needed	Supports available
		1 2 3 4 5 none few many	1 2 3 4 5 not so-so great good		
		1 2 3 4 5 none few many	1 2 3 4 5 not so-so great good		
		1 2 3 4 5 none few many	1 2 3 4 5 not so-so great good		
		1 2 3 4 5 none few many	1 2 3 4 5 not so-so great good		
		1 2 3 4 5 none few many	1 2 3 4 5 not so-so great good		
		1 2 3 4 5 none few many	1 2 3 4 5 not so-so great good		
		1 2 3 4 5 none few many	1 2 3 4 5 not so-so great good		
		1 2 3 4 5 none few many	1 2 3 4 5 not so-so great good		

Form 9.2.   Social Opportunities Chart.

The Transition Handbook: Strategies High School Teachers Use that Work!
by Carolyn Hughes, Ph.D., and Erik W. Carter, M.Ed.
© 2000 by Paul H. Brookes Publishing Co., Baltimore

Peer Buddy Social Skills Teaching Checklist

Student: _____   **Time start:** _____

Date: _____   **Time stop:** _____

Observer: _____   **Number of minutes:** _____

Peer buddy: _____   **Location:** _____

Rationale

☐ **1.** Peer buddy explains that he or she wants to help student learn to talk to his or her friends at school.

☐ **2.** Peer buddy explains that he or she is going to teach student a way to talk.

Training Sequence

☐ **3.** Peer buddy models using the book.

☐ **4.** Peer buddy goes through all of the pictures in the book.

☐ **5.** Peer buddy looks at each picture and asks the question.

☐ **6.** Peer buddy instructs student while student uses book to ask questions.

☐ **7.** Student uses book to ask questions.

☐ **8.** Peer buddy provides lots of verbal praise for using book.

☐ **9.** Peer buddy corrects student if student misses a step.

☐ **10.** Peer buddy prompts student to use book.

Reminder

☐ **11.** Peer buddy reminds student to use book when student wants to talk to somebody.

☐ **12.** Peer buddy reminds student to start talking and do all of the talking when student talks to his or her next friend.

Comments: _____

_____

_____

_____

_____

Form 9.3.   Peer Buddy Social Skills Teaching Checklist. (From Hughes, C., Harmer, M.L., Killian, D.J., & Niarhos, F. [1995]. The effects of multiple exemplar self-instructional training on high school students' generalized conversational interactions. *Journal of Applied Behavior Analysis, 28,* 206–207. Copyright *Journal of Applied Behavior Analysis;* adapted by permission.)

The Transition Handbook: Strategies High School Teachers Use that Work!
by Carolyn Hughes, Ph.D., and Erik W. Carter, M.Ed.
© 2000 by Paul H. Brookes Publishing Co., Baltimore

Peer Perception Questionnaire

Student: _____   **Date:** _____

Partner: _____   **Location:** _____

INSTRUCTIONS: Please circle the number that best represents the way you feel about the interaction you just experienced with your partner.

	Never	Rarely	Sometimes	Usually	Always
Did you feel that your partner interacted with you appropriately?	1	2	3	4	5
Did you enjoy this interaction?	1	2	3	4	5
Would you like to have this kind of interaction again?	1	2	3	4	5
Do you think that your partner enjoyed this interaction?	1	2	3	4	5
When you are with your friends, do you have similar interactions?	1	2	3	4	5

Comments: _____

_____

_____

Form 9.4.   Peer Perception Questionnaire.

The Transition Handbook: Strategies High School Teachers Use that Work!
by Carolyn Hughes, Ph.D., and Erik W. Carter, M.Ed.
© 2000 by Paul H. Brookes Publishing Co., Baltimore

R e s o u r c e s

Assessment
Books
Instruments
Videotapes

Careers and Employment
Books
Resource Guides
Videotapes

Collaboration and Family Involvement
Books
Curriculum
Videotapes

Community Living
Books
Resource Guides
Videotapes

Diversity Awareness
Books
Videotapes

Inclusion
Books
Resource Guides
Videotapes

Legislation
Books
Videotapes

Leisure and Recreation
Books

Self-Determination
Books
Curricula
Resource Guides
Videotapes

Social Support
Books
Curricula
Videotapes

Technology and Augmentative Communication
Books
Videotapes

Transition Planning
Books
Resource Guides

Journals and Newsletters

Publishers

Organizations

Transition Link Web Site

ASSESSMENT

Books

Bigge, J.L., Stump, C.S., Spagna, M.E., & Silberman, R.K. (1999). *Curriculum, assessment, and instruction for students with disabilities.* Belmont, CA: Wadsworth.

Browder, D.M. (1991). *Assessment of individuals with severe disabilities: An applied behavior approach to life skills assessment* (2nd ed.). Baltimore: Paul H. Brookes Publishing Co.

Bullis, M., & Davis, C.D. (Eds.). (1999). *Functional assessment in transition and rehabilitation for adolescents and adults with learning disorders.* Austin, TX: PRO-ED.

Burns, E. (1998). *Test accommodations for students with disabilities.* Springfield, IL: Charles C Thomas.

Choate, J.S., Enright, B.E., Miller, L.J., Poteet, J.A., & Rakes, T.A. (1995). *Curriculum-based assessment and programming* (3rd ed.). Needham Heights, MA: Allyn & Bacon.

Clark, G.M. (1998). *Assessment for transition planning: A guide for special education teachers and related service personnel* (PRO-ED series on transition). Austin, TX: PRO-ED.

Dais, T.A., & Kohler, P.D. (1995). *Review of transition-related assessment instruments.* Champaign: University of Illinois at Urbana–Champaign, Transition Research Institute.

DuPaul, G.J., & Stoner, G. (1994). *ADHD in the schools: Assessment and intervention strategies.* New York: Guilford Press.

Gupta, R.M., & Coxhead, P. (Eds.). (1988). *Cultural diversity and learning efficiency: Recent developments in assessment.* New York: St. Martin's Press.

Maddox, T. (Ed.). (1997). *Tests: A comprehensive reference for assessments in psychology, education, and business* (4th ed.). Austin, TX: PRO-ED.

Overton, T. (1996). *Assessment in special education: An applied approach* (2nd ed.). Upper Saddle River, NJ: Prentice-Hall.

Power, P.W. (1991). *A guide to vocational assessment* (2nd ed.). Austin, TX: PRO-ED.

Repp, A.C., & Horner, R.H. (1999). *Functional analysis of problem behavior: From effective assessment to effective support.* Belmont, CA: Wadsworth.

Sitlington, P.L., Neubert, D.A., Begun, W., Lombard, R.C., & Leconte, P.J. (1996). *Assess for success: Handbook on transition assessment.* Reston, VA: Council for Exceptional Children, Division on Career Development and Transition.

Taylor, R.L. (1997). *Assessment of exceptional students: Educational and psychological procedures* (4th ed.). Needham Heights, MA: Allyn & Bacon.

Taylor, R.L. (Ed.). (1997). *Assessment of individuals with mental retardation.* San Diego: Singular Publishing Group.

Instruments

Brigance, A.H. (1995). *BRIGANCE Life Skills Inventory.* North Billerica, MA: Curriculum Associates.

Brolin, D.E. (1992). *Life-Centered Career Education (LCCE) Competency Assessment Knowledge Batteries.* Reston, VA: Council for Exceptional Children.

Brolin, D.E. (1992). *Life-Centered Career Education (LCCE) Competency Assessment Performance Batteries.* Reston, VA: Council for Exceptional Children.

Bruininks, R.H., Hill, B.K., Weatherman, R.F., & Woodcock, R.W. (1986). *Inventory for Client and Agency Planning (ICAP).* Allen, TX: DLM Teaching Resources.

Bruininks, R.H., Woodcock, R.W., Weatherman, R.F., & Hill, B.K. (1996). *Scales of Independent Behavior–Revised* (SIB–R). Chicago: Riverside.

Bullis, M. (1998). *Community-based social skill performance assessment tool.* Santa Barbara, CA: James Stanfield.

Clark, G.M., & Patton, J.R. (1997). *Transition planning inventory* (TPI). Austin, TX: PRO-ED.

Enderle, J., & Severson, S. (1996). *Enderle-Severson Transition Rating Scales–Revised* (ESTR–R). Moorhead, MN: Practical Press.

Gilliam, J.E. (1994). *Work adjustment inventory (WAI): Measures of job-related temperament.* Austin, TX: PRO-ED.

McCarney, S.B. (1989). *Transition behavior scale* (TBS). Columbia, MO: Hawthorne Educational Service.

Parker, R.M. (1991). *Occupational aptitude survey and interest schedule* (2nd ed.). Austin, TX: PRO-ED.

Sparrow, S.S., Balla, D.A., & Cicchetti, D.V. (1984). *Vineland Adaptive Behavior Scales.* Circle Pines, MN: American Guidance Service.

Videotapes

Ruesch, G., & Hartwig, E. (1998). *Functional behavioral assessments: How to do them right!* [Videotape]. (Available from LRP Publications, 747 Dresher Road, Suite 500, Post Office Box 980, Horsham, PA 19044-0980)

CAREERS AND EMPLOYMENT

Books

Benz, M.R., & Lindstrom, L.E. (1997). *Building school-to-work programs: Strategies for youth with special needs.* Austin, TX: PRO-ED.

Bragman, R.S. (1992). *Employment for individuals with disabilities: What every job-seeker with a disability needs to know.* Indian Rocks Beach, FL: Phillip Roy.

Brooke, V., Inge, K.J., Armstrong, A.J., & Wehman, P. (Eds.). (1997). *Supported employment handbook: A customer-driven approach for persons with significant disabilities.* Richmond: Virginia Commonwealth University.

Callahan, M.J., & Garner, J.B. (1997). *Keys to the workplace: Skills and supports for people with disabilities.* Baltimore: Paul H. Brookes Publishing Co.

Clark, G.M., & Kolstoe, O.P. (1995). *Career development and transition education for adolescents with disabilities* (2nd ed.). Needham Heights, MA: Allyn & Bacon.

DiLeo, D., Luecking, R., & Hathaway, S. (1995). *Natural supports in action: Strategies to facilitate employer supports of workers with disabilities.* St. Augustine, FL: Training Resources Network.

Hagner, D., & DiLeo, D. (1993). *Working together: Workplace culture, supported employment, and persons with disabilities.* Cambridge, MA: Brookline Books.

Kiernan, W.E., & Schalock, R.L. (Eds.). (1997). *Integrated employment: Current status and future directions.* Washington, DC: American Association on Mental Retardation.

Murphy, S.T., & Rogan, P.M. (1994). *Developing natural supports in the workplace: A practitioner's guide.* St. Augustine, FL: Training Resource Network.

Rusch, F.R. (1990). *Supported employment: Models, methods, and issues.* Pacific Grove, CA: Brooks/Cole.

Smith, M.D., Belcher, R.G., & Juhrs, P.D. (1995). *A guide to successful employment for individuals with autism.* Baltimore: Paul H. Brookes Publishing Co.

Szymanski, E.M., & Parker, R.M. (Eds.). (1996). *Work and disability: Issues and strategies in career development and job placement.* Austin, TX: PRO-ED.

Thuli, K.G., & Hong, E. (1998). *Employer toolkit.* Washington, DC: National Transition Alliance for Youth with Disabilities, Academy for Educational Development.

Wehman, P., & Kregel, J. (Eds.). (1998). *More than a job: Securing satisfying careers for people with disabilities.* Baltimore: Paul H. Brookes Publishing Co.

Wehman, P., Sale, P., & Parent, W. (1992). *Supported employment: Strategies for integration of workers with disabilities.* Austin, TX: PRO-ED.

Wolffe, K.E. (1997). *Career counseling for people with disabilities: A practical guide to finding employment.* Austin, TX: PRO-ED.

Resource Guides

Boevers, J., Erickson, R., Johnson, D., & Mangan, T. (1992). *Going to work: Profiles in supported employment.* Minneapolis: University of Minnesota, Institute on Community Integration.

HEATH Center. (1996). *HEATH national resource directory on postsecondary education and disability.* Washington, DC: Author.

Krawetz, N., & Wallace, T. (1994). *Exemplary programs for persons with disabilities in transition, supported employment, and parent–professional collaboration.* Minneapolis: University of Minnesota, Institute on Community Integration.

Supported Employment Parents Transition and Technical Assistance Project. (1996). *Supported employment and transition resources.* Minneapolis, MN: PACER.

Technical Assistance on Transition and the Rehabilitation Act Project. (1996). *Vocational Rehabilitation Resources Directory.* Minneapolis, MN: PACER.

University Affiliated Program of Rhode Island. (1997). *Employing people with disabilities: A resource guide for employers.* Providence: Rhode Island Supported Employment Program and University Affiliated Program of Rhode Island College.

Videotapes

The Arc (Producer). (1989). *Everybody wins! Tips for supervising the employee with mental retardation* [Videotape]. (Available from The Arc, 500 East Border Street, Suite 300, Arlington, TX 76010)

Attainment Company (Producer). (1996). *Every one can work: A look at successes in supported employment* [Videotape]. (Available from Paul H. Brookes Publishing Co., Post Office Box 10624, Baltimore, MD 21285-0624)

Films for the Humanities (Producer). (1991). *Disabilities in the workplace* [Videotape]. (Available from Program Development Associates, 5620 Business Avenue, Suite B, Cicero, NY 13039)

James Brodie Productions (Producer). (1997). *A different way of learning: The employee with a learning disability* [Videotape]. (Available from Paul H. Brookes Publishing Co., Post Office Box 10624, Baltimore, MD 21285-0624)

Mesa Developmental Services. (1999). *Training for job success: An employer's guide to training new employees with developmental disabilities* [Videotape]. (Available from Training Resource Network, Inc., Post Office Box 439, St. Augustine, FL 32085-0439)

Penn State Public Broadcasting (Producer). (1996). *Life link: A transition lab* [Videotape]. (Available from Program Development Associates, 5620 Business Avenue, Suite B, Cicero, NY 13039)

Working with pride: A video about the Rehabilitation Act [Videotape]. (1996). (Available from PACER Center, 4826 Chicago Avenue, Minneapolis, MN 55417)

WPSX-TV, Penn State Television (Producer), & Kranich, K. (Director). (1996). *The wild dream team* [Videotape]. (Available from MediaSales, Pennsylvania State University, 118 Wagner Building, University Park, PA 16802)

COLLABORATION AND FAMILY INVOLVEMENT

Books

Blalock, G., & Benz, M. (1999). *Using community transition teams to improve transition services* (PRO-ED series on transition). Austin, TX: PRO-ED.

Covert, S. (1997). *Whatever it takes! Excellence in family support: When families experience a disability.* St. Augustine, FL: Training Resource Network.

Cozzens, G., Dowdy, C., & Smith, T.E.C. (1999). *Adult agencies: Linkages for adolescents in transition* (PRO-ED series on transition). Austin, TX: PRO-ED.

Cramer, S.F. (1997). *Collaboration: A success strategy for special educators.* Needham Heights, MA: Allyn & Bacon.

DeFur, S., & Patton, J.R. (1999). *Transition and school-based services: Interdisciplinary perspectives for enhancing the transition process.* Austin, TX: PRO-ED.

Dettner, P., Dyck, N., & Thurston, L.P. (1999). *Consultation, collaboration, and teamwork for students with special needs* (3rd ed.). Needham Heights, MA: Allyn & Bacon.

Fabian, E.S., Luecking, R.G., & Tilson, G.P. (1996). *A working relationship: The job development specialist's guide to successful partnerships with business.* Baltimore: Paul H. Brookes Publishing Co.

Fishbaugh, M.S.E. (1997). *Models of collaboration.* Needham Heights, MA: Allyn & Bacon.

Friend, M., & Cook, L. (1995). *Interactions: Collaboration skills for school professionals* (2nd ed.). New York: Longman.

Fuller, M.L., & Olsen, G. (Eds.). (1998). *Home–school relations: Working successfully with parents and families.* Needham Heights, MA: Allyn & Bacon.

Harry, B., Kalyanpur, M., & Day, M. (1999). *Building cultural reciprocity with families: Case studies in special education.* Baltimore: Paul H. Brookes Publlishing Co.

Idol, L., Nevin, A., & Paolucci-Whitcomb, P. (1994). *Collaborative consultation* (2nd ed.). Austin, TX: PRO-ED.

Johnson, D., Kaufman, P., & Thompson, S. (1990). *Interagency planning for transition: Quality standards for improvement.* Minneapolis: University of Minnesota, Institute on Community Integration.

Kalyanpur, M., & Harry, B. (1999). *Culture in special education: Building reciprocal family–professional relationships.* Baltimore: Paul H. Brookes Publishing Co.

Mostert, M.P. (1998). *Interprofessional collaboration in schools: Practical action in the classroom.* Needham Heights, MA: Allyn & Bacon.

Rainforth, B., & York-Barr, J. (1997). *Collaborative teams for students with severe disabilities: Integrating therapy and educational services* (2nd ed.). Baltimore: Paul H. Brookes Publishing Co.

Rioux, J.W., & Berla, N. (1993). *Library of innovations series: Innovations in parent and family involvement.* Larchmont, NY: Eye on Education.

Rosenfield, S.A., & Gravois, T. (1996). *Instructional consultation teams: Collaborating for change.* New York: Guilford Press.

Shea, T.M., & Bauer, A.M. (1991). *Parents and teachers of children with exceptionalities: A handbook for collaboration* (2nd ed.). Needham Heights, MA: Allyn & Bacon.

Singer, G.H.S., Powers, L.E., & Olson, A.L. (Eds.). (1996). *Redefining family support: Innovations in public–private partnerships.* Baltimore: Paul H. Brookes Publishing Co.

Thomas, C.C., Correa, V.I., & Morsink, C.V. (1995). *Interactive teaming: Consultation and collaboration in special programs* (2nd ed.). Englewood Cliffs, NJ: Merrill.

Wehmeyer, M.L., Morningstar, M., & Husted, D. (1999). *Family involvement in transition planning* (PRO-ED series on transition). Austin, TX: PRO-ED.

Curriculum

West, J.F., Idol, L., & Cannon, G. (1989). *Collaboration in the schools: An inservice and preservice curriculum for teachers, support staff, and administrators.* Austin, TX: PRO-ED.

Videotapes

DO-IT (Producer). (1995). *Working together: Faculty and students with disabilities* [Videotape]. (Available from DO-IT, Box 354842, Seattle, WA 98195)

Horwath, A., & Banks, S. (1993). *A family focus* [Videotape]. Honolulu: University of Hawaii, Hawaii University Affiliated Program for Developmental Disabilities.

San Francisco Unified School District (Producer). (1997). *Collaborating for change: Creating an inclusive school* [Videotape]. (Available from Paul H. Brookes Publishing Co., Post Office Box 10624, Baltimore, MD 21285-0624)

COMMUNITY LIVING

Books

Allen, S.M., & Mor, V. (Eds.). (1998). *Living in the community with disability: Service needs, use and systems.* New York: Springer-Verlag.

Falvey, M.A. (1994). *Community-based curriculum: Instructional strategies for students with severe handicaps* (2nd ed.). Baltimore: Paul H. Brookes Publishing Co.

Hall, M., & Lambert, P. (1998). *Faith communities and inclusion of people with developmental disabilities.* Syracuse, NY: Syracuse University, Center on Human Policy.

Nadel, L., & Rosenthal, D. (Eds.). (1995). *Down syndrome: Living and learning in the community.* New York: John Wiley & Sons.

O'Brien, J., & O'Brien, C.L. (1996). *Members of each other: Building community in company with people with developmental disabilities.* Toronto, Ontario, Canada: Inclusion Press.

O'Brien, J., O'Brien, C.L., & Jacob, G. (1998). *Celebrating the ordinary: The emergence of options in community living as a thoughtful organization.* Toronto, Ontario, Canada: Inclusion Press.

Racino, J.A., Walker, P., O'Conner, S., & Taylor, S.J. (Eds.). (1993). *Housing, support, and community: Choices and strategies for adults with disabilities.* Baltimore: Paul H. Brookes Publishing Co.

Schalock, R.L. (Ed.). (1996–1997). *Quality of life* (Vols. 1 & 2). Washington, DC: American Association on Mental Retardation.

Thornburgh, G. (1997). *That all may worship: An interfaith welcome to people with disabilities.* Washington, DC: National Organization on Disability.

Resource Guides

American Network of Community Options & Resources. (1997). *Annotated bibliography: Life in the community.* Annandale, VA: Author.

The Arc. (1996). *Supported living resource list.* Arlington, TX: Author.

Hall, M., & Walker, P. (Eds.). (1998). *Annotated bibliography on community integration* (3rd ed.). Syracuse, NY: Syracuse University, Center on Human Policy.

Hewitt, S., Larson, S., & Lakin, K.C. (1997). *A guide to high quality direct service training resources* (2nd ed.). Minneapolis: University of Minnesota, Institute on Community Integration.

Hulgin, K., Shoultz, B., Walker, P., & Drake, S. (Eds.). (1996). *Innovative practices in supported living: An overview of organizations, issues, and resource materials.* Syracuse, NY: Syracuse University, Center on Human Policy.

Videotapes

Institute on Disability/UAP. (1994). *A home of my own* [Videotape]. (Available from Institute on Disability/UAP, 7 Leavitt Lane, Suite 101, Durham, NH 03824)

PennyCorner Press (Producer). (1996). *Fred's story* [Videotape]. (Available from Program Development Associates, 5620 Business Avenue, Suite B, Cicero, NY 13039)

DIVERSITY AWARENESS

Books

Banks, J.A. (1997). *Educating citizens in a multicultural society.* New York: Teachers College Press.

Deshler, D., Schumaker, J., Harris, K., & Graham, S. (Eds.). (1998). *Advances in teaching and learning series: Teaching every adolescent every day. Learning in diverse high school classrooms.* Cambridge, MA: Brookline Books.

Durán, E. (1992). *Vocational training and employment of the moderately and severely handicapped and autistic adolescent with particular emphasis to bilingual special education.* Springfield, IL: Charles C Thomas.

Durán, E. (1996). *Teaching students with moderate/severe disabilities, including autism: Strategies for second language learners in inclusive settings* (2nd ed.). Springfield, IL: Charles C Thomas.

Ford, B.A. (Ed.). (1997). *Multiple voices for ethnically diverse exceptional learners.* Reston, VA: Council for Exceptional Children, Division for Culturally and Linguistically Diverse Exceptional Learners.

Garcia, S.B. (Ed.). (1994). *Addressing cultural and linguistic diversity in special education: Issues and trends.* Reston, VA: Council for Exceptional Children, Division for Culturally and Linguistically Diverse Exceptional Learners.

Grossman, H. (1998). *Ending discrimination in special education.* Springfield, IL: Charles C Thomas.

Harry, B. (1997). *A teacher's handbook for cultural diversity, families, and the special education system: Communication and empowerment.* New York: Teachers College Press.

Kuehn, M.L. (1998). *Cultural diversity and disability: An annotated bibliography.* (Available from National Maternal and Child Health Clearinghouse, 2070 Chain Bridge Road, Suite 450, Vienna, VA 22182-2536)

Lynch, E.W., & Hanson, M.J. (Eds.). (1998). *Developing cross-cultural competence: A guide to working with children and their families* (2nd ed.). Baltimore: Paul H. Brookes Publishing Co.

Miller, N.B., & Sammons, C.C. (1999). *Everybody's different: Understanding and changing our reactions to disabilities.* Baltimore: Paul H. Brookes Publishing Co.

O'Conner, S. (1993). *Multiculturalism and disability: A collection of resources.* Syracuse, NY: Syracuse University, Center on Human Policy.

Roseberry-McKibbin, C. (1995). *Multicultural students with special language needs: Practical strategies for assessment and instruction.* Oceanside, CA: Academic Communication Associates.

Screen, R.M., & Anderson, N.B. (1994). *Multicultural perspectives in communication disorders.* San Diego: Singular Publishing Group.

Walker, S., Turner, K.A., Haile-Michael, M., Vincent, A., & Miles, M.D. (1995). *Disability and diversity: New leadership for a new era.* Syracuse, NY: Syracuse University, Center on Human Policy.

Walsh, J. (1995). *Mastering diversity: Managing for success under ADA & other anti-discrimination laws (Taking control).* Santa Monica, CA: Merritt.

Videotapes

Advocating Change Together (Producer). (1996). *Tools for change: Shaking off stereotypes* [Videotape]. (Available from Advocating Change Together, 1821 University Avenue, Suite 306 South, St. Paul, MN 55104)

Chen, D., Brekken, L., Chan, S., & Guarneri, G. (1997). *Project CRAFT: Culturally responsive and family focused training* [Videotape]. (Available from Paul H. Brookes Publishing Co., Post Office Box 10624, Baltimore, MD 21285-0624)

Films for the Humanities (Producer). (1996). *Without pity: A film about abilities* [Videotape]. (Available from Program Development Associates, 5620 Business Avenue, Suite B, Cicero, NY 13039)

Idea Bank (Producer), & Lambert, R. (Director). (1993). *A videoguide to (dis)ability awareness* [Videotape]. (Available from Program Development Associates, 5620 Business Avenue, Suite B, Cicero, NY 13039)

Marlin Westwood Training (Producer). (1991). *Breaking the attitude barrier: Learning to value people with disabilities* [Videotape]. (Available from MTI Film & Video, 108 Wilmont Road, Deerfield, IL 60015)

World Interdependence Fund (Producer). (1995). *Interdependence* [Videotape]. (Available from Inclusion Press, 24 Thome Crescent, Toronto, Ontario M6H 2S5, Canada)

INCLUSION

Books

Coutinho, M.J., & Repp, A.C. (Eds.). (1999). *Inclusion: The integration of students with disabilities.* Belmont, CA: Wadsworth.

Downing, J.E. (1996). *Including students with severe and multiple disabilities in typical classrooms: Practical strategies for teachers.* Baltimore: Paul H. Brookes Publishing Co.

Doyle, M.B. (1997). *The paraprofessional's guide to the inclusive classroom: Working as a team.* Baltimore: Paul H. Brookes Publishing Co.

Falvey, M.A. (Ed.). (1995). *Inclusive and heterogeneous schooling: Assessment, curriculum, and instruction.* Baltimore: Paul H. Brookes Publishing Co.

Fisher, D., Sax, C., & Pumpian, I. (1999). *Inclusive high schools: Learning from contemporary classrooms.* Baltimore: Paul H. Brookes Publishing Co.

Friend, M., & Bursuck, W.D. (1999). *Including students with special needs: A practical guide for classroom teachers* (2nd ed.). Needham Heights, MA: Allyn & Bacon.

Giangreco, M.F. (Ed.). (1997). *Quick-guides to inclusion: Ideas for educating students with disabilities.* Baltimore: Paul H. Brookes Publishing Co.

Giangreco, M.F. (Ed.). (1998). *Quick-guides to inclusion 2: Ideas for educating students with disabilities.* Baltimore: Paul H. Brookes Publishing Co.

Haring, N.G., & Romer, L.T. (Eds.). (1995). *Welcoming students who are deaf-blind into typical classrooms: Facilitating school participation, learning, and friendships.* Baltimore: Paul H. Brookes Publishing Co.

Jorgensen, C.M. (1997). *Restructuring high schools for all students: Taking inclusion to the next level.* Baltimore: Paul H. Brookes Publishing Co.

Lipsky, D.K., & Gartner, A. (1997). *Inclusion and school reform: Transforming America's class-rooms.* Baltimore: Paul H. Brookes Publishing Co.

Putnam, J.W. (Ed.). (1998). *Cooperative learning and strategies for inclusion: Celebrating diversity in the classroom* (2nd ed.). Baltimore: Paul H. Brookes Publishing Co.

Sage, D.D. (Ed.). (1997). *Inclusion in secondary schools: Bold initiatives challenging change.* Port Chester, NY: National Professional Resources.

Sapon-Shevin, M. (1999). *Because we can change the world: A practical guide to building cooperative, inclusive classroom communities.* Needham Heights, MA: Allyn & Bacon.

Smith, T.E.C., Polloway, E.A., Patton, J.R., & Dowdy, C.A. (1998). *Teaching students with special needs in inclusive settings* (2nd ed.). Needham Heights, MA: Allyn & Bacon.

Stainback, S., & Stainback, W. (Eds.). (1996). *Inclusion: A guide for educators.* Baltimore: Paul H. Brookes Publishing Co.

York-Barr, J. (Ed.). (1996). *Creating inclusive school communities: A staff development series for general and special educators.* Baltimore: Paul H. Brookes Publishing Co.

Zionts, P. (1997). *Inclusion strategies for students with learning and behavior problems: Perspectives, experiences, and best practices.* Austin, TX: PRO-ED.

Resource Guides

Doyle, M.B., Vandercook, T., Walz, L., Wolff, S., & York, J. (1995). *Inclusive education for learners with severe disabilities: Print and media resources.* Minneapolis: University of Minnesota, Institute on Community Integration.

Klauber, J., & Klauber, A. (1996). *Inclusion & parent advocacy: A resource guide.* Centereach, NY: Disability Resources.

Kronberg, R. (Ed.). (1996). *From vision to practice: Ideas for implementing inclusive education.* Minneapolis: University of Minnesota, Institute on Community Integration.

Kronberg, R., & York-Barr, J. (1998). *Differentiated teaching and learning in heterogeneous classrooms: Strategies for meeting the needs of all students.* Minneapolis: University of Minnesota, Institute on Community Integration.

Vandercook, T., Wolff, S., & York, J. (1989). *Learning together: Stories and strategies.* Minneapolis: University of Minnesota, Institute on Community Integration.

Videotapes

Comforty Media Concepts (Producer). (1991). *Choices* [Videotape]. (Available from Program Development Associates, 5620 Business Avenue, Suite B, Cicero, NY 13039)

Dover, W. (1995). *Teacher inclusion video series: Lesson plans and modifications for inclusion and collaborative classrooms* [Videotape]. (Available from Strategies for Educational Change, 11 Whitby Court, Mount Holly, NJ 08060)

Dover, W. (1996). *The training video series for the paraprofessional* [Videotape]. (Available from Peytral Publications, Post Office Box 1162, Minnetonka, MN 55345)

Jorgensen, C.M., Mroczka, M.M., & Williams, S. (1997). *Class of '96: An inclusive community of learners* [Videotape]. (Available from Institute on Disability/UAP, 7 Leavitt Lane, Suite 101, Durham, NH 03824)

Lipsky, D.K., & Gartner, A. (1998). *Standards & inclusion: Can we have both?* [Videotape]. (Available from National Professional Resources, 25 South Regent Street, Port Chester, NY 10573)

Maloney, M. (1995). *Inclusion: Heaven or hell?* [Videotape]. (Available from LRP Publications, 747 Dresher Road, Suite 500, Post Office Box 980, Horsham, PA 19044-0980)

Maloney, M. (1995). *Special education for regular educators* [Videotape]. (Available from LRP Publications, 747 Dresher Road, Suite 500, Post Office Box 980, Horsham, PA 19044-0980)

Rief, S.F. (1995). *ADHD: Inclusive instruction and collaborative practices* [Videotape]. (Available from National Professional Resources, 25 South Regent Street, Port Chester, NY 10573)

Tashie, C., Shapiro-Barnard, S., & Crabtree, J. (1998). *Petroglyphs* [Videotape]. (Available from Institute on Disability/UAP, 7 Leavitt Lane, Suite 101, Durham, NH 03824)

Vargo, J., & Vargo, R. (1995). *The face of inclusion—A parent's perspective* [Videotape]. (Available from LRP Publications, 747 Dresher Road, Suite 500, Post Office Box 980, Horsham, PA 19044-0980)

Winebrenner, S. (1989). *Teaching gifted kids in the regular classroom* [Videotape]. (Available from Free Spirit, 400 First Avenue North, Suite 616, Minneapolis, MN 55401)

LEGISLATION

Books

Blanck, P.D. (1998). *The Americans with Disabilities Act and the emerging workforce: Employment of people with mental retardation.* Washington, DC: American Association on Mental Retardation.

Boyer, C., & Wendling, D. (1996). *NARIC guide to resources for the Americans with Disabilities Act (ADA)* (2nd ed.). Silver Spring, MD: National Rehabilitation Information Center.

Bruyère, S.M., & Golden, T.P. (Eds.). (1996). *The job developer's guide to the Americans with Disabilities Act: Using the ADA to promote job opportunities for people with disabilities.* St. Augustine, FL: Training Resource Network.

CEC Public Policy Unit. (1998). *IDEA 1997: Let's make it work.* Reston, VA: Council for Exceptional Children.

Gordon, M., & Keiser, S. (Eds.). (1998). *Accommodations in higher education under the Americans with Disabilities Act (ADA): A no-nonsense guide for clinicians, educators, administrators, and lawyers.* New York: Guilford Press.

Friel, J. (1997). *Children with special needs: Assessment, law and practice: Caught in the acts* (4th ed.). London: Jessica Kingsley.

Jones, N.L., & Aleman, S.R. (1997). *The 1997 IDEA amendments: A guide for educators, parents and attorneys.* Horsham, PA: LRP Publications.

Miller, L., & Newbill, C. (1998). *Section 504 in the classroom: How to design and implement accommodation plans.* Austin, TX: PRO-ED.

Osborn, A.G. (1996). *Legal issues in special education.* Needham Heights, MA: Allyn & Bacon.

Rothstein, L.F. (1995). *Special education law* (2nd ed.). Reading, MA: Addison Wesley Longman.

Ruesch, G.M. (Ed.). (1996). *Special education law and practice: A manual for the special education practitioner.* Horsham, PA: LRP Publications.

Smith, T.E.C., & Patton, J.R. (1998). *Section 504 and the public schools: A practical guide to determining eligibility, developing accommodation plans, and documenting compliance.* Austin, TX: PRO-ED.

Turnbull, H.R., & Turnbull, A. (1998). *Free appropriate public education: The law and children with disabilities* (5th ed.). Denver, CO: Love Publishing.

Underwood, J.K., & Mead, J.F. (1995). *Legal aspects of special education and pupil services.* Needham Heights, MA: Allyn & Bacon.

Yell, M.L. (1998). *The law and special education* (4th ed.). Upper Saddle River, NJ: Prentice-Hall.

Videotapes

AFB ADA Consulting Group (Producer). (1992). *Making the ADA work for you: A video training seminar* [Videotape]. (Available from AFB Press, 11 Penn Plaza, Suite 300, New York, NY 10001)

The Arc. (1991). *The Americans with Disabilities Act at work* [Videotape]. (Available from The Arc, 500 East Border Street, Suite 300, Arlington, TX 76010)

Cynthia Kay/Wayne Glatz Film & Video (Producer). (1992). *ADA facts and fears video* [Videotape]. (Available from The Association for Persons in Supported Employment, 1627 Monument Avenue, Richmond, VA 23220)

Hanlon, G.M. (1998). *A new IDEA for special education: Understanding the system and the new law* [Videotape]. (Available from Edvantage Media, 740 River Road, Suite 301, Fair Haven, NJ 07704)

Maloney, M. (1997). *The new IDEA: What are your responsibilities?* [Videotape]. (Available from LRP Publications, 747 Dresher Road, Suite 500, Post Office Box 980, Horsham, PA 19044-0980)

Maloney, M. (1997). *The new IDEA: What regular educators need to know* [Videotape]. (Available from LRP Publications, 747 Dresher Road, Suite 500, Post Office Box 980, Horsham, PA 19044-0980)

Parent Educational Advocacy Training Center (PEATC). (1997). *What a great IDEA!* [Videotape]. (Available from PEATC, 10340 Democracy Lane, Suite 206, Fairfax, VA 22030)

School of Industrial and Labor Relations, Cornell University (Producer). (1996). *No barriers for business: Implementing the Americans with Disabilities Act* [Videotape]. (Available from Program Development Associates, Post Office Box 2038, Syracuse, NY 13220-2038)

LEISURE AND RECREATION

Books

Block, M.E. (1994). *A teacher's guide to including students with disabilities in regular physical education.* Baltimore: Paul H. Brookes Publishing Co.

Bullock, C., & Mahon, M. (1997). *Introduction to recreation services for people with disabilities: A person-centered approach.* Champaign, IL: Sagamore.

Dattilo, J. (1994). *Inclusive leisure services: Responding to the rights of people with disabilities.* State College, PA: Venture Publishing.

Heyne, L., Rynders, J., Schleien, S.J., & Tabourne, C. (Eds.). (1995). *Powerful partnerships: Parents & professionals building inclusive recreation programs together.* Minneapolis: University of Minnesota, Institute on Community Integration.

Heyne, L., Schleien, S.J., & McAvoy, L. (1993). *Making friends: Using recreation activities to promote friendship between children with and without disabilities.* Minneapolis: University of Minnesota, School of Kinesiology and Leisure Studies.

Komissar, C., Hart, D., Friedlander, R., Tufts, S., & Paiewonsky, M. (1997). *Don't forget the fun: Developing inclusive recreation.* Boston: Institute for Community Inclusion.

Paciorek, M.J., & Jones, J.A. (1995). *Sports and recreation for the disabled* (2nd ed.). Champaign, IL: Sagamore.

Peniston, L. (1997). *Developing recreation skills: For individuals with learning disabilities.* Champaign, IL: Sagamore.

Rynders, J.E., & Schleien, S.J. (1991). *Together successfully: Creating recreational and educational programs that integrate people with and without disabilities.* Arlington, TX: The Arc.

Schleien, S.J., Meyer, L.H., Heyne, L.A., & Brandt, B.B. (1995). *Lifelong leisure skills and lifestyles for persons with developmental disabilities.* Baltimore: Paul H. Brookes Publishing Co.

Schleien, S.J., Ray, M.T., & Green, F.P. (1997). *Community recreation and people with disabilities: Strategies for inclusion* (2nd ed.). Baltimore: Paul H. Brookes Publishing Co.

Smith, R.W., Austin, D.R., & Kennedy, D.W. (1996). *Inclusive and special recreation: Opportunities for persons with disabilities* (3rd ed.). Madison, WI: Brown & Benchmark.

SELF-DETERMINATION

Books

Agran, M. (Ed.). (1997). *Student-directed learning: Teaching self-determination skills.* Pacific Grove, CA: Brooks/Cole.

Dybwad, G., & Bersani, H. (Eds.). (1996). *New voices: Self-advocacy by people with disabilities.* Cambridge, MA: Brookline Books.

Field, S., Hoffman, A., & Spezia, S. (1998). *Self-determination strategies for adolescents in transition* (PRO-ED series on transition). Austin, TX: PRO-ED.

Field, S., Martin, J., Miller, R., Ward, M., & Wehmeyer, M. (1998). *A practical guide for teaching self-determination.* Reston, VA: Council for Exceptional Children.

Goldman, C.D. (1991). *Disability rights guide: Practical solutions affecting people with disabilities* (2nd ed.). Lincoln, NE: Media Publishing.

Goode, B. (1997). *The beliefs, values, and principles of self-advocacy.* Cambridge, MA: Brookline Books.

Ordover, E.L., & Boundy, K.B. (1991). *Educational rights for children with disabilities: A primer for advocates.* Washington, DC: Center for Law and Education.

Powers, L.E., Singer, G.H.S., & Sowers, J. (Eds.). (1996). *On the road to autonomy: Promoting self-competence in children and youth with disabilities.* Baltimore: Paul H. Brookes Publishing Co.

Sands, D.J., & Wehmeyer, M.L. (Eds.). (1996). *Self-determination across the life span: Independence and choice for people with disabilities.* Baltimore: Paul H. Brookes Publishing Co.

Shapiro, E.S., & Cole, C.L. (1994). *Behavior change in the classroom: Self-management interventions.* New York: Guilford Press.

Wehmeyer, M.L., Agran, M., & Hughes, C. (1997). *Teaching self-determination to students with disabilities: Basic skills for successful transition.* Baltimore: Paul H. Brookes Publishing Co.

Wehmeyer, M., & Kelchner, K. (1995). *The Arc's self-determination scale: Adolescent version.* Arlington, TX: The Arc.

Wehmeyer, M.L., & Sands, D.J. (Eds.). (1998). *Making it happen: Student involvement in educational planning, decision making, and instruction.* Baltimore: Paul H. Brookes Publishing Co.

Workman, E.A., & Katz, A.M. (1995). *Teaching behavioral self-control to students* (2nd ed.). Austin, TX: PRO-ED.

Curricula

Abery, B., Arndt, K., Greger, P., Tetu, L., Eggebeen, A., Barosko, J., Hinga, A., McBride, M., Peterson, K., & Rudrud, L. (1994). *Self-determination for youth with disabilities: A family education curriculum*. Minneapolis: University of Minnesota, Institute on Community Integration.

Carpenter, W.D. (1994). *Become your own expert: Self-advocacy curriculum for individuals with learning disabilities*. Little Canada: Minnesota Education Services.

Field, S., & Hoffman, A. (1996). *Steps to self-determination: A curriculum to help adolescents learn to achieve their goals*. Austin, TX: PRO-ED.

Fullerton, A. (1994). *Putting feet on my dreams: A program in self-determination for adolescents and young adults*. Portland, OR: Portland State University.

Halpern, A.S., Herr, C.M., Wolf, N.K., Lawson, J.D., Doren, B., Johnson, M.D., & Lawson, J.D. (1997). *Next S.T.E.P.: Student transition and educational planning*. Austin, TX: PRO-ED.

Marshall, L.H., & Martin, J. (1997). *Choosing employment goals*. Longmont, CO: Sopris West.

Martin, J., & Marshall, L.H. (1996). *Self-directed IEP*. Longmont, CO: Sopris West.

Martin, J.E., Marshall, L., Maxson, L., & Jerman, P. (1996). *ChoiceMaker self-determination curriculum*. Longmont, CO: Sopris West.

National Information Center for Children and Youth with Disabilities. (1995). *A student's guide to the IEP* [Book and audiotape]. Washington, DC: Author.

Powers, L. (1993). *TAKE CHARGE for the future*. Portland: Oregon Health Sciences University.

Vandercook, T., York, J., & Forest, M. (1989). The McGill Action Planning System (MAPS): A strategy for building the vision. *Journal of The Association for Persons with Severe Handicaps, 14*, 205–215.

VanReusen, A.K., Bos, C.S., Schumaker, J.B., & Deshler, D.D. (1994). *Self-advocacy strategy for education and transition planning*. Lawrence, KS: Edge Enterprises.

Wehmeyer, M., & Kelchner, K. (1995). *Whose future is it, anyway? A student-directed transition planning process*. Arlington, TX: The Arc.

Resource Guides

The Arc. (1998). *Self-advocacy bibliography*. (Available from The Arc, 500 East Border Street, Suite 300, Arlington, TX 76010)

The Arc's Self-Advocacy Committee. (1998). *Directory of self-advocacy programs*. (Available from The Arc, 500 East Border Street, Suite 300, Arlington, TX 76010)

Hayden, M., Fijas, B., & Koeper, E. (1995). *Self-advocacy print and media resources/1995–1996*. Minneapolis: University of Minnesota, Institute on Community Integration.

Hayden, M.F., & Ward, N. (Eds.). (1994). *IMPACT: Feature issue on self-advocacy*. Minneapolis: University of Minnesota, Institute on Community Integration.

Longhurst, N.A. (1994). *The self-advocacy movement by people with developmental disabilities: A demographic study and directory of self-advocacy groups in the United States*. Washington, DC: American Association on Mental Retardation.

Lovett, H. (1996). *The positive behavior supports project bibliography*. Durham, NH: Institute on Disability/UAP.

Videotapes

Advocating Change Together (Producer). (1996). *Tools for change: Freedom, equality, and justice for all* [Videotape]. (Available from Human Policy Press, 805 South Crouse Avenue, Syracuse, NY 13244)

Advocating Change Together (Producer). (1997). *Self advocates becoming empowered* [Video-tape]. (Available from Human Policy Press, 805 South Crouse Avenue, Syracuse, NY 13244)

Advocating Change Together (Producer). (1997). *Whose decision is it anyway?* [Videotape]. (Available from Program Development Associates, 5620 Business Avenue, Suite B, Cicero, NY 13039)

Advocating Change Together (Producer). (1999). *Tools for change: Lasting leadership* [Video-tape]. (Available from Program Development Associates, 5620 Business Avenue, Suite B, Cicero, NY 13039)

Advocating Change Together (Producer). (1999). *Tools for change: My choice, your decision* [Videotape]. (Available from Program Development Associates, 5620 Business Avenue, Suite B, Cicero, NY 13039)

American Foundation for the Blind (Producer). (1997). *Brief encounters of the right kind: Or, how to make your point as an advocate in 10 minutes or less* [Videotape]. (Available from American Foundation for the Blind, 11 Penn Plaza, Suite 300, New York, NY 10001)

The Arc & The Arc of New Mexico. (1992). *Self-advocacy: Supporting the vision* [Videotape]. (Available from The Arc, 500 East Border Street, Suite 300, Arlington, TX 76010)

Eaton, H., & Coull, L. (1997). *Transitions from high school to postsecondary learning: School and life self-advocacy skills for students with learning disabilities and/or ADD/ADHD* [Videotape]. (Available from Eaton Coull Learning Group, Ltd., 3541 West 16th Avenue, Vancouver, British Columbia V6R 3C2, Canada)

Eaton, H., & Coull, L. (1998). *Moving on to high school: School and life self-advocacy skills for students with learning disabilities and/or ADD/ADHD* [Videotape]. (Available from Eaton Coull Learning Group, Ltd., 3541 West 16th Avenue, Vancouver, British Columbia V6R 3C2, Canada)

Institute on Disability/UAP & The Robert Wood Johnson Foundation. (1996). *Self-determination for persons with developmental disabilities* [Videotape]. (Available from Institute on Disability/UAP, 7 Leavitt Lane, Suite 101, Durham, NH 03824-3522)

Irene M. Ward and Associates. (1997). *What is self-determination and how to make it work* [Videotape]. (Available from Program Development Associates, 5620 Business Avenue, Suite B, Cicero, NY 13039)

James Brodie Productions (Producer). (1997). *The road you take is yours* [Videotape]. (Available from Paul H. Brookes Publishing Co., Post Office Box 10624, Baltimore, MD 21285-0624)

SOCIAL SUPPORT

Books

Bradley, V.J., Ashbaugh, J.W., & Blaney, B.C. (Eds.). (1994). *Creating individual supports for people with developmental disabilities: A mandate for change at many levels.* Baltimore: Paul H. Brookes Publishing Co.

Burton, M., Kagan, C., & Clements, P. (1995). *Social skills for people with learning disabilities—A social capability approach.* San Diego: Stanley Thornes.

Elksnin, L.K., & Elksnin, N. (1995). *Assessment and instruction of social skills: Across the life-span and the curriculum* (2nd ed.). San Diego: Singular Publishing Group.

Elksnin, N., & Elksnin, L.K. (1998). *Teaching occupational social skills* (PRO-ED series on transition). Austin, TX: PRO-ED.

Elliot, S.N., & Gresham, F.M. (1991). *Social skills intervention guide: Practical strategies for social skills training.* Circle Pines, MN: American Guidance Service.

Gresham, F.M., & Elliot, S.N. (1990). *Social skills rating system (SSRS)*. Circle Pines, MN: American Guidance Service.

Jackson, D.A., Jackson, N.F., & Bennett, M.L. (1998). *Teaching social competence to youth and adults with developmental disabilities: A comprehensive program*. Austin, TX: PRO-ED.

Knapczyk, D.R., & Rodes, P. (1996). *Teaching social competence: A practical approach for improving social skills in students at-risk*. Pacific Grove, CA: Brooks/Cole.

Murphy, S.T., & Rogan, P.M. (1994). *Developing natural supports in the workplace: A practitioner's guide*. St. Augustine, FL: Training Resource Network.

Nevil, N.F., Beatty, M.L., & Moxley, D.P. (1997). *Socialization games for persons with disabilities: Structured group activities for social and interpersonal development*. Springfield, IL: Charles C Thomas.

Riches, V.C. (1996). *Everyday social interaction: A program for people with disabilities* (2nd ed.). Baltimore: Paul H. Brookes Publishing Co.

Rutherford, R., Chipman, J., DiGangi, S., & Anderson, K. (1992). *Teaching social skills: A practical instructional approach*. Reston, VA: Council for Exceptional Children.

Sargent, L.R. (Ed.). (1998). *Social skills in the school and community: Systematic instruction for children and youth with cognitive delays*. Reston, VA: Council for Exceptional Children.

Stengle, L.J. (1996). *Laying community foundations for your child with a disability: How to establish relationships that will support your child after you're gone*. Bethesda, MD: Woodbine House.

Curricula

Dygdon, J.A. (1997). *The culture and lifestyle appropriate social skills intervention curriculum (CLASSIC): A program for socially valid social skills training*. Austin, TX: PRO-ED.

Waksman, S., & Waksman, D.D. (1998). *The Waksman social skills curriculum for adolescents: An assertive behavior program* (4th ed.). Austin, TX: PRO-ED.

Videotapes

Attainment Company, Inc. (Producer). (1993). *It's all part of the job: Social skills for success at work* [Videotape]. (Available from Paul H. Brookes Publishing Co., Post Office Box 10624, Baltimore, MD 21285-0624)

Institute on Disability/UAP. (1992). *Dream catchers* [Videotape]. (Available from Institute on Disability/UAP, 7 Leavitt Lane, Suite 101, Durham, NH 03824)

Institute on Disability/UAP. (1996). *Voices of friendship* [Videotape]. (Available from Institute on Disability/UAP, 7 Leavitt Lane, Suite 101, Durham, NH 03824)

Warger, C.L., & Rutherford, R. (1996). *A collaborative approach to social skills instruction* [Videotape]. (Available from Council for Exceptional Children, 1920 Association Drive, Reston, VA 20191)

TECHNOLOGY AND AUGMENTATIVE COMMUNICATION

Books

Alliance for Technology Access. (1997). *Computer resources for people with disabilities: A guide to exploring today's assistive technology* (2nd ed.). Oakland, CA: Hunter House.

Beukelman, D.R., & Mirenda, P. (1998). *Augmentative and alternative communication: Management of severe communication disorders in children and adults* (2nd ed.). Baltimore: Paul H. Brookes Publishing Co.

Chambers, A.C. (1997). *Has technology been considered? A guide for IEP teams.* Reston, VA: Council for Exceptional Children, Administrators of Special Education, Technology and Media Division.

Flippo, K.F., Inge, K.J., & Barcus, J.M. (Eds.). (1995). *Assistive technology: A resource for school, work, and community.* Baltimore: Paul H. Brookes Publishing Co.

Glennen, S.L., & DeCoste, D.C. (1996). *Handbook of augmentative and alternative communication.* San Diego: Singular Publishing Group.

Gray, D.B., Quatrano, L.A., & Lieberman, M.L. (Eds.). (1998). *Designing and using assistive technology: The human perspective.* Baltimore: Paul H. Brookes Publishing Co.

Kelker, K., Holt, R., & Sullivan, J. (1998). *Family guide to assistive technology.* Cambridge, MA: Brookline Books.

Lewis, R.B. (1993). *Special education technology: Classroom applications.* Pacific Grove, CA: Brooks/Cole.

Light, J., & Binger, C. (1997). *Building communicative competence with individuals who use augmentative and alternative communication.* Baltimore: Paul H. Brookes Publishing Co.

Lindsey, J.D. (Ed.). (1999). *Technology and exceptional individuals* (3rd ed.). Austin, TX: PRO-ED.

Male, M. (1996). *Technology for inclusion: Meeting the special needs of all students* (3rd ed.). Needham Heights, MA: Allyn & Bacon.

McCarthy, C.F., McLean, L.K., Miller, J.F., Paul-Brown, D., Romski, M.A., Rourk, J.D., & Yoder, D.E. (1998). *Communication supports checklist for programs serving individuals with severe disabilities.* Baltimore: Paul H. Brookes Publishing Co.

Roulstone, A. (1998). *Enabling technology: Disabled people, work, and new technology (Disability, human rights, and society).* Buckingham, England: Open University Press.

Scherer, M.J. (1996). *Living in the state of stuck: How technology impacts the lives of people with disabilities* (2nd ed.). Cambridge, MA: Brookline Books.

Von Tetzchner, S., & Jensen, M.H. (1996). *Augmentative and alternative communication: European perspectives.* San Diego: Singular Publishing Group.

Videotapes

Canter & Associates, Inc. (Producer). (1998). *Technology in today's classroom (Video series): Skip Stahl on technology and students with special needs* [Videotape]. (Available from Canter & Associates, Inc., Post Office Box 2113, Santa Monica, CA 90407)

DO-IT (Producer). (1995). *Working together: People with disabilities and computer technology* [Videotape]. (Available from DO-IT, Box 354842, Seattle, WA 98195)

Northern Light Productions (Producer). (1992). *Equal access* [Videotape]. (Available from Center for Applied Special Technology, 39 Cross Street, Suite 201, Peabody, MA 01960)

Rochester Institute of Technology (Producer). (1995). *The EASI guide to adaptive technology for people with disabilities* [Videotape]. (Available from Equal Access to Software and Information, Post Office Box 18928, Rochester, NY 14618)

TRANSITION PLANNING

Books

Bishop, B., Blue-Banning, M., Holt, F., Irving, J., & Martel, T. (1992). *Planning for life after high school: A handbook of information and resources for families and young adults with disabilities.* Lawrence, KS: Full Citizenship.

Brolin, D.E. (1997). *Life centered career education: A competency based approach* (5th ed.). Reston, VA: Council for Exceptional Children.

Everson, J.M. (1993). *Youth with disabilities: Strategies for interagency transition programs.* Austin, TX: PRO-ED.

Garfinkel, L. (1995). *Legal issues in transitioning students.* Horsham, PA: LRP Publications.

Giangreco, M.F., Cloninger, C.J., & Iverson, V.S. (1997). *Choosing options and accommodations for children (COACH): A guide to educational planning for students with disabilities* (2nd ed.). Baltimore: Paul H. Brookes Publishing Co.

McDonnell, J., Mathot-Buckner, C., & Ferguson, B. (1996). *Transition programs for students with moderate/severe disabilities.* Pacific Grove, CA: Brooks/Cole.

Morningstar, M.E. (1995). *Planning for the future: A workbook to help young adults with disabilities, their families and professionals to plan for living, working, and participating in the community.* Lawrence: University of Kansas, Department of Special Education.

Patton, J.R., & Blalock, G. (Eds.). (1996). *Transition and students with learning disabilities: Facilitating the movement from school to adult life.* Austin, TX: PRO-ED.

Patton, J.R., & Dunn, C. (1998). *Transition from school to young adulthood: Basic concepts and recommended practices.* Austin, TX: PRO-ED.

Pierangelo, R., & Crane, R. (1997). *Complete guide to special education transition services: Ready-to-use help and materials for successful transitions from school to adulthood.* West Nyack, NY: Center for Applied Research in Education.

Rosenfeld, L.R. (1994). *Your child and health care: A "dollars & sense" guide for families with special needs.* Baltimore: Paul H. Brookes Publishing Co.

Rusch, F.R., & Chadsey, J.G. (Eds.). (1998). *Beyond high school: Transition from school to work.* Belmont, CA: Wadsworth.

Wehman, P. (1995). *Individual transition plans: The teacher's curriculum guide for helping youth with special needs.* Austin, TX: PRO-ED.

Wehman, P. (1996). *Life beyond the classroom: Transition strategies for young people with disabilities* (2nd ed.). Baltimore: Paul H. Brookes Publishing Co.

Wehman, P., & Targett, P.S. (1999). *Vocational curriculum for individuals with special needs: Transition from school to adulthood.* Austin, TX: PRO-ED.

West, L.L., Corbey, S., Boyer-Stephens, A., Jones, B., Miller, R.J., & Sarkees-Wircenski, M. (1992). *Integrating transition planning into the IEP process.* Reston, VA: Council for Exceptional Children, Division on Career Development and Transition.

Resource Guides

The Arc. (1997). *Future planning resources.* (Available from The Arc, 500 East Border Street, Suite 300, Arlington, TX 76010)

Corbey, S., Miller, R., Severson, S., & Enderle, J. (1993). *Identifying individual transition needs: A resource guide for special educators working with students in their transition from school to adult life.* St. Paul: Minnesota Department of Education.

Mathie, B., & Thompson, S. (1991). *Transition strategies that work: Vol. I. Profiles of successful high school transition programs.* Minneapolis: University of Minnesota, Institute on Community Integration.

Stenjhem, P.H., & da Gama, G. (1997). *Communities of vision & action: Systems change through Minnesota's community transition interagency committees.* Minneapolis: University of Minnesota, Institute on Community Integration.

JOURNALS AND NEWSLETTERS

Ability
Post Office Box 10655
Costa Mesa, CA 92627
Telephone: (714) 854-8700
Fax: (714) 548-5966
E-mail: subscriptions@abilitymagazine.com
http://www.abilitymagazine.com
Published bimonthly

The Able Informer
1130 Sunset Drive
Clyde, TX 79510
Telephone: (915) 893-4513; (915) 893-3078
E-mail: snuffyj@camalott.com
On-line newsletter: http://www.sasquatch.com/ableinfo

The Advance
The Association for Persons in Supported Employment (APSE)
1627 Monument Avenue
Richmond, VA 23220
Telephone: (804) 278-9187
Fax: (804) 278-9377
E-mail: apse@apse.org
http://www.apse.org
Published quarterly

The Advocate
Autism Society of America
7910 Woodmont Avenue
Suite 300
Bethesda, MD 20814-3015
Telephone: (800) 3-AUTISM; (301) 657-0881
Fax: (301) 657-0869
http://www.autism-society.org
Published bimonthly

Advocate Update
Advocates Across America
Post Office Box 754
Chandler, AZ 85244-0754
Telephone: (602) 917-0955
Fax: (602) 814-9404
E-mail: support@axa.org
http://www.axa.org
Published quarterly

Alliance
National Transition Alliance for Youth with Disabilities
Academy for Educational Development
1875 Connecticut Avenue NW
Suite 900
Washington, DC 20009-1202
Telephone: (202) 884-8183
Fax: (202) 884-9344
E-mail: nta@aed.org
http://www.dssc.org/nta
Published quarterly

Alternatively Speaking
Augmentative Communication, Inc.
One Surf Way
Suite 215
Monterey, CA 93940
Telephone: (408) 649-3050
Fax: (408) 646-5428
E-mail: sarahblack@aol.com
Published quarterly

American Journal of Occupational Therapy (AJOT)
American Occupational Therapy Association (AOTA)
4720 Montgomery Lane
Bethesda, MD 20814-3425
Telephone: (301) 652-2682
Fax: (301) 652-7711
E-mail: praota@aota.org
http://www.aota.org
Published bimonthly

The American Journal on Mental Retardation (AJMR)
American Association on Mental Retardation (AAMR)
444 North Capitol Street NW
Suite 846
Washington, DC 20001-1512
Telephone: (800) 424-3688; (202) 387-1968
Fax: (202) 387-2193
E-mail: mailbox@aamr.org
http://www.aamr.org
Published six times per year

Augmentative and Alternative Communication (AAC)
University of British Columbia
Faculty of Education
2125 Main Mall
Vancouver, British Columbia
V6T 1Z4

Canada
Telephone: (604) 253-1929
Fax: (604) 251-1057
E-mail: rbutus@uniserve.com
http://www.isaac-online.com
Published quarterly

Augmentative Communication News
Augmentative Communication, Inc.
One Surf Way
Suite 215
Monterey, CA 93940
Telephone: (408) 649-3050
Fax: (408) 646-5428
E-mail: sarahblack@aol.com
Published bimonthly

Behavioral Disorders
Council for Children with Behavioral Disorders (CCBD)
Council for Exceptional Children (CEC)
1920 Association Drive
Reston, VA 20191-1589
Telephone: (888) 232-7733
Fax: (703) 264-9494
E-mail: service@cec.sped.org
http://www.cec.sped.org
Published quarterly

Career Development for Exceptional Individuals (CDEI)
Council for Exceptional Children (CEC)
Division on Career Development and Transition (DCDT)
1920 Association Drive
Reston, VA 20191-1589
Telephone: (888) 232-7733
Fax: (703) 264-9494
E-mail: service@cec.sped.org
http://www.ed.uiuc.edu/SPED/dcdt
Published twice yearly

Common Sense
National Program Office on Self-Determination
3700 Riverside Drive
Post Office Box 21322
Columbus, OH 43221-0322
Telephone: (614) 777-1575
Fax: (614) 777-0414
E-mail: ksherida@columbus.rr.com
Published three times per year

Community Advocacy Press
Capabilities Unlimited, Inc.
2495 Eric Avenue
Cincinnati, OH 45208
Telephone: (800) 871-2186
Fax: (513) 871-5893
Email: countusin@brugold.com
http://brugold.com/cui.htm
Published quarterly

DCDT Network
Division on Career Development and Transition for Exceptional Individuals
Special Education
Moorhead State University
Moorhead, MN 56563
Telephone: (218) 236-3527
Fax: (218) 299-5850
E-mail: severson@mhd1.moorhead.msus.edu
http://www.ed.uiuc.edu/sped/dcdt
Published three times per year

Diagnostique
Council for Education Diagnostic Services (CEOS)
Council for Exceptional Children (CEC)
1920 Association Drive
Reston, VA 20191-1589
Telephone: (888) 232-7733
Fax: (703) 264-9494
E-mail: service@cec.sped.org
http://www.cec.sped.org
Published quarterly

Disability & Society
Carfax Publishing
47 Runway Road
Suite G
Levittown, PA 10957-4900
Telephone: (215) 269-0400
Fax: (215) 269-0363
E-mail: sales@carfax.co.uk
http://www.carfax.co.uk
Published six times per year

Disability Compliance Bulletin
LRP Publications
747 Dresher Road, Suite 500
Post Office Box 980
Horsham, PA 19044-0980
Telephone: (800) 341-7874

Fax: (215) 784-9639
E-mail: custserve@lrp.com
http://www.lrp.com
Published 22 times per year

Disability International
Disabled Peoples' International
101-7 Evergreen Place
Winnipeg, Manitoba
R3L 2T3
Canada
Telephone: (800) 749-7773; (204) 287-8010
Fax: (204) 453-1367
E-mail: dpi@dpi.org
On-line magazine: http://www.dpi.org
Published 4 times per year

DO-IT News
Disabilities, Opportunities, Internetworking, and Technology (DO-IT)
University of Washington
Box 354842
Seattle, WA 98195-4842
Telephone: (206) 685-DOIT
Fax: (206) 221-4171
E-mail: doit@u.washington.edu
http://weber.u.washington.edu/~doit
Published quarterly

Education and Training in Mental Retardation and Developmental Disabilities
Division on Mental Retardation and Developmental Disabilities (MRDD)
Council for Exceptional Children (CEC)
1920 Association Drive
Reston, VA 20191-1589
Telephone: (888) 232-7733
Fax: (703) 264-9494
E-mail: service@cec.sped.org
http://www.cec.sped.org
Published quarterly

Exceptional Children
Council for Exceptional Children (CEC)
1920 Association Drive
Reston, VA 20191-1589
Telephone: (888) 232-7733
Fax: (703) 264-9494
E-mail: service@cec.sped.org
http://www.cec.sped.org
Published four times per year

Exceptional Parent Magazine
555 Kinderkamack Road
Oradell, NJ 07649-1517
Telephone: (201) 634-6550
Fax: (201) 634-6599
E-mail: vieparent@concentric.net
http://www.eparent.com
Published monthly

Exceptionality
Lawrence Erlbaum Associates, Inc.
10 Industrial Avenue
Mahwah, NJ 07430-2262
Telephone: (800) 9BOOKS9
Fax: (201) 236-0072
E-mail: orders@erlbaum.com
http://www.erlbaum.com
Published quarterly

Families and Disability Newsletter
Beach Center on Families and Disability
University of Kansas
3111 Haworth Hall
Lawrence, KS 66045-7516
Telephone: (785) 864-7600
Fax: (785) 864-7605
E-mail: beach@dole.lsi.ukansas.edu
http://www.lsi.ukans.edu/beach/beachhp.htm
Published three times per year

Focus on Autism and Other Developmental Disabilities
PRO-ED Publishing Company
8700 Shoal Creek Boulevard
Austin, TX 78757-6897
Telephone: (800) 897-3202; (512) 451-3246
Fax: (800) 397-7633; (512) 451-8542
E-mail: proed1@aol.com
http://www.proedinc.com
Published quarterly

Fostering Access, Communication, and Technology Supports (FACTS)
Center on Community Inclusion
University of Maine/UAP
5717 Corbett Hall, Room 114
Orono, MA 04469-5717
Telephone: (207) 581-1084
Fax: (207) 581-1231
E-mail: susan_scott@umit.maine.edu
http://www.ume.maine.edu/~cci
Published quarterly

Government Reporter
Governmental Affairs Office of The Arc
1730 K Street NW
Suite 1212
Washington, DC 20006
Telephone: (202) 785-3388
Fax: (202) 467-4179
E-mail: arcga@radix.net
http://www.thearc.org
Published semimonthly

IMPACT
Institutes on Community Integration
University of Minnesota
109 Pattee Hall
150 Pillsbury Drive SE
Minneapolis, MN 55455
Telephone: (612) 624-4512
Fax: (612) 624-9344
E-mail: ici@mailici.coled.umn.edu
http://ici.coled.umn.edu
Published quarterly

Inclusion News
Inclusion Press International
24 Thome Crescent
Toronto, Ontario
M6H 255
Canada
Telephone: (416) 658-5363
Fax: (416) 658-5067
E-mail: includer@idirect.com
http://www.inclusion.com
Published annually

Inclusion Times
National Professional Resources, Inc.
25 South Regent Street
Port Chester, NY 10573
Telephone: (800) 453-7461
Fax: (914) 937-9327
E-mail: info@nprinc.com
http://www.npinc.com
Published five times per year

Inclusive Education Programs (IEP)
LRP Publications
747 Dresher Road
Suite 500

Post Office Box 980
Horsham, PA 19044-0980
Telephone: (800) 341-7874
Fax: (215) 784-9639
E-mail: custserve@lrp.com
http://www.lrp.com
Published 12 times per year

Journal for Education of the Gifted (JEG)
The Association for the Gifted
Council for Exceptional Children (CEC)
Prufrock Press
Post Office Box 8813
Waco, TX 76714-8813
Telephone: (800) 998-2208
Fax: (800) 240-0333
E-mail: McElhannon@prufrock.com
http://www.prufrock.com
Published quarterly

Journal of Emotional and Behavioral Disorders (JEBD)
PRO-ED Publishing Company
8700 Shoal Creek Boulevard
Austin, TX 78757-6897
Telephone: (800) 897-3202; (512) 451-3246
Fax: (800) 397-7633; (512) 451-8542
E-mail: proed1@aol.com
http://www.proedinc.com
Published quarterly

Journal of Learning Disabilities (JLD)
PRO-ED Publishing Company
8700 Shoal Creek Boulevard
Austin, TX 78757-6897
Telephone: (800) 897-3202; (512) 451-3246
Fax: (800) 397-7633; (512) 451-8542
E-mail: proed1@aol.com
http://www.proedinc.com
Published bimonthly

Journal of Secondary Gifted Education (JSGE)
Prufrock Press
Post Office Box 8813
Waco, TX 76714-8813
Telephone: (800) 998-2208
Fax: (800) 240-0333
E-mail: Bates@prufrock.com
http://www.prufrock.com
Published quarterly

The Journal of Special Education (JSE)
PRO-ED Publishing Company
8700 Shoal Creek Boulevard
Austin, TX 78757-6897
Telephone: (800) 897-3202; (512) 451-3246
Fax: (800) 397-7633; (512) 451-8542
E-mail: proed1@aol.com
http://www.proedinc.com
Published quarterly

Journal of The Association for Persons with Severe Handicaps (JASH)
TASH (formerly The Association for Persons with Severe Handicaps)
29 West Susquehanna Avenue
Suite 210
Baltimore, MD 21204
Telephone: (410) 828-8274
Fax: (410) 828-6706
E-mail: info@tash.org
http://www.tash.org
Published quarterly

Journal of Visual Impairment and Blindness (JVIB)
American Foundation for the Blind (AFB)
Sheridan Press
450 Fame Avenue
Hanover, PA 17331
Telephone: (800) 877-2693; (717) 632-3535
Fax: (518) 436-7433
E-mail: pubsvc@tsp.sheridan.com
http://www.afb.org
Published monthly

Journal of Vocational Rehabilitation
Elsevier Science
Post Office Box 945
New York, NY 10159-0945
Telephone: (888) 427-4636; (212) 633-3730
Fax: (212) 633-3680
E-mail: usinfo-f@elsevier.com
http://www.elsevier.com
Published six times per year

Learning Disabilities: Research & Practice
Division for Learning Disabilities
Council for Exceptional Children (CEC)
Lawrence Erlbaum Associates, Inc.
10 Industrial Avenue
Mahwah, NJ 07430-2262
Telephone: (800) 9BOOKS9

Fax: (201) 236-0072
E-mail: orders@erlbaum.com
http://www.erlbaum.com
Published quarterly

Mainstream Magazine
2973 Beech Street
Suite I
San Diego, CA 92102
Telephone: (619) 234-3138
Fax: (619) 234-3155
E-mail: editor@mainstream-mag.com
Mainstream Online: http://www.mainstream-mag.com
Published monthly

Mental Retardation
American Association on Mental Retardation (AAMR)
444 North Capitol Street NW
Suite 846
Washington, DC 20001-1512
Telephone: (800) 424-3688; (202) 387-1968
Fax: (202) 387-2193
E-mail: mailbox@aamr.org
http://www.aamr.org
Published bimonthly

National Disability Law Reporter
LRP Publications
747 Dresher Road
Suite 500
Post Office Box 980
Horsham, PA 19044-0980
Telephone: (800) 341-7874
Fax: (215) 784-9639
E-mail: custserve@lrp.com
http://www.lrp.com
Published 22 times per year

Network News
National Transition Network
Institute on Community Integration
University of Minnesota
430 Wulling Hall
86 Pleasant Street SE
Minneapolis, MN 55455
Telephone: (612) 627-4008
Fax: (612) 627-1998
E-mail: ntn@mail.ici.coled.umn.edu

http://www.ici.coled.umn.edu/ntn
Published quarterly

New Mobility Magazine
Post Office Box 220
Horsham, PA 19044
Telephone: (215) 675-9133
Fax: (215) 675-9376
E-mail: ginal@jvlconard.com
On-line magazine: http://www.newmobility.com
Published monthly

Opening Doors: A Housing Publication for the Disability Community
Technical Assistance Collaborative, Inc.
One Center Plaza
Suite 310
Boston, MA 02108-2207
Telephone: (617) 742-5657
Fax: (617) 742-0509
E-mail: info@tacinc.org
http://c-c-d.org/doors.html
Published quarterly

People First Newsletter
People First of Washington
Post Office Box 648
Clarkston, WA 99403
Telephone: (800) 758-1123
Published quarterly

Ragged Edge
Advocado Press, Inc.
Post Office Box 145
Louisville, KY 40201
Telephone: (502) 894-9492
Fax: (502) 899-9562
E-mail: editor@ragged-edge-mag.com
http://www.ragged-edge-mag.com
Published bimonthly

Remedial and Special Education (RASE)
PRO-ED Publishing Company
8700 Shoal Creek Boulevard
Austin, TX 78757-6897
Telephone: (800) 897-3202; (512) 451-3246
Fax: (800) 397-7633; (512) 451-8542
E-mail: proed1@aol.com
http://www.proedinc.com
Published semiannually

Rural Special Education Quarterly
American Council on Rural Special Education (ACRSE)
2323 Anderson Avenue
Suite 225
Manhattan, KS 66502
Telephone: (785) 532-5717
Fax: (785) 532-7732
E-mail: acres@k-state.edu
http://www.ksu.edu/acres/about.html
Published quarterly

Special Education Law Monthly
LRP Publications
747 Dresher Road
Suite 500
Post Office Box 980
Horsham, PA 19044-0980
Telephone: (800) 341-7874
Fax: (215) 784-9639
E-mail: custserve@lrp.com
http://www.lrp.com
Published monthly

Special Education Report
Capitol Publications
110 King Street
Suite 444
Alexandria, VA 22314
Telephone: (703) 683-4100
Fax: (703) 739-6517
http://www.educationdaily.com
Published biweekly

The Special Educator (TSE)
LRP Publications
747 Dresher Road
Suite 500
Post Office Box 980
Horsham, PA 19044-0980
Telephone: (800) 341-7874
Fax: (215) 784-9639
E-mail: custserve@lrp.com
http://www.lrp.com
Published 22 times per year

Supported Employment InfoLines
Training Resource Network, Inc.
Post Office Box 439
St. Augustine, FL 32085-0439

Telephone: (904) 823-9800
Fax: (904) 823-3554
E-mail: trninc@aol.com
http://www.trninc.com/infolines.htm
Published 10 times per year

TEACHING Exceptional Children (TEC)
Council for Exceptional Children (CEC)
1920 Association Drive
Reston, VA 20191-1589
Telephone: (888) 232-7733
Fax: (703) 264-9494
E-mail: service@cec.sped.org
http://www.cec.sped.org
Published six times per year

Technology & Disability
Elsevier Science
Post Office Box 945
New York, NY 10159-0945
Telephone: (888) 427-4636; (212) 633-3730
Fax: (212) 633-3680
E-mail: usinfo-f@elsevier.com
http://www.elsevier.com
Published quarterly

Technology & Inclusion News
Post Office Box 150878
Austin, TX 78715-0878
Telephone: (512) 280-7235
Fax: (512) 891-9288
E-mail: greetings@taicenter.com
http://www.taicenter.com/tainews.html
Published quarterly

Washington Watch
United Cerebral Palsy Association (UCP)
1660 L Street NW
Suite 700
Washington, DC 20036
Telephone: (800) 872-5827
Fax: (202) 776-0414
E-mail: Rforeman@ucpa.org
http://www.ucpa.org
Published bimonthly

What's Working in Transition
Transition Technical Assistance Project
Institute on Community Integration
University of Minnesota

109 Pattee Hall
150 Pillsbury Drive SE
Minneapolis, MN 55455
Telephone: (612) 624-4512
Fax: (612) 624-9344
E-mail: ici@mail.ici.coled.umn.edu
http://www.ici.coled.umn.edu/ici
Published quarterly

PUBLISHERS

Academic Communication Associates, Inc.
4149 Avenida de la Plata
Department 317
Post Office Box 586249
Oceanside, CA 92058-6249
Telephone: (760) 758-9593
Fax: (760) 758-1604
E-mail: acom@acadcom.com
http://www.acadcom.com

Academic Therapy Publications/Ann Arbor Publishers
20 Commercial Boulevard
Novato, CA 94949-6191
Telephone: (800) 422-7249; (415) 883-3314
Fax: (415) 883-3720
E-mail: atpub@aol.com
http://www.atpub.com

Allyn & Bacon
160 Gould Street
Needham Heights, MA 02494
Telephone: (800) 666-9433; (515) 284-6751
Fax: (515) 284-2607
E-mail: simon@neodata.com
http://www.abacon.com

American Association on Mental Retardation (AAMR)
444 North Capitol Street NW
Suite 846
Washington, DC 20001-1512
Telephone: (800) 424-3688; (202) 387-1968
Fax: (202) 387-2193
E-mail: mailbox@aamr.org
http://www.aamr.org

American Foundation for the Blind (AFB Press)
11 Penn Plaza
Suite 300
New York, NY 10001

Telephone: (800) 232-3044
Fax: (212) 507-7774
E-mail: bkatzen@afb.org
http://www.afb.org

American Guidance Service (AGS)
4201 Woodland Road
Circle Pines, MN 55014-1796
Telephone: (800) 328-2560; (612) 786-4343
Fax: (800) 471-8457; (612) 786-9077
E-mail: agsmail@agsnet.com
http://www.agsnet.com

The Arc
500 East Border Street
Suite 300
Arlington, TX 76010
Telephone: (817) 261-6003
Fax: (817) 277-3499
E-mail: thearc@metronet.com
http://www.thearc.org

Attainment Company, Inc.
Post Office Box 930160
Verona, WI 53593-0160
Telephone: (800) 327-4269
Fax: (800) 942-3865
E-mail: info@attainment-inc.com
http://www.attainment-inc.com

Brookline Books
Post Office Box 1047
Cambridge, MA 02238-1047
Telephone: (800) 666-2665; (617) 868-0360
Fax: (617) 868-1772
E-mail: brooklinebks@delphi.com
http://people.delphi.com/brooklinebks

Brooks/Cole Publishing Company
511 Forest Lodge Road
Pacific Grove, CA 93950
Telephone: (800) 354-9706
Fax: (800) 487-8488
E-mail: info@brookscole.com
http://www.brookscole.com

Center for Applied Research in Education
Prentice-Hall
Post Office Box 11071
Des Moines, IA 50336
Telephone: (800) 372-9400

Fax: (515) 284-2607
http://www.phdirect.com

Charles C Thomas Publisher, Ltd.
2600 South First Street
Springfield, IL 62704
Telephone: (800) 258-8980; (217) 789-8980
Fax: (217) 789-9130
E-mail: books@ccthomas.com
http://www.ccthomas.com

Council for Exceptional Children—CEC Publications
1920 Association Drive
Department K7082
Reston, VA 20191-1589
Telephone: (888) 232-7733
Fax: (703) 264-9494
E-mail: service@cec.sped.org
http://www.cec.sped.org

Delmar Publishers
3 Columbia Circle
Albany, NY 12212
Telephone: (800) 865-5840
Fax: (800) 880-9496
E-mail: info@delmar.com
http://www.delmar.com

Disability Resources, Inc.
4 Glatter Lane
Centereach, NY 11720-1032
Telephone: (516) 585-0290
Fax: (516) 585-0290
E-mail: info@disabilityresources.org
http://www.disabilityresources.org

Diverse City Press Inc.
BM 272, 33 des Floralies
Eastman, Québec
J0E 1P0
Canada
Telephone: (450) 297-3080
Fax: (450) 297-3080
E-mail: diversec@interlinx.qc.ca
http://www.diverse-city.com

Edmark
Post Office Box 97021
Redmond, WA 98073-9721
Telephone: (800) 362-2890; (425) 556-8430

Fax: (425) 556-8400
E-mail: edmarkteam@edmark.com
http://www.edmark.com

Eye on Education
6 Depot Way West
Suite 106
Larchmont, NY 10538
Telephone: (914) 833-0551
Fax: (914) 833-0761
E-mail: info@eyeoneducation.com
http://www.eyeoneducation.com

Future Horizons
720 North Fielder
Arlington, TX 76012
Telephone: (800) 489-0727
Fax: (817) 277-2270
E-mail: edfuture@onramp.net
http://www.futurehorizons-autism.com

Gallaudet University Press
800 Florida Avenue NE
Washington, DC 20002-3695
Telephone: (800) 621-2736; (773) 568-1550
Fax: (800) 621-8476
E-mail: pubnet@202-5280
http://gupress.gallaudet.edu

Guilford Publications
72 Spring Street
New York, NY 10012
Telephone: (800) 365-7006; (212) 431-9800
Fax: (212) 966-6708
E-mail: info@guilford.com
http://www.guilford.com

Haworth Press, Inc.
10 Alice Street
Binghamton, NY 13904-1580
Telephone: (800) 542-1673; (573) 874-1710
Fax: (800) 442-9509
E-mail: getinfo@haworthpressinc.com
http://www.haworthpressinc.com

Hawthorne Educational Services, Inc.
800 Gray Oak Drive
Columbia, MO 65201
Telephone: (800) 542-1673; (573) 874-1710
Fax: (800) 442-9509

Human Policy Press
Center on Human Policy
805 South Crouse Avenue
Syracuse, NY 13244-2280
Telephone: (800) 894-0826; (315) 443-3851
Fax: (315) 443-4338
E-mail: thechp@sued.syr.edu
http://soeweb.syr.edu/thechp

Inclusion Press International
24 Thome Crescent
Toronto, Ontario
M6H 2S5
Canada
Telephone: (416) 658-5363
Fax: (416) 658-5067
E-mail: includer@idirect.com
http://www.inclusion.com

Institute on Disability/UAP
University of New Hampshire
7 Leavitt Lane
Suite 101
Durham, NH 03824-3522
Telephone: (603) 862-4320
Fax: (603) 862-0555
E-mail: institute.disability@unh.edu
http://iod.unh.edu

James Stanfield Publishing Company
Drawer WWW
Post Office Box 41058
Santa Barbara, CA 93140
Telephone: (800) 421-6534
Fax: (805) 897-1187
E-mail: stanfield@stanfield.com
http://www.stanfield.com

Jessica Kingsley Publishers
116 Pentonville Road
London N1 9JB
Telephone: 44 171 833 2307
Fax: 44 171 837 2917
E-mail: post@jkp.com
http://www.jkp.com

LRP Publications
747 Dresher Road
Suite 500
Post Office Box 980

Horsham, PA 19044-0980
Telephone: (800) 341-7874
Fax: (215) 784-9639
E-mail: custserve@lrp.com
http://www.lrp.com

National Professional Resources, Inc.
25 South Regent Street
Port Chester, NY 10573
Telephone: (800) 453-7461
Fax: (914) 937-9327
E-mail: info@nprinc.com
http://www.nprinc.com

Paul H. Brookes Publishing Company
Post Office Box 10624
Baltimore, MD 21285-0624
Telephone: (800) 638-3775; (410) 337-9580
Fax: (410) 337-8539
E-mail: custserv@brookespublishing.com
http://www.brookespublishing.com

PCI Educational Publishing
Post Office Box 34270
San Antonio, TX 78265-4270
Telephone: (800) 594-4263
Fax: (888) 259-8284
E-mail: info@pcicatalog.com
http://www.pcicatalog.com

Peytral Publications, Inc.
Post Office Box 1162
Suite 100
Minnetonka, MN 55345
Telephone: (877) PEYTRAL; (612) 949-8707
Fax: (612) 906-9777
E-mail: helpline@peytral.com
http://www.peytral.com

Phillip Roy, Inc.
Post Office Box 130
Indian Rocks Beach, FL 33785
Telephone: (800) 255-9085; (813) 593-2700
Fax: (813) 595-2685
E-mail: phillipr@gte.net
http://www.phillip-roy.com

Practical Press
Post Office Box 455
Moorhead, MN 56561-0455

Telephone: (218) 233-2842
Fax: (218) 236-5199
E-mail: ppress@rrnet.com
http://rrnet.com/~ppress

PRO-ED Publishing Company
8700 Shoal Creek Boulevard
Austin, TX 78757-6897
Telephone: (800) 897-3202
Fax: (800) 397-7633
E-mail: books@proedinc.com
http://www.proedinc.com

Program Development Associates
5620 Business Avenue
Suite B
Cicero, NY 13039-9576
Telephone: (800) 543-2119
Fax: (315) 452-0710
E-mail: pdassoc@servtech.com
http://www.pdassoc.com

Prufrock Press
Post Office Box 8813
Waco, TX 76714-8813
Telephone: (800) 998-2208
Fax: (800) 240-0333
E-mail: Bates@prufrock.com
http://www.prufrock.com

Research Press Company
Department 991
Post Office Box 9177
Champaign, IL 61826
Telephone: (800) 519-2707
Fax: (217) 352-1221
E-mail: rp@researchpress.com
http://www.researchpress.com

Singular Publishing Group, Inc.
401 West A Street
Suite 325
San Diego, CA 92101-7904
Telephone: (800) 521-8545; (619) 238-6777
Fax: (619) 238-6789
E-mail: singpub@singpub.com
http://www.singpub.com

Sopris West
4093 Specialty Place
Longmont, CO 80504
Telephone: (800) 547-6747; (303) 651-2829
Fax: (303) 776-5934
E-mail: prodinfo@sopriswest.com
http://www.sopriswest.com

Special Needs Project
3463 State Street
Suite 282
Santa Barbara, CA 93105
Telephone: (800) 333-6867; (805) 962-8087
Fax: (805) 962-5087
E-mail: books@specialneeds.com
http://www.specialneeds.com

Teachers College Press
Post Office Box 20
Williston, VT 05495-0020
Telephone: (800) 575-6566
Fax: (802) 864-7626
E-mail: tcpress@www.tc.columbia.edu
http://www.tc.columbia.edu/~tcpress

Training Resource Network, Inc.
Post Office Box 439
St. Augustine, FL 32085-0439
Telephone: (904) 823-9800
Fax: (904) 823-3554
E-mail: trninc@aol.com
http://www.trninc.com

Wadsworth Publishing Company
10 Davis Drive
Belmont, CA 94002
Telephone: (650) 595-2350
Fax: (650) 592-9081
E-mail: webmaster@wadsworth.com
http://www.wadsworth.com

Woodbine House
6510 Bells Mill Road
Bethesda, MD 20817
Telephone: (800) 843-7323; (301) 897-3570
Fax: (301) 897-5838
E-mail: info@woodbinehouse.com
http://www.woodbinehouse.com

ORGANIZATIONS

ABLEDATA
8401 Colesville Road
Suite 200
Silver Spring, MD 20910
Telephone: (800) 227-0216; (301) 608-8998
Fax: (301) 608-8958
E-mail: kableknap@aol.com
http://www.abledata.com

ADA Technical Assistance Program
8455 Colesville Road
Suite 935
Silver Spring, MD 20910-3319
Telephone: (800) 949-4232
E-mail: adata@adata@org
http://www.adata.org

Adaptive Technology Resource Centre (ATRC)
J.P. Robarts Library
First Floor
University of Toronto Information Commons
130 St. George Street
Toronto, Ontario
M5S 3H1
Canada
Telephone: (416) 978-4360
Fax: (416) 971-2629
E-mail: iris.neher@utoronto.ca
http://www.utoronto.ca/atrc/

Administration on Developmental Disabilities (ADD)
Administration for Children and Families
U.S. Department of Health and Human Services
200 Independence Avenue SW
Washington, DC 20201
Telephone: (202) 690-6590
Fax: (202) 690-6904
E-mail: add@acf.dhhs.gov
http://www.acf.dhhs.gov/programs/add/index.htm

Advocates Across America, Inc.
Post Office Box 754
Chandler, AZ 85244-0754
Telephone: (602) 917-0955
Fax: (602) 814-9404
E-mail: support@axa.org
http://www.axa.org

Alliance for Technology Access (ATA)
2175 East Francisco Boulevard
Suite L
San Rafael, CA 94901
Telephone: (415) 455-4575
Fax: (415) 455-0654
E-mail: atainfo@ataccess.org
http://www.ataccess.org

American Association for Leisure and Recreation (AALR)
1900 Association Drive
Reston, VA 20191-1599
Telephone: (800) 213-7193; (703) 476-3472
Fax: (703) 476-9527
E-mail: aalr@aahperd.org
http://www.aahperd.org/aalr/aalr.html

American Association of People with Disabilities (AAPD)
1819 H Street NW
Suite 330
Washington, DC 20006
Telephone: (800) 840-8844
Fax: (202) 457-0473
E-mail: aapd@aol.com
http://aapd-dc.org

American Association of University Affiliated Programs for Persons with Developmental
    Disabilities (AAUAP)
8630 Fenton Street
Suite 410
Silver Spring, MD 20910
Telephone: (301) 588-8252
Fax: (301) 588-2842
E-mail: info@aauap.org
http://www.aauap.org

American Association on Mental Retardation (AAMR)
444 North Capitol Street NW
Suite 846
Washington, DC 20001-1512
Telephone: (800) 424-3688; (202) 387-1968
Fax: (202) 387-2193
E-mail: mailbox@aamr.org
http://www.aamr.org

American Council of the Blind (ACB)
1155 15th Street NW
Suite 720
Washington, DC 20005
Telephone: (800) 424-8666; (202) 467-5081

Fax: (202) 467-5085
E-mail: webmaster@acb.org
http://www.acb.org

American Disability Association
2201 6th Avenue South
Birmingham, AL 35233
Telephone: (205) 323-0088
Fax: (205) 251-7417
E-mail: adanet@sisonline.com
http://www.adanet.org

American Foundation for the Blind (AFB)
11 Penn Plaza
Suite 300
New York, NY 10001
Telephone: (800) 232-5463; (212) 502-7600
Fax: (212) 502-7777
E-mail: afbinfo@afb.org
http://www.afb.org

American Network of Community Options & Resources (ANCOR)
4200 Evergreen Lane
Suite 315
Annandale, VA 22003
Telephone: (703) 642-6614
Fax: (703) 642-0497
E-mail: ancor@radix.net
http://www.ancor.org

American Speech-Language-Hearing Association (ASHA)
10801 Rockville Pike
Rockville, MD 20852
Telephone: (888) 821-ASHA; (301) 897-5700
Fax: (301) 571-0457
E-mail: actioncenter@asha.org
http://www.asha.org

The Arc
500 East Border Street
Suite 300
Arlington, TX 76010
Telephone: (817) 261-6003
Fax: (817) 277-3491
E-mail: thearc@metronet.com
http://www.thearc.org

Association of Persons in Supported Employment (APSE)
1627 Monument Avenue
Richmond, VA 23220
Telephone: (804) 278-9187

Fax: (804) 278-9377
E-mail: apse@apse.org
http://www.apse.org

Association on Higher Education and Disability (AHEAD)
Post Office Box 21192
Columbus, OH 43221-0192
Telephone: (614) 488-4972
Fax: (614) 488-1174
E-mail: ahead@postbox.acs.ohio-state.edu
http://www.ahead.org

Autism Society of America
7910 Woodmont Avenue
Suite 300
Bethesda, MD 20814-3015
Telephone: (800) 328-8476; (301) 657-0881
Fax: (301) 657-0869
E-mail: ben.dorman@home.com
http://www.autism-society.org

Barkley Augmentative and Alternative Communication Lab
University of Nebraska–Lincoln
Barkley Memorial Center, Room 202
Lincoln, NE 68583
Telephone: (402) 472-5463
Fax: (402) 472-7697
E-mail: drb@unlinfo.unl.edu
http://aac.unl.edu

Beach Center on Families & Disability
University of Kansas
3111 Haworth Hall
Lawrence, KS 66045
Telephone: (785) 864-7600
Fax: (785) 864-7605
E-mail: beach@dole.lsi.ukans.edu
http://www.lsi.ukans.edu/beach/beachhp.htm

Center for Applied Special Technology (CAST)
39 Cross Street
Suite 201
Peabody, MA 01960
Telephone: (978) 531-8555
Fax: (978) 531-0192
E-mail: cast@cast.org
http://www.cast.org

Center for Information Technology Accommodation (CITA)
1800 F Street NW, Room 1234
Washington, DC 20405

Telephone: (202) 501-4906
Fax: (202) 501-6269
E-mail: susan.brummel@gsa.gov
http://www.itpolicy.gsa.gov/coca/index.htm

Center for Law and Education (CLE)
1875 Connecticut Avenue NW
Suite 510
Washington, DC 20009
Telephone: (202) 986-3000
Fax: (202) 986-6648
E-mail: cle@cleweb.org
http://www.cleweb.org

Center for Recreation and Disability Studies (CRDS)
Center for Leisure Studies & Recreation Administration
CB #3185
730 Airport Road
Suite 204
University of North Carolina
Chapel Hill, NC 27599-3185
Telephone: (919) 962-0534
Fax: (919) 962-1233
E-mail: kluken@email.unc.edu
http://www.unc.edu/depts/recreate

Center on Human Policy
Syracuse University, School of Education
805 South Crouse Avenue
Syracuse, NY 13244-2280
Telephone: (800) 894-0826; (315) 443-3851
Fax: (315) 443-4338
E-mail: thechp@sued.syr.edu
http://soeweb.syr.edu/thechp

Consortium on Inclusive Schooling Practices (CISP)
Allegheny University of the Health Sciences
Child and Family Studies Program
1 Allegheny Center
Suite 510
Pittsburgh, PA 15212
Telephone: (412) 359-1600
Fax: (412) 359-1601
E-mail: menuit@pgh.auhs.edu
http://www.pgh.auhs.edu/CISP/brochure/abtcons.htm

Council for Exceptional Children (CEC)
1920 Association Drive
Reston, VA 20191-1589

Telephone: (888) 232-7733
Fax: (703) 264-9494
E-mail: service@cec.sped.org
http://www.cec.sped.org

Council on Quality and Leadership in Supports for People with Disabilities
100 West Road
Suite 406
Towson, MD 21204
Telephone: (410) 583-0600
Fax: (410) 583-0063
E-mail: info@thecouncil.org
http://www.thecouncil.org

Disabilities, Opportunities, Internetworking, and Technology (DO-IT)
University of Washington
4545 15th Avenue NE
Seattle, WA 98105
Telephone: (206) 685-DOIT
Fax: (206) 685-4054
E-mail: doit@u.washington.edu
http://weber.u.washington.edu/~doit

Disability Rights Education & Defense Fund (DREDF)
2212 Sixth Street
Berkeley, CA 94710
Telephone: (800) 466-4232; (510) 644-2555
Fax: (510) 841-8645
E-mail: dredf@dredf.org
http://www.dredf.org

Disabled Peoples' International
101-7 Evergreen Place
Winnepeg, Manitoba
R3L 2T3
Canada
Telephone: (204) 287-8010
Fax: (204) 453-1367
E-mail: dpi@dpi.org
http://www.dpi.org

Division of Career Development and Transition (DCDT)
Council for Exceptional Children (CEC)
1920 Association Drive
Reston, VA 22091
Telephone: (888) 232-7733; (703) 620-3660
Fax: (703) 264-9494
E-mail: bvtc@unicorn.net
http://www.ed.uiuc.edu/SPED/dcdt/

ERIC Clearinghouse on Disabilities and Gifted Education
1920 Association Drive
Reston, VA 20191-1589
Telephone: (800) 328-0272; (703) 620-3660
Fax: (703) 264-9494
E-mail: ericec@cec.sped.org
http://www.cec.sped.org/ericec.htm

Federal Resource Center for Special Education
1875 Connecticut Avenue NW
Suite 900
Washington, DC 20009
Telephone: (202) 884-8215
Fax: (202) 884-8442
E-mail: frc@aed.org
http://www.dssc.org/frc

HEATH Resource Center
National Clearinghouse on Postsecondary Education for Individuals with Disabilities
American Council on Education
1 Dupont Circle NW
Suite 800
Washington, DC 20036-1193
Telephone: (800) 544-3284; (202) 939-9320
Fax: (202) 833-4760
E-mail: heath@ace.nche.edu
http://www.acenet.edu

Independent Living Research Utilization Project (ILRU)
The Institute for Rehabilitation Research
2323 South Shepherd
Suite 1000
Houston, TX 77019
Telephone: (713) 520-0232
Fax: (713) 520-5785
E-mail: ilru@ilru.org
http://www.ilru.org

Institute for Community Inclusion (ICI)
300 Longwood Avenue
Boston, MA 02115
Telephone: (617) 355-6506
Fax: (617) 355-7940
E-mail: ici@a1.tch.harvard.edu
http://web1.tch.harvard.edu/ici

Institute on Community Integration
University of Minnesota
109 Pattee Hall
150 Pillsbury Drive SE

Minneapolis, MN 55455
Telephone: (612) 624-4512
Fax: (612) 624-9344
E-mail: ici@mail.ici.coled.umn.edu
http://www.ici.coled.umn.edu/ici

Institute on Disability/UAP
University of New Hampshire
7 Leavitt Lane
Suite 101
Durham, NH 03824
Telephone: (603) 862-4320
Fax: (603) 862-0555
E-mail: institute.disability@unh.edu
http://iod.unh.edu

International Society for Augmentative and Alternative Communication (ISAAC)
49 The Donway West
Suite 308
Toronto, Ontario
M3C 3M9
Canada
Telephone: (416) 385-0351
Fax: (416) 385-0352
E-mail: isaac_mail@mail.cepp.org
http://www.isaac-online.org

Interwork Institute
5850 Hardy Avenue
Suite 112
San Diego, CA 92182-5313
Telephone: (619) 594-4220
Fax: (619) 594-4208
E-mail: webmaster@interwork.sdsu.edu
http://interwork.sdsu.edu

Job Accommodation Network (JAN)
West Virginia University
918 Chestnut Ridge Road
Morgantown, WV 26506-6080
Telephone: (800) 232-9675; (800) 526-7234
Fax: (304) 293-5407
E-mail: jan@jan.icdi.wvu.edu
http://www.jan.wvu.edu

National Alliance of Business
1201 New York Avenue NW
Suite 700
Washington, DC 20005-6143
Telephone: (202) 289-2888

Fax: (202) 289-1303
E-mail: info@nab.com
http://www.nab.com

National Alliance of the DisAbled, Inc. (NAOTD)
1352 Sioux Street
Orange Park, FL 32065
Telephone: (904) 276-2169
Fax: (904) 276-2169
E-mail: naotd@aol.com
http://www.naotd.org

National Arts and Disability Center (NADC)
300 UCLA Medical Plaza
Suite 3330
Los Angeles, CA 90095-6967
Telephone: (310) 794-1141
Fax: (310) 794-1143
E-mail: oraynor@mednet.ucla.edu
http://www.dcp.ucla.edu/nadc

National Association of Developmental Disabilities Councils (NADDC)
1234 Massachusetts Avenue NW
Suite 103
Washington, DC 20005
Telephone: (202) 347-1234
Fax: (202) 347-4023
E-mail: naddc@igc.apc.org
http://www.igc.org/NADDC/index4.html

National Association of Protection and Advocacy Systems (NAPAS)
900 2nd Street NE
Suite 211
Washington, DC 20002
Telephone: (202) 408-9514
Fax: (202) 408-9520
E-mail: napas@earthlink.net
http://www.protectionandadvocacy.com

National Association of Vocational Education Special Needs Personnel (NAVESNP)
614 Penridge Road
Pittsburgh, PA 15211
Telephone: (404) 549-2362
Fax: (412) 675-9067
E-mail: eeb6@psu.edu
http://www.erc.mk.psu.edu/navesnp.htm

National Center for Youth with Disabilities (NCYD)
University of Minnesota
Box 721

420 Delaware Street SE
Minneapolis, MN 55455-0392
Telephone: (800) 333-6293; (612) 626-2825
Fax: (612) 626-2134
E-mail: neyd@gold.tc.umn.edu
http://www.peds.umn.edu/centers/ncyd

National Center on Educational Restructuring and Inclusion
City University of New York
The Graduate School and University Center
33 West 42nd Street
New York, NY 10036
Telephone: (212) 642-2656; (212) 642-2151
Fax: (212) 642-1972

National Clearinghouse for Professions in Special Education (NCPSE)
Council for Exceptional Children (CEC)
1920 Association Drive
Reston, VA 20191-1589
Telephone: (800) 641-7824; (703) 264-9476
Fax: (703) 264-9480
E-mail: ncpse@cec.sped.org
http://www.cec.sped.org/ncpse.htm

National Council on Disability (NCD)
1331 F Street NW
Suite 1050
Washington, DC 20004-1107
Telephone: (202) 272-2004
Fax: (202) 272-2022
E-mail: mquigley@ncd.gov
http://www.ncd.gov

National Council on Independent Living (NCIL)
2111 Wilson Boulevard
Suite 405
Arlington, VA 22201
Telephone: (703) 525-3406
Fax: (703) 525-3409
E-mail: ncil@tsbbs08.tnet.com

National Down Syndrome Society (NDSS)
666 Broadway
8th Floor
New York, NY 10012-2317
Telephone: (800) 221-4602; (212) 460-9330
Fax: (212) 979-2873
E-mail: info@ndss.org
http://www.ndss.org

National Easter Seal Society
230 West Monroe Street
Suite 1800
Chicago, IL 60606-4802
Telephone: (800) 221-6827; (312) 726-6200
Fax: (312) 726-1494
E-mail: info@easter-seals.org
http://www.seals.com

National Information Center for Children and Youth with Disabilities (NICHCY)
Post Office Box 1492
Washington, DC 20013-1492
Telephone: (800) 695-0285; (202) 884-8200
Fax: (202) 884-8441
E-mail: nichcy@aed.org
http://www.nichcy.org

National Information Center on Deafness (NICD)
Gallaudet University
800 Florida Avenue NE
Washington, DC 20002-3695
Telephone: (202) 651-5051
E-mail: nicd@gallux.gallaudet.edu
http://www.gallaudet.edu/~nicd

National Library Service for the Blind and Physically Handicapped
Library of Congress
1291 Taylor Street NW
Washington, DC 20542
Telephone: (800) 424-8567; (202) 707-5100
Fax: (202) 707-0712
E-mail: nls@loc.gov
http://lcweb.loc.gov/nls/nls.html

National Organization on Disability (NOD)
910 16th Street NW
Suite 600
Washington, DC 20006
Telephone: (202) 293-5960
Fax: (202) 293-7999
E-mail: ability@nod.org
http://www.nod.org

National Parent Network on Disability (NPND)
1130 17th Street NW
Suite 400
Washington, DC 20036
Telephone: (202) 463-2299
Fax: (202) 463-9403
E-mail: npnd@cs.net
http://www.npnd.org

National Rehabilitation Information Center (NARIC)
1010 Wayne Avenue
Suite 800
Silver Spring, MD 20910-3319
Telephone: (800) 346-2742; (301) 562-2400
Fax: (301) 562-2401
E-mail: naricinfo@kra.com
http://www.naric.com/naric

National Resource Center on Supported Living and Choice
The Center on Human Policy
805 South Crouse Avenue
Syracuse, NY 13244-2280
Telephone: (800) 894-0826; (315) 443-4338
Fax: (315) 443-4338
E-mail: thechp@sued.syr.edu
http://soeweb.syr.edu/thechp/chpact.htm

National School-to-Work Learning & Information Center
400 Virginia Avenue SW
Room 150
Washington, DC 20024
Telephone: (800) 251-7236; (202) 401-6222
Fax: (202) 401-6211
E-mail: stw-lc@ed.gov
http://www.stw.ed.gov

National Transition Alliance for Youth with Disabilities (NTA)
Transition Research Institute at Illinois
113 Children's Research Center
51 Gerty Drive
Champaign, IL 61820
Telephone: (217) 333-2325
Fax: (217) 244-0851
E-mail: nta@aed.org
http://www.dssc.org/nta

Office of Special Education and Rehabilitative Services (OSERS)
330 C Street SW
Switzer Building
Room 3132
Washington, DC 20202-2524
Telephone: (202) 205-8241
Fax: (202) 401-2608
http://www.ed.gov/offices/osers

Office of the Americans with Disabilities Act
Civil Rights Division
U.S. Department of Justice
Post Office Box 66118
Washington, DC 20035-6118

Telephone: (800) 514-0301; (202) 514-0301
http://www.usdoj.gov/crt/ada/adahom1.htm

Parent Advocacy Coalition for Educational Rights (PACER)
4826 Chicago Avenue South
Minneapolis, MN 55417-1098
Telephone: (612) 827-2966
Fax: (612) 827-3065
E-mail: webster@pacer.org
http://www.pacer.org

PEAK Parent Center, Inc.
6055 Lehman Drive
Suite 101
Colorado Springs, CO 80918
Telephone: (719) 531-9400
Fax: (719) 531-9452
E-mail: info@peakparent.org
http://www.peakparent.org

People First, International
Post Office Box 12642
Salem, OR 97309
Telephone: (503) 362-0336
Fax: (503) 585-0287
E-mail: heathd@open.org
http://www.open.org/people1

Pike Institute on Law and Disability
Boston University School of Law
765 Commonwealth Avenue
Boston, MA 02215
Telephone: (617) 353-2904
Fax: (617) 353-2906
E-mail: pikeinst@bu.edu
http://www.bu.edu/pike/home.html

President's Committee on Employment of People with Disabilities
1331 F Street NW
Suite 300
Washington, DC 20004-1107
Telephone: (202) 376-6200
Fax: (202) 376-6219
E-mail: info@pceped.gov
http://www.pcepd.gov

Research & Training Center on Independent Living (RTC-IL)
University of Kansas
4089 Dole Building
Lawrence, KS 66045-2930

Telephone: (913) 864-4095
Fax: (913) 864-5063
E-mail: rtcil@ukans.edu
http://www.lsi.ukans.edu/rtcil/rtcil.htm

Self Advocates Becoming Empowered (SABE)
Post Office Box 105C1
New Fairfield, CT 06812
E-mail: netsabe@aol.com
http://members.aol.com/netsabe/netsabe.html

Sibling Information Network
University of Connecticut
A.J. Pappanikou Center
249 Glenbrook Road, U-64
Storrs, CT 06269-2064
Telephone: (860) 486-4985
Fax: (860) 486-5037
E-mail: spendmol@uconnvm.uconn.edu

Special Needs Advocates for Parents (SNAP)
1801 Avenue of the Stars, #410
Century City, CA 90067
Telephone: (888) 310-9889; (310) 201-9614
Fax: (310) 201-9899
E-mail: info@snapinfo.org
http://www.snapinfo.org

TASH (formerly The Association for Persons with Severe Handicaps)
29 West Susquehanna Avenue
Suite 210
Baltimore, MD 21204
Telephone: (410) 828-8274
Fax: (410) 828-6706
E-mail: info@tash.org
http://www.tash.org

Trace Research & Development Center
University of Wisconsin–Madison
5901 Research Park Boulevard
Madison, WI 53719-1252
Telephone: (608) 262-6966
Fax: (608) 262-8848
E-mail: info@trace.wisc.edu
http://www.trace.wisc.edu

Unified Sports
Special Olympics, Inc.
1326 G Street NW
Suite 500

Washington, DC 20005
Telephone: (202) 628-3630
Fax: (202) 824-0200
http://www.specialolympics.com

Very Special Arts
1300 Connecticut Avenue NW
Suite 700
Washington, DC 20036
Telephone: (202) 628-2800
Fax: (202) 737-0725
E-mail: webmaster@vsarts.org
http://www.vsarts.org

World Institute on Disability
510 16th Avenue
Suite 100
Oakland, CA 94612-1500
Telephone: (510) 763-4100
Fax: (510) 763-4109
E-mail: wid@wid.org
http://www.wid.org

TRANSITION LINK WEB SITE

Make sure to visit the companion web site to *The Transition Handbook* at
www.transitionlink.com. This interactive site contains practical information, updated references, useful stategies, and links to a multitude of transition resources.
Features of Transition Link include

- *On-line strategies:* Visitors to Transition Link can submit effective strategies
  of their own or search from a growing database of field-tested strategies
  used by teachers, family members, and employment specialists around
  the country.
- *Valuable resources:* Need additional information or resources on a specific
  topic in the area of transition? In addition to the numerous resources listed
  in *The Transition Handbook*, an extensive listing of books, journals, newsletters, organizations, conferences, and related web sites is maintained at
  Transition Link. Link directly to these sources, or suggest your own links.
- *Transition programs:* Find out what other schools, communities, and employers are doing to help students make the transition from school to life
  in the community! Post information about your own program or get ideas
  from transition programs around the country.

Index of Support Strategies

Social support(s)
   communicating needs for, 118–123
   conducting assessments of, 111–114
   evaluating social opportunities and, 274
   existing, gaining access to, 131–136
   identifying, 110, 111–117
   incorporating into instruction, 129–131
   increasing, 110–136
Social support plan, developing, 123–131
   individualizing and, 123–129
Standardized assessment
   using, 164–166
   see also Assessment
Statements, self-instruction, formulating, 200–201
Strengths
   assessing, 155–166
   collecting data on, 143–147
   communicating, 166–171
   identifying, 140
   matching self-management strategies to, 190
   observing performance and, 141–150
   pointing out to employers and co-workers, 32
   promoting, 139–177
   stressing, 47–50, 139–140
Student(s)
   choices of, *see* Choice(s)
   educating, about self-determination, 182–185
   environmental support needs of, communicating to others, 82, 90–92
   evaluations of, reviewing, 150–154
   increasing social participation by, 62–64
   instructing
      incorporating environmental supports into, 97, 99
      incorporating social supports into, 129–131
   interactions of, *see* Social interactions
   interviewing
      about social supports, 135–136
      about strengths and needs, 171
   in need of support, identifying, 7
   performance of
      assessing preferences using, 240–241
      observing, 80–82, 83–89, 141–150
      see also Strengths
   promoting competence in, 140
   providing information about, 42–47
   rotating leadership among, 282
   social support needs of
      collaborating about, 120–123
      communicating to others, 118–120
   teaching skills that support acceptance to, 54–57
   see also Peer(s)
Student Job History, assessing choices with, 231–232, 234
Student-directed individualized education program (IEP), supporting, 245–246, 247
Support(s)
   educational, considering, 8
   environmental
      communicating needs for, 82, 90–92

   developing, 12
   developing for individual, 94–99
   gaining access to, 100–102
   identifying, 92–93
   increasing, 70–107
   gaining access to, 100–102, 131–136
   model of
      creating, 4–7
      organizing strategies based on, 17–19
      understanding premises of, 301–304
   public, increasing, 52–54
   social
      communicating needs for, 118–123
      developing for individual, 123–129
      evaluating social opportunities and, 274
      gaining access to, 131–136
      increasing, 109–136
   students in need of, identifying, 7
   see also specific type
Support strategies
   combining, 21
   compiling, 11–12
   forms for applying, 19, 309–352
   organizing, 17–19, 21–25
   research-based
      field-testing, 10–11
      identifying, 10
   "right," locating, 19–21
   sharing, 16–17
   see also specific strategies
Survey, environmental
   completing, 72, 74–75, 76–79, 81
   using to identify preferences, 232–233
   using to identify social supports, 114, 116
Switches, activation of, assessing preferences using, 237–239

Target behavior
   teaching self-instruction for, 198–201, 202
   teaching steps of, 196–197
Task analysis
   combining pictures with, as permanent prompts, 204–208
   conducting, 73, 79
      observing interactions and, 116
      observing strengths and, 146, 147, 151
   modifying, teaching new skills and, 177
Teacher(s)
   collaborating with, 35–42
      social interactions and, 283, 284
      strengths and needs and, 166–170
      students' choices and, 241–244
   communicating environmental support needs to, 90–92
   communicating social support needs to, 118, 119–120
   fading involvement of, 100
   field-testing strategies with, 11
   interacting with researchers, 9–10, 16
   teaching skills that support acceptance to, 57–58

Index of Student Skills